Teach
Yourself
MICROSOFT®
FRONTPAGE™
98

in 24 Hours

Teach Yourself
MICROSOFT®
FRONTPAGE™ 98
in 24 Hours

Andy Shafran

201 West 103rd Street
Indianapolis, Indiana 46290

International Standard Book Number: 1-57521-367-2

Library of Congress Catalog Card Number: 97-68738

2000   99   4

Interpretation of the printing code: the rightmost double-digit number is the year of the book's printing; the rightmost single digit is the number of the book's printing. For example, a printing code of 97-1 shows that the first printing of the book occurred in 1997.

Composed in AGaramond and MCPdigital by Macmillan Computer Publishing

Printed in the United States of America

Trademarks

President   Richard K. Swadley

Publisher and Director of Acquisitions   Jordan Gold

Director of Product Development   Dean Miller

Executive Editor   Beverly M. Eppink

Managing Editor   Jodi Jensen

Indexing Manager   Johnna L. VanHoose

Director of Marketing   Kelli S. Spencer

Product Marketing Manager   Wendy Gilbride

Acquisitions Editor
David B. Mayhew

Development Editor
Scott D. Meyers

Production Editor
Tonya R. Simpson

Copy Editors
Kimberly K. Hannel
Bart Reed

Indexer
Kelly Talbot

Technical Reviewer
Brad Meyers

Editorial Coordinators
Mandie Rowell
Katie Wise

Marketing Coordinator
Linda Beckwith

Technical Edit Coordinator
Lorraine E. Schaffer

Editorial Assistants
Carol Ackerman
Andi Richter
Rhonda Tinch-Mize
Karen Williams

Cover Designer
Karen Ruggles

Book Designer
Gary Adair

Copy Writer
David Reichwein

Production Team Supervisors
Brad Chinn
Andrew Stone

Production
Cyndi Davis-Hubler
Lana Dominguez
Chris Livengood
Ian Smith

Overview

Contents

Acknowledgments

Although my name goes on the cover, this book wouldn't be a reality without the hard work and dedication of countless people. First and foremost, I'd like to acknowledge my wife Liz, who is busy herself in grad school but found the time to edit, research, and help me out on this project.

There are several individuals at Sams.net who deserve to be thanked as well. Beverly Eppink and David Mayhew were extraordinarily patient and supportive—the best set of editors I've worked with. Tonya Simpson guided this book through the publishing process, and the rest of the crew—Bart, Brad, Kim, and Scott—helped make this book a high-quality publication.

About the Author

Andy Shafran has been writing computer books for several years. He actually enjoys working with the Internet, World Wide Web, and related information technologies such as Lotus Notes. Born in Columbus, Ohio, Andy recently graduated from The Ohio State University with a degree in Computer Science Engineering. He now lives in Cincinnati, the Queen City, and is an avid Reds and baseball fan.

He has written several other computer books, including *Creating Your Own Web Pages*, *Creating Your Own Web Graphics*, and others.

When he's not writing he enjoys live theater, particularly Broadway shows. He also loves traveling abroad and is constantly making excuses to buy yet another plane ticket to a foreign country. You can talk to Andy via e-mail at andy@shafran.com or visit his WWW page at http://www.shafran.com.

Tell Us What You Think!

As a reader, you are the most important critic and commentator of our books. We value your opinion and want to know what we're doing right, what we could do better, what areas you'd like to see us publish in, and any other words of wisdom you're willing to pass our way. You can help us make strong books that meet your needs and give you the computer guidance you require.

Do you have access to the World Wide Web? Then check out our site at http://www.mcp.com.

JUST A MINUTE

> If you have a technical question about this book, call the technical support line at 317-581-3833, or send e-mail to support@mcp.com.

As the team leader of the group that created this book, I welcome your comments. You can fax, e-mail, or write me directly to let me know what you did or didn't like about this book—as well as what we can do to make our books stronger. Here's the information:

Fax: 317-581-4669

E-mail: Beverly M. Eppink   mset_mgr@sams.mcp.com

Mail: Beverly M. Eppink
          Comments Department
          Sams Publishing
          201 W. 103rd Street
          Indianapolis, IN 46290

Introduction

The Internet and World Wide Web are phenomenal innovations. Anytime, anywhere, you can communicate with anyone in the world. You can send e-mail, visit Web sites, or even chat directly through your computer. The Internet has revolutionized the way people can communicate and exchange information with one another.

Blazing the Internet's brazen path has been the World Wide Web (WWW). The WWW is what's commonly called a *killer app* in computer talk. A killer app is a program or innovation that single-handedly changes the way computers are used and justifies their purchase, education, and use. Killer apps are few and far between—Lotus 123, Microsoft Windows, and WordPerfect are just a few. The World Wide Web and its accompanying software, Web browsers, are the killer apps in today's world.

Using your browser, you can access the WWW and shop for groceries, learn about your favorite movies, see a baseball game, or get live news coverage. The WWW is so popular because it is so easy to use; and more importantly, so easy to add on to. Anyone in the world can create their own strands of the WWW and interlink them with other related pieces.

This book is all about building your own section of the Web. Over the next 24 hours (or 24 1-hour sessions) you'll learn all about using the best program out there for creating sites on the WWW. Microsoft FrontPage is a fantastic program that lets you build world-class Web sites without becoming a professional programmer or techno afficionado.

This book is structured to teach you the basics of Microsoft FrontPage 98. It is broken into 24 easy-to-digest chapters that all focus on teaching you a new piece or concept of building a Web site using FrontPage 98. This book is all about creating a personalized corner on the WWW as soon as possible—in a painless manner.

You'll enjoy the friendly writing and goal-oriented nature of the book, and you won't waste time learning unimportant details that won't make your site better and more enjoyable to the thousands of people you hope will stop by.

The first section of the book introduces you to some of the important concepts that will help you digest the next 24 hours. You'll learn how the book is structured, get a tentative roadmap to some of the most important sections, and learn what to expect from the next few hundred pages. So read on and enjoy *Teach Yourself Microsoft FrontPage 98 in 24 Hours*!

Accompanying Web Site

Because this book is about creating Web sites with Microsoft FrontPage, it's only appropriate to have an accompanying site that's geared toward you, the reader:

`http://www.shafran.com/frontpage98`

This Web site has updated information about Microsoft FrontPage and important Web-related sites that are of interest to you. You'll find all the examples described in this book, a listing of important resources that will help you build your site, and important graphics and tools to make your job easier. This companion Web site goes hand in hand with the book and should be visited by everyone.

How to Use This Book

This book was written so you could read it one chapter at a time and learn all about FrontPage 98. By reading it from cover to cover, you'll know all about making great Web sites and publishing to the WWW. Realistically though, you probably aren't going to sit down and read this book straight through. With that in mind, here are four possible alternative paths through this book. Each path is geared toward a different type of user with a different goal.

1. "I just bought FrontPage 98 and don't know a thing about HTML or the WWW." This path will teach you the basics of Web publishing and help you get a simple site out there immediately.

   ☐ Read Hour 1, "Welcome to Web Publishing."

   ☐ Read Hour 2, "Installing and Using FrontPage."

   ☐ Read Hour 4, "FrontPage Editor Basics."

   ☐ Now create your first FrontPage Web (a few small pages).

   ☐ Read Hour 17, "Publishing to the WWW."

2. "I'm familiar with a Web browser and very simple HTML, but I want to create more exciting pages than I have today." This path leads you through adding some of the fun stuff to your Web site.

   ☐ Read Hour 2, "Installing and Using FrontPage."

   ☐ Read Hour 5, "Adding Style to Your Text."

   ☐ Skim Hour 7, "Constructing Tables."

   ☐ Read Hour 9, "Understanding and Using Web Graphics."

   ☐ Update your Web page using these new techniques. Make sure you incorporate colors and tables.

   ☐ Finish up with a bang and read Hour 21, "Applying Web Themes."

3. "I'm experienced with FrontPage 97 and want to learn FrontPage 98's new features." This path is a highlight of the best new features in FrontPage 98—you won't be disappointed.

☐ Read Hour 11, "Working with Image Composer."

☐ Read Hour 13, "Framing Your Web Page."

☐ Read Hour 18, "Enabling Style Sheets."

☐ Read Hour 21, "Applying Web Themes."

☐ Jazz up your existing site. Make sure you use some custom-built graphics and learn about style sheets.

☐ Blow your visitors away by skimming through Hour 24, "Finale: Building a Home Page from Scratch."

☐ Finish up by reading Hour 22, "Site Design Tips."

4. "I need to create an interactive site where I exchange information with my visitors." This path leads you through the chapters that describe visitor interaction.

☐ Start out with Hour 2, "Installing and Using FrontPage."

☐ Carefully read Hour 3, "Quickstart: Using the FrontPage Templates."

☐ Read Hour 12, "Imagemap Education."

☐ Read Hour 23, "Forms."

☐ Create your interactive Web site. Use a template and include a discussion site and even an interactive form or two.

☐ Finish this path by reading Hour 22, "Site Design Tips," and then carefully reading Hour 19, "Managing Your Web Site."

Special Highlighted Elements

There are several special sections and asides included in this book. Many have their own icon or pointer that helps draw your eye to an important or related piece of information. This section describes each of the different special sections you'll encounter while reading this book.

 This icon is used whenever a new or complicated term is introduced. You'll see a definition and proper usage of the term described in this box.

TIME SAVER

Time Savers are cool tips or tricks on how you can save time when stepping through a process.

JUST A MINUTE

This is an important or extended discussion on a specific topic for creating Web pages. You might learn the history behind a product or a special related technique germane to the discussion.

COFFEE BREAK

Coffee Breaks are entertaining asides and related information that might be useful to know, but are not directly applicable to learning FrontPage or creating a Web site.

Q&A, Quizzes, and Activities

At the end of each hour there are three important sections: Questions and Answers, Quizzes, and Activities. The Q&A section answers several questions that you might have thought of while reading through the hour. The Quiz section is a reminder of the chapter you just read, and it highlights the important concepts.

Finally, the Activities section provides a roadmap for which next steps you should take after successfully finishing the current hour.

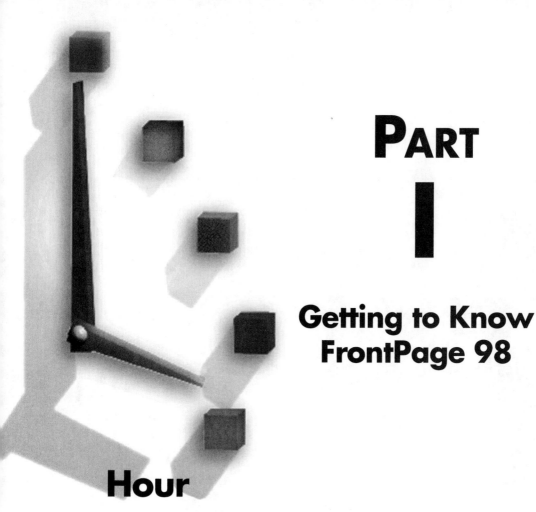

PART
I

Getting to Know FrontPage 98

Hour

Hour 1

Welcome to Web Publishing

The advent of the World Wide Web (WWW), which is only a few years old, has revolutionized how people communicate electronically with each other. Now, rather than send e-mail across the world, you can visit a person's or a company's Web site. This flexibility enables everyone to create their own custom information and make it available to anyone with a Web browser.

In this hour you'll learn some history behind Web publishing and see how Microsoft FrontPage makes it easier than ever for you to build your own personal presence on the Web.

Before you can start publishing on the Web or use FrontPage, you should first spend some time browsing. By using either Netscape Navigator/Communicator or Microsoft Internet Explorer (IE), visit various places on the Internet to see some examples of different Web sites.

If you are new to the World Wide Web, here a few sites you'll want to stop by before publishing on the Web. These sites will give you an idea of some of the different types of places you can visit—and possibly build.

- ☐ `http://www.yahoo.com`
- ☐ `http://www.microsoft.com`
- ☐ `http://www.samspublishing.com`
- ☐ `http://www.shafran.com`

In this hour you'll learn about the following topics:

- ☐ How the WWW started and the first few generations of Web publishing tools
- ☐ Simple HTML file creation and usage
- ☐ How FrontPage 98 fits into the publishing paradigm

History of Web Publishing

 The *Web* is a global network made up of thousands of different computers constantly talking to one another. Each computer on the WWW is called a *Web server* and contains many different HTML files.

One of the most basic features of the Web is the capability for one HTML file to link to another. This embedded hyperlink enables you to connect two pieces of information even if they sit on different Web servers across the world from each other. Therefore, you could link the *National Geographic*'s home page (`http://www.nationalgeographic.com`) to a home page in Sudan that talks about wildlife and expeditions. You as a user wouldn't know—or even care—where the different files are located as long as they are linked properly.

It doesn't take much imagination to see where the Web got its name. With hyperlinks pointing back and forth across the world, if you were to draw each link on a map of the world, they would quickly make the world look like a gigantic spider's home.

Web pages have been around since 1991, when the World Wide Web was invented. Back then, a group of individuals collaborated to create several standards that enabled computers around the world to talk to each other electronically. One of the most important standards they created was HTML, which stands for *Hypertext Markup Language*. HTML, the programming language behind each and every Web page, controls exactly how text and graphics are displayed.

HTML was a tremendous innovation because all of a sudden anyone, anywhere could create a page of information and make it available to anyone else, anywhere else in the world. Practically overnight, the Web publishing industry started booming.

HTML files are commonly referred to as *Web pages*. Currently, literally millions of different Web pages make up the WWW.

The other important innovation besides HTML was the Web browser. *Web browsers* read HTML files and decide how they should be displayed in a graphical manner. Browsers turn the boring and standard HTML files into dazzling and interactive sites that include different colors, cool images, and even multimedia sound and audio snippets. Browsers were the glue that made HTML and the Web so popular.

Today, you're probably familiar with two important browsers: Microsoft Internet Explorer (IE) and Netscape Navigator/Communicator (often just referred to as "Netscape's browser"). IE is free software—anyone around the world can use it without charge—and you can download a trial version of the Netscape browser, which you then are supposed to pay for.

More recently, a third important innovation has hastened the popularity of Web publishing—the HTML editor. Before the HTML editor, creating a Web page required in-depth knowledge of HTML, because you had to type each specific code individually into a simple text editor such as WordPad or Notepad. Now, several high-quality HTML editors are out there, of which Microsoft FrontPage is the best of the breed.

These three components—HTML, browsers, and HTML editors—are all important to understanding how Web publishing works. This section gives you more information on how these different pieces are interrelated and work with each other to create Web pages.

HTML History

HTML is a markup language that describes how something should logically appear on a computer screen. HTML is stored as special tags inside regular text files. In fact, the only way you can tell HTML files apart from text files without looking inside them is by looking at their file extension—usually .HTM or .HTML instead of .TXT for text files or .DOC for Microsoft Word files.

As mentioned before, HTML files require a separate program to read through them and then decide how to display that. This separate HTML interpreter is called a Web browser. Today, there are two popular Web browsers—Microsoft Internet Explorer and Netscape Navigator/ Communicator. In simple terms, WWW browsers read HTML files and decide how to display the logical markup tags that are included within them.

If you read through an HTML file (and you will during Hour 20, "Under the Hood with HTML"), you'll find it somewhat readable. For example, to make a piece of text appear bold within a browser, you would use the following line of HTML:

```
<B>This text appears bold</B>
```

You probably understand that text surround by the <B> and </B> tags means that it should appear as bold text on-screen. Notice how that is all the information an HTML file gives about displaying bold text. It doesn't tell you what font or size text to use, nor does it explicitly describe any special traits of bold text. How to render the bold text within the tags is completely up to the browser.

CAUTION

Because of the way Web browsers interpret HTML tags, Web pages might look slightly different when viewed with different browsers. This difference is because of the way HTML is geared toward logical formatting. HTML simply uses the <B> tag to indicate that something is important enough to be marked for emphasis. It lets the browser take care of the physical formatting of interpreting the logical HTML tags.

For example, Netscape might make bold text appear darker than bold text within Internet Explorer. There are several subtle differences between IE and Netscape when displaying individual snippets of HTML. However, the biggest worry are *browser-specific* tags, or pieces of HTML code that work only with a single Web browser. Usually introduced by a single company, browser-specific tags will work only within either IE or Netscape.

One prime example is the Microsoft-introduced Marquee tag. The Marquee tag scrolls text across the screen so that it rolls like an old-style marquee. Netscape does not support this tag; therefore, a Web page using this tag looks significantly different in one browser versus the other.

In general, all tags work within the popular Web browsers with just a few subtle differences in how they appear, but you'll want to be careful to always look at your Web sites with IE and Netscape to make sure each page is acceptable, because you can't control what the browser visitors will be using when they stop by your pages.

The HTML language is defined by a worldwide standards organization that continually seeks to improve the language. Over the years, HTML has undergone several revisions and changes as new tags are introduced and new features included within the language. The current HTML standard is level 4.0. You can keep up-to-date on the trials and tribulations of the HTML standard by visiting the World Wide Web Consortium (W3C) home page at http://www.w3.org/pub/WWW/ (see Figure 1.1).

1

Figure 1.1.
The Web Consortium is where HTML began.

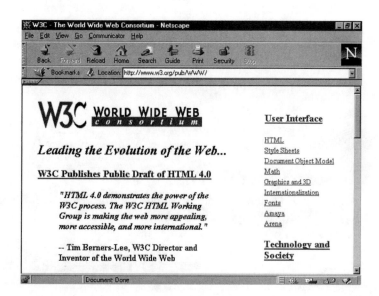

There are many different components of HTML besides controlling how text should appear within a browser. HTML also enables you to add graphics to a Web page, build bulleted lists, and create simple and complex tables. The crown jewel of HTML is the capability to embed hyperlinks to other pages across the world. Any file can contain a link to another Web page if it uses the correct tag.

Browser Background

Browsers are a key ingredient to the WWW working properly. Without Web browsers, no one could see the special markup tags that are inside HTML files.

Web browsers are the software that everyone must have on their desktops to explore the Internet. When reading HTML files, browsers must communicate with one of the thousands of Web servers that make up the WWW. For example, point your Web browser to http://www.shafran.com/index.htm. You are actually telling your browser to find the computer www.shafran.com and asking it to send back the file named index.htm. When it is contacted, the Web server looks for the requested file and then zips it right back to the browser. It also sends back any graphics included within index.htm so that the page can be displayed properly. Every time you visit a different site on the WWW, this same process repeats itself over and over again.

To use Microsoft FrontPage, you must have a current version of Internet Explorer or Netscape Communicator. Use the following links to download a current release of your Web browser:

☐ Microsoft Internet Explorer

http://www.microsoft.com/ie

☐ Netscape Communicator

http://www.netscape.com/download

Creating HTML Files

When HTML was originally designed, it could be built only with a simple text editor. You simply typed in all your text and then retyped and added the proper HTML tags. Figure 1.2 shows an HTML file being edited in Notepad.

Figure 1.2.

Using Notepad is not the easiest way to create HTML files.

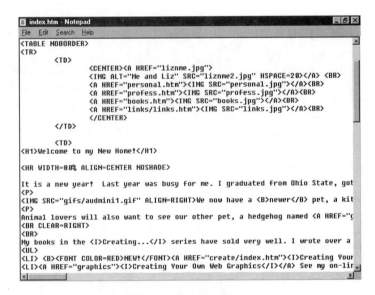

As you can imagine, learning how to build Web sites with these types of simple HTML tools takes some time and effort.

Since then, several programs have been created that aid in the creation of Web sites, Microsoft FrontPage being one of the best.

When using FrontPage, you don't need to know any HTML because FrontPage takes care of all the difficult work for you. In FrontPage, if you want a line to appear bold, you simply highlight it with your mouse and click the Bold icon.

1

In the background, FrontPage takes care of generating all the HTML code required. Therefore, when you save a specific Web page from FrontPage, you are really creating a textual HTML file. Then, you use your favorite Web browser to read that HTML and interpret each individual tag. FrontPage lets you go under the covers and edit your HTML directly, but nearly 99 percent of the time, you'll use FrontPage's graphical interface when you build Web sites. Figure 1.3 shows a Web page being edited with FrontPage.

Figure 1.3.

Usually, you don't see a hint of HTML when editing with FrontPage.

The Future of Web Publishing

As the WWW, HTML, Web browsers, and Web editors continue to evolve, you'll find that programs such as Microsoft FrontPage will become more robust, easier to use, and much more like a full-fledged word processor such as Microsoft Word, or even a desktop publishing tool such as Adobe PageMaker.

FrontPage is a good harbinger of how in the future you'll have a Web editor, Web management tool, graphics creation tool, and publishing tool all rolled together as a complete package. These different tools will continue to be integrated. Also, they will be easier for beginners to use and will contain more powerful automated options for the power user.

Other Web enhancements you can expect to see are new ways to add multimedia clips into pages as well as continued improvements of Java, a new programming language developed by Sun.

Introducing FrontPage 98

Now that you understand a little of the history of HTML and Web publishing, it's time to look a little closer at Microsoft FrontPage 98. This book focuses on showing you how to use all the features within FrontPage 98 to create a great-looking Web site without being a professional HTML programmer. You'll find that FrontPage is an excellent, easy-to-use program that simplifies what used to be a complex job of lining up hundreds of different tags per page.

The first lesson to learn about is FrontPage's terminology. In FrontPage, a group of Web pages that are related to one another—often called a Web site—is always referred to as a *FrontPage Web*. This is different than the World Wide Web (WWW), which is usually referred to in the phrase "browsing the Web." That "Web" is the set of computers all linked to one another around the world that send pages of HTML back and forth as individuals and users request them.

Actually, FrontPage isn't just one program, but rather a suite of related programs that all work together and make Web publishing as easy as possible. Just as you use the different components of Microsoft Office in certain situations, you'll find yourself working with all of the different pieces of FrontPage interchangeably.

Here's a list of the different FrontPage components:

- ☐ FrontPage Explorer
- ☐ FrontPage Editor
- ☐ Task Manager
- ☐ Image Composer
- ☐ Publishing Wizard

During the next hour, you'll get a much closer look at installing and using these different—but important—components of FrontPage 98.

Each of these different components contribute individual pieces to publishing a Web site. But the best part of FrontPage is how they all work together. For example, you have much more than a good HTML editor at your fingertips with FrontPage. You have a separate tool to help you manage large and complicated sites—the FrontPage Explorer—and another tool that keeps track of what pages are finished and which ones need more work—the Task Manager.

In addition, a complete Web graphics creation and editing program—Image Composer—eliminates most of your need to purchase and use a separate nonintegrated program such as Adobe Photoshop. And, finally, FrontPage comes with all the tools necessary to copy your Web pages from your computer onto the Internet. All together, FrontPage is the pinnacle in Web publishing tools and is a great value for your money.

The First Step: Planning Your Web

Before you can start creating your own Web site or even learning Microsoft FrontPage, the very first step in Web publishing is coming up with a plan. You don't need a complex plan or detailed blueprints for your entire Web site, but here are a few questions you might want to think about when creating your plan:

- ☐ What's my goal behind creating this Web site: selling products? advertising? personal use?

- ☐ Who's going to see/use this site?

- ☐ How much time do I have to create and then maintain this site? A lot? Only a few hours?

Coming up with a plan for your Web site helps you identify what type of information you are going to include and how your site will be organized.

For example, if you are building a personal site for yourself or your family, you'll want to start with some background on who you are, where you work, and maybe include pictures of your family. Look at Figure 1.4. It's a personal Web page and simply starts with background information and a picture.

Figure 1.4.

You can visit James's page for yourself at http://www.qtm.net/~springsteen/.

On the other hand, you might be trying to sell products or offer support to customers with your Web page like Jasc software does at http://www.jasc.com (see Figure 1.5). As the maker of a shareware graphics tool called Paint Shop Pro, Jasc gets thousands of hits from people who want to buy its products or get technical help. You can tell Jasc has an entirely different focus for its Web page than simply providing information about its company.

Figure 1.5.

Jasc's home page sells software, offers technical help, and serves as a shopping mall for its entire suite of products.

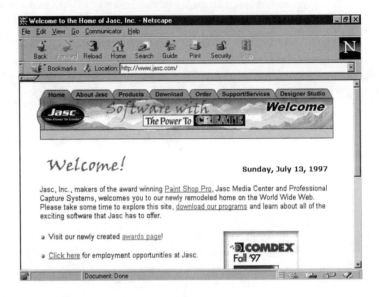

Don't be afraid to explore the WWW and browse different individual and corporate sites to get ideas for how you can plan and design your Web site.

When you have a few ideas in your mind, the next step is to draw on paper what you would like the site to look like. Do you have a picture of yourself or a logo you want included? Sketch it on the paper. Write out any large headlines and jot down a note or two about the information you must make sure you cover. Will you need to have separate pages that link together? Draw each page individually and connect the ones that point to each other.

After you've had a chance to sketch out your initial site, it's time to move on and start learning FrontPage so that you can build each of these pages. Always keep your plans handy so you can scribble changes or add notes as you continue to think about your site.

Summary

This first hour introduced you to a lot of background information that you needed to know before you could start using FrontPage to build your own Web site. HTML, the WWW, browsers, and editors are all important pieces in the Web publishing equation once you know how they all fit together. You should be comfortable with how Web publishing works and how FrontPage 98 comes with all the necessary tools.

1

Q&A

Q **Why do all the sites I visit start with a www, as in www.shafran.com?**

A Before the Web was created, the Internet was still around, and each computer had its own unique name—shafran.com, mcp.com, and so on. This unique name was used for a variety of purposes, such as helping e-mail route its way to the proper person. When the WWW was invented, the originators wanted some standard way of separating it as a different type of Internet service from e-mail, gopher, newsgroups, and the others. So, by default, all sites on the Internet who put up their own Web server just added a www to their unique name. Today, most sites don't need the www to find them, but they still regularly use it. If you point to http://jasc.com, it takes you to the same place as http://www.jasc.com.

Q **Microsoft sometimes advertises that FrontPage is a third-generation editing tool. What were the first two generations and is the third much better?**

A HTML editors have been maturing very quickly over the past few years. When they were first released, HTML editors were nothing much more than Notepad with a few extra buttons that would add the HTML tags when you clicked them. You would have to read through your text file and you still needed to understand how all the tags worked with one another.

The second generation of editors was the first to be called WYSIWYG (What You See Is What You Get). They offered a graphical look and feel and displayed text as it was supposed to look within a browser, and they also hid most of the HTML from you. They were a gigantic step forward in making Web publishing accessible to normal everyday users.

FrontPage 98 is a third-generation tool. It still has much of the same look and feel as its previous version—but only when it comes to the HTML editing. What makes FrontPage 98 so special is the integration of all the other tools that ease the publishing process. For example, FrontPage lets you add a standard header, footer, or navigation bar to all your pages, and it will keep them up-to-date as various pages change. This type of automation and assistance of Web publishing makes FrontPage a fantastic tool. Who knows what the next release will bring!

Workshop

The Workshop contains quiz questions and an Activities section to help reinforce what you've learned in this hour. Try not to look at the quiz answers until you've tried to work them out yourself!

Quiz

1. Give your own definition of the World Wide Web. Explain the difference between the WWW and the Internet.

2. Who substantiates and validates HTML and ratifies new additions to the language?

3. What's the first step in creating a Web site?

Answers

1. The WWW is a global network of computers that all link back and forth to one another and can be accessed with a special piece of software called a browser.

   The Internet is the physical set of computers and their communications line between each other, whereas the Web is software that runs on top of most computers connected to the Internet.

2. The Web Consortium (`http://www.w3.org/pub/WWW/`) is in charge of all versions of HTML. Future enhancements are voted on by this standards-setting organization.

3. Making a solid plan. Explore the Web and decide what type of site you want to build, and then write it down on paper. You'll be significantly more successful when you have a goal in mind for your overall site.

Activities

This hour covered only the basics of Web publishing and FrontPage. Read Hour 2, "Installing and Using FrontPage," for a detailed description of each of the various FrontPage components and how they work with each other.

Do you want to get started and build a Web site quickly? Go to Hour 3, "Quickstart: Using the FrontPage Templates," and you'll see how you can make a complete site from scratch in a short time.

No matter how advanced FrontPage is, you'll still need to know the basics of HTML and how it is used to build Web pages. There are many, many books available in a bookstore about HTML, or you can read some of them for free on-line at the Macmillan Computer Publishing Web site. Visit the Personal Bookshelf at `http://www.mcp.com/personal/` for more information.

Hour 2

Installing and Using FrontPage

During this hour, you'll learn how to install and recognize the various FrontPage components. Although these components are easy to install, there are a handful of installation options that you might want to take advantage of that are not normally selected. Then, after installation is complete, there are a few important details that you must understand before FrontPage will work properly on your computer.

The most important part of this hour is the virtual tour of all the components and tools FrontPage has to offer. You'll learn how to recognize the FrontPage Explorer, Editor, Image Composer, and more. Specifically in this hour, you'll learn how to do the following:

- ☐ Customize your FrontPage installation to meet your specific needs
- ☐ Run FrontPage for the first time and configure your personal Web server
- ☐ Use and recognize each separate FrontPage component

Installing FrontPage

When you purchased FrontPage, you probably got a simple installation manual that leads you through the basics of adding FrontPage to your computer. In general, the manual indicates that you should insert the FrontPage 98 CD-ROM into your computer and then follow the installation instructions that appear automatically. If your installation instructions don't pop up, you can install FrontPage 98 by clicking the Start button and choosing Run. In the Run dialog box, type e:\setup.exe (see Figure 2.1).

Replace the e with the proper letter of your CD-ROM drive (this is often d).

Figure 2.1.

If FrontPage 98 doesn't install automatically, the Run dialog box triggers the setup program.

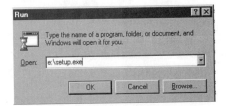

For the most part, the FrontPage 98 installation is self-guiding and easy to follow. FrontPage first asks you for your name and company and then requires you to read the standard license agreement from Microsoft. Keep clicking the Next button until you arrive at the Setup Type dialog box shown in Figure 2.2.

Figure 2.2.

Choose the FrontPage installation you want to use.

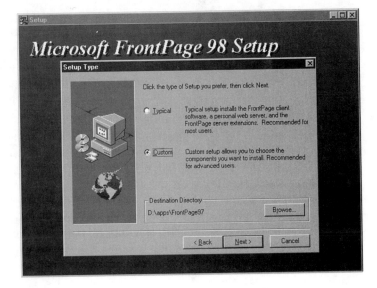

By default, if you click the Next button, FrontPage will install the basic FrontPage program on your computer. All the important components will be included, but you will be missing several important details. Click the Custom radio button and then the Next button to see all the goodies you miss by choosing the default FrontPage 98 installation.

FrontPage brings up the Select Components dialog box, as shown in Figure 2.3. Notice there are several components that are not selected to be installed. You'll want two of them—Additional FrontPage Themes and Additional Clipart—for your own use when building sites. You'll learn more about clipart and themes later in this book, but you definitely want them installed. Select these two components and then click the Next button.

Figure 2.3.

Pick the important pieces of FrontPage you want to install on your computer.

TIME SAVER

You can also change the default location on your computer where FrontPage 98 gets installed from the Select Components dialog box. You might want to change the default installation path if you have additional disk space on another drive or keep all of your programs together under a special subdirectory.

CAUTION

If you are extremely tight on disk space, you might not want to install the extra FrontPage 98 components. Although they are very useful, they can suck up several additional megabytes of space on a computer's hard drive. Make sure you have enough room to install all the components you select, and make sure you have at least 40MB of free space left over after installation.

FrontPage then starts copying and installing files onto your computer. Finally, when you're nearly finished with the installation, FrontPage brings up the dialog box shown in Figure 2.4.

Figure 2.4.

You must type a username and password so that FrontPage will recognize you.

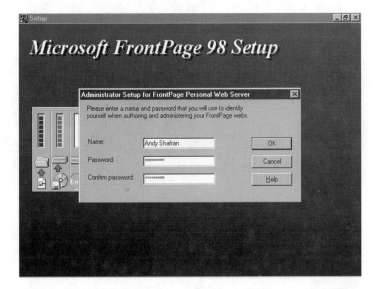

FrontPage 98 uses this dialog box to validate you each time you start editing a Web. You must have a username and password. Write down your case-sensitive username and password on a scrap of paper in case you forget them. Don't forget to store that paper in a secure location.

FrontPage usernames and passwords are also used when uploading your pages to the Web. You'll not be able to create or edit FrontPage Webs without the proper FrontPage name and password for your computer.

JUST A MINUTE

Did you forget your password? You can always uninstall and then reinstall FrontPage 98. Don't forget to copy all your existing FrontPage Webs to another directory before uninstalling FrontPage.

2

After you click OK, FrontPage finishes the installation.

Running for the First Time

Before running FrontPage for the first time, you must have your own Internet connection set up and configured on your computer. If you can explore the Internet using a Web browser, your Internet connection is already established. Connecting to the Internet requires an *Internet provider*—such as America Online, CompuServe, or one of hundreds of companies around the world.

When installation is complete, it's time to start FrontPage for the first time. To start FrontPage 98, choose Programs | Microsoft FrontPage from the Windows 95 Start button.

Your Computer's Hostname

TCP/IP settings are complicated configuration variables that control exactly how your computer connects and communicates with other computers on the Internet.

NEW TERM   The first time you start FrontPage, several one-time configuration settings are set. FrontPage brings up a simple dialog box that tells you it will look into your TCP/IP settings to determine some important information (see Figure 2.5).

Click OK to continue, and a few moments later, FrontPage returns with an important message: your computer's hostname (see Figure 2.6). This hostname is the name of your

Figure 2.5.

This message just lets you know FrontPage might be searching your computer for a few minutes.

computer using the FrontPage Personal Web Server. The Personal Web Server lets you test and explore your FrontPage sites using a browser, just as if you were talking to one of the computers on the Internet. So instead of pointing your browser to a default Web URL such as `http://www.shafran.com`, you point your browser to your computer's Personal Web Server.

Figure 2.6.

Write down the hostname FrontPage tells you.

In this example, this computer's hostname is *none*. So, to point to the Personal Web Server that comes with FrontPage, you'd point your browser to http://none. You'll see this concept in action later in the chapter.

COFFEE BREAK

By this point, you're probably asking, "What's really happening with all this talk of TCP/IP addresses and hostnames?" Here is a long-winded, but thorough explanation of TCP/IP addresses, hostnames, and how they relate to you.

Each computer on the Internet has its own unique way to identify itself among other computers around the world. This unique number is called the *TCP/IP address*. TCP/IP works basically the same way as your mail address. There are several different components, and no computer in the world can share the same TCP/IP address. These addresses are cryptic looking—125.12.0.1, 199.88.17.3, and so on.

Using your browser, you can retrieve any Web site by pointing to a TCP/IP address. But that is really confusing. No one understands where 182.13.99.0 points to—it's not as descriptive as saying "44 West Main Street, Cincinnati, OH 45202."

To solve this problem, the Internet community created the concept of a *hostname*, or an easy-to-remember shortcut for each TCP/IP address across the world. Using a hostname, you can point to http://www.mcp.com, and let the computers on the Internet (called *domain name servers*) translate that URL into the complicated TCP/IP address.

Whew! Now on to the important stuff—what does all this mean to you as you use FrontPage 98? One important component of FrontPage 98 is the Personal Web Server. The *Personal Web Server* is special software that receives URL requests and properly sends pages back to the requesting browser. Therefore, using your browser, you can point to your own Personal Web Server and test and explore any FrontPage Web you create. In fact, that's how you see any page you create—by pointing toward your Personal Web Server.

Well, your Personal Web Server must have its own hostname so that you can properly point to it, instead of to a different computer elsewhere in the world. So, FrontPage looks through your TCP/IP settings, determined when you set up your Internet connection, and finds a name for you. Want to see your hostname for yourself? Follow these steps:

1. Click the Start button and choose Settings I Control Panel.
2. Double-click the icon labeled Network to bring up the Network dialog box.
3. Double-click the component labeled TCP/IP to bring up the TCP/IP Properties dialog box.
4. Click the tab marked DNS Configuration and look in the box labeled Host. You'll notice that the host configured for you is the exact same name as the host of your FrontPage Personal Web Server.

This topic is pretty complicated and you don't need to worry about it too much when creating Web sites. If you are interested in learning more about TCP/IP and hostnames, check out *The Internet Unleashed*, a comprehensive reference to the Internet, published by Sams.net.

Creating a Web

After you've settled your computer's hostname, FrontPage brings up the Getting Started dialog box (see Figure 2.7). From here, you can create a new FrontPage Web from scratch or edit an existing set of pages.

Figure 2.7.

Now you're ready to create a Web!

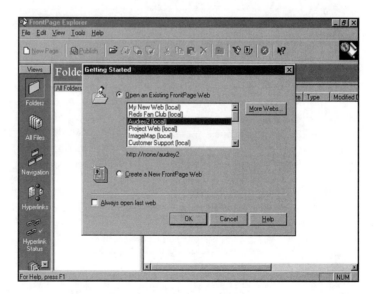

Hour 3, "Quickstart: Using the FrontPage Templates," teaches you all about creating a new Web from scratch. The rest of this hour assumes that you are editing an existing Web site so you can learn the various FrontPage components.

Select the FrontPage Web you want to open, and click OK. FrontPage will immediately start the Personal Web Server component and prompt you for your user ID and password (see Figure 2.8).

Figure 2.8.

Remember the password you wrote down earlier? Here's where you use it.

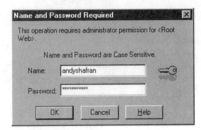

Getting to Know FrontPage

When you started FrontPage, you actually started up the FrontPage Explorer, the main component from which all the other pieces are controlled.

This section describes how the FrontPage Explorer works and shows you all the other important components that come along with the FrontPage package.

Starting the FrontPage Explorer

The FrontPage Explorer is the center of operations for the whole Web creation process. From here you can call up the other components of FrontPage, including the Page Editor, the To Do list, the Image Composer, and more. You'll always have the FrontPage Explorer open when you're editing or creating any aspect of a Web.

Besides calling the other features, the FrontPage Explorer is also used to manage and control Webwide options. It offers several different graphical views of all the pages within your Web. Each of these views is important because it shows different information about the various pages within the entire Web site.

Before you learn about the different components of FrontPage, it is important to become familiar with the seven different views that can be displayed inside Explorer. You can switch between the seven different views by clicking each labeled icon on the left side of the FrontPage Explorer.

JUST A MINUTE

Don't confuse the FrontPage Explorer with the default Windows 95 File Explorer. The FrontPage Explorer only lets you see and manipulate files that are stored within different FrontPage Webs. The Windows Explorer lets you browse through your computer's hard drive and move files from one directory to another.

2

Folders and All Files Views

The most common view you'll use in FrontPage is the Folders view. This view shows how the entire Web is organized. All HTML files and images are displayed and can be organized into various subdirectories.

Figure 2.9 shows the Folders view looking at a FrontPage Web site. Notice how there are several HTML files displayed as well as an images subdirectory, where all the Web graphics are stored.

Figure 2.9.

Most of your time in the FrontPage Explorer will be spent within the Folders view.

Folders view icon

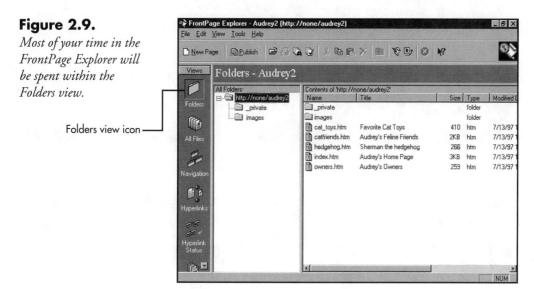

Similar to the Folders view, the All Files view simply lists every file in the entire Web, not sorted and organized by the folder they are within. Figure 2.10 shows the All Files view for the same Web.

Navigation View

The Navigation view is used to build automated navigation bars between Web pages. Navigation bars are advanced and powerful features discussed briefly during Hour 19, "Managing Your Web Site."

Figure 2.10.
The All Files view gives you a complete inventory of the entire Web site.

All Files view icon ——

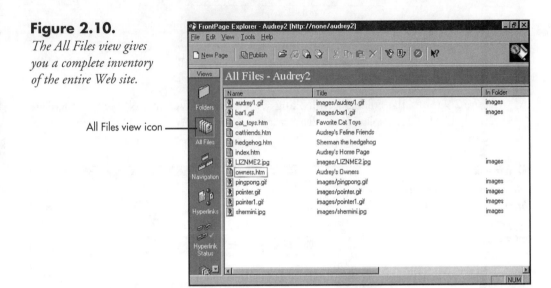

Figure 2.11 shows a simple navigation scheme for this FrontPage Web.

Figure 2.11.
Not too complicated, the navigation scheme is very structured.

Navigation view icon ——

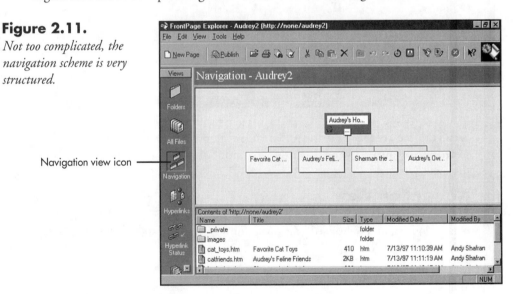

Hyperlinks and Hyperlink Status Views

The Hyperlinks view offers a graphical representation of how each file in your Web is linked to one another. By using a hierarchical system, FrontPage draws lines between linked files.

Figure 2.12 shows how each link comes from the main page in this Web. You'll learn more about building hyperlinks between documents in Hour 8, "Linking Pages Together."

Figure 2.12.

Every link in your entire Web is graphically represented in this view.

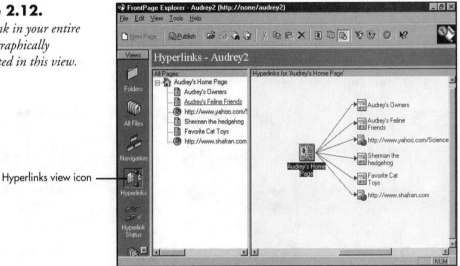

Hyperlinks view icon ————

In a large Web site, managing your hyperlinks can be challenging and confusing—old links can be out of date, pages can be deleted, or filenames can change.

Figure 2.13 shows the Explorer's Hyperlink Status view, where FrontPage keeps track of each link within the Web. FrontPage lets you automatically verify each link in your Web for correctness.

Figure 2.13.
When you have dozens of links in your Web, the Hyperlink Status view becomes a crucial crutch.

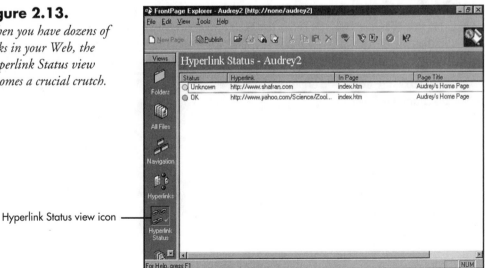

Hyperlink Status view icon ————

Themes View

The Themes view is the most entertaining view in the Explorer. Here you can set Webwide themes. A FrontPage theme is where you can choose an entire motif for your site—text color, headline graphics, background images, and more. FrontPage lets you select from over two dozen different innovative and exciting themes (see Figure 2.14).

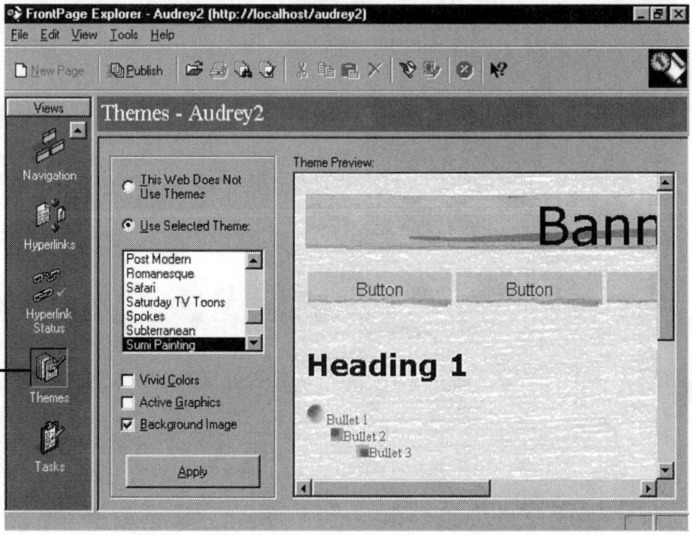

Figure 2.14.

FrontPage shows you each theme as you select it.

Tasks View

The final Explorer view shows a listing of all the tasks you've assigned to be completed. Throughout the process of building your Web, you can often make notes of tasks that should be completed before the Web is finished.

These tasks are stored and organized in the Task view (shown in Figure 2.15) and can be read and completed one at a time.

Figure 2.15.

This electronic task manager ensures that important details won't be forgotten.

Tasks view icon ——

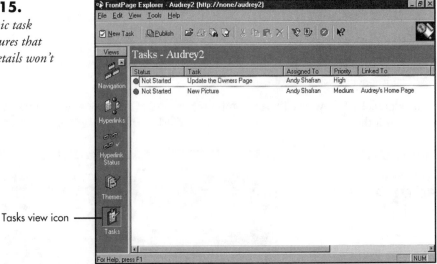

Using the FrontPage Editor

 With all seven Explorer views out of the way, the next important component to learn about is the FrontPage Editor. The Editor is where you actually edit and modify each individual page within your site.

You can start the Editor component of FrontPage by choosing Tools | Show FrontPage Editor from the menu bar. Figure 2.16 shows the Editor in action. You'll learn a great deal more about using the Editor beginning in Hour 4, "FrontPage Editor Basics."

Figure 2.16.

The Editor is the critical piece for building each individual page.

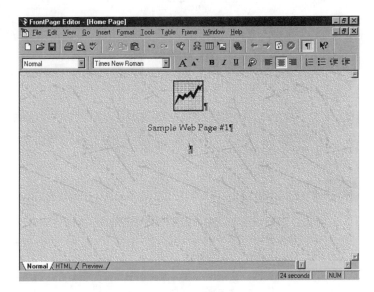

Microsoft Image Composer

 The final FrontPage component you'll learn about in this hour is the Image Composer. This important component lets you create and update graphics specifically geared toward your Web page. Using several included tools, the Image Composer is an important component in the Web creation process.

Figure 2.17 shows the Image Composer working with some Web graphics. You'll learn all about the Image Composer in Hour 11, "Working with Image Composer."

Figure 2.17.

Edit, manipulate, and create images with the Image Composer.

Summary

This hour stepped you through the installation process for FrontPage 98. There are several important details and options you should be aware of while installing FrontPage, and you should understand what happens when you start the Explorer for the first time.

Most importantly, this hour introduced the three most important components of FrontPage: the Explorer, the Editor, and the Image Composer. These three components work interchangeably, and all must be used in order to build a fantastic-looking Web site.

Q&A

Q What are some other components of FrontPage, and when are they used?

A Besides the Explorer, the Editor, and the Image Composer, FrontPage includes a handful of other pieces. First and foremost is the Web Publishing component. This important piece of FrontPage helps upload pages from your computer to the Internet and is discussed in Hour 17, "Publishing to the WWW." In addition, the FrontPage Task Manager is another popular component that manages each task listed in the Task view inside of the FrontPage Explorer.

Q I'm still not sure why the hostname is important to me. How do I use it with my browser?

A When the FrontPage Personal Web Server is running, you can point your browser to any Web that is saved on your computer. To start the Personal Web Server, start FrontPage and open an existing Web. Then point your Web browser to the hostname FrontPage told you about when you started it for the first time. If your hostname is `computer`, then you would point your browser to `http://computer`. You can then explore the various Webs saved within FrontPage.

Workshop

The Workshop contains quiz questions and an Activities section to help reinforce what you've learned in this hour. Try not to look at the quiz answers until you've tried to work them out yourself!

Quiz

1. Name the seven different views within the FrontPage Explorer.
2. How can you change your FrontPage password?
3. What are the two ways to switch between views in the FrontPage Explorer?

Answers

1. The seven views are Folders, All Files, Navigation, Hyperlinks, Hyperlink Status, Themes, and Tasks.
2. You can update your FrontPage password at any time by choosing Tools | Change Password from the menu bar.
3. You can click each icon on the left side of the Editor window or choose the view you want to see from the View menu bar.

Activities

1. This hour should have whetted your appetite to learn more about building Web pages. Jump right into Hour 3, a "quickstart" chapter that describes how to build complete sites with FrontPage templates.
2. Learn how to build each page one at a time by reading Hour 4. This important chapter discusses the techniques and flexibility available when making a Web.

Hour **3**

Quickstart: Using the FrontPage Templates

When it comes to Web-building tools, FrontPage is the complete package. During the first two hours, you learned how to install and get around the basic—and important—FrontPage features. During this hour, you'll learn how to use a complete FrontPage template to create an entire site from scratch.

FrontPage comes with a dozen templates and wizards that automatically build certain pages, add graphics, and dynamically generate links. These templates let you build a site within a few minutes and immediately get a Web presence.

In this hour, you'll learn how to

☐ Identify and use the default FrontPage templates and wizards.

☐ Use templates and wizards to save time and create an attractive Web site

☐ Quickly use some of the site-building and managing tools that FrontPage has to offer

Understanding FrontPage Templates

NEW TERM A *template* is a set of default, blank Web pages that are formatted and customized but contain no actual information or data. A template is really a skeleton of a Web site, and you are expected to flesh out each specific page. For example, a template might contain a Product Information page that creates links to related pages automatically, adds standard header and footer information, and uses a certain font and color scheme. You must type in the product name and specific information such as pricing, availability, and other details. In other words, a template controls how a page appears but not each piece of data that is on it.

The quickest way to get up and running when creating a Web site is to use one of the default FrontPage wizards or templates. FrontPage comes with nearly a dozen different templates that you can use for a variety of different Web sites.

FrontPage will build a Web site automatically by using either a template or a wizard. Templates and wizards are similar but have one major difference. When you're building a site from a wizard, FrontPage asks you a series of informational questions about the site you want to create and then, based on your answers, builds all the pages you require. It's really a great process and works extremely well for simple, good-looking Web sites. Templates simply create a default set of pages automatically, giving you no choices for customization.

This section introduces you to the FrontPage templates and helps you decide when to use a template and identify which one fits your particular needs.

How Templates Work

As you start using FrontPage, normally you'll create your Web site one page at a time. With the FrontPage Editor, you'll type the text you want to appear, add an image or two, and then link your page to another within your Web site or elsewhere on the WWW.

You'll repeat this process several times until you've covered everything that you want to appear on your Web site. Many Web sites are only a single page, whereas others are quite large. Either way, most are built the same way the Egyptian pyramids were: one block at a time.

Templates change that paradigm significantly by giving you the entire framework for your site in one fell swoop. Then, filling in the details on top of that framework and customizing it to fit your particular site is up to you. So, rather than build the Eiffel Tower one level at a time, you start with the complete shell of the building and simply need to add the interior decoration.

As you can imagine, quite a lot of work is still required to customize the framework you get from a template into an attractive site—but not nearly what is required when you create each page from scratch. In addition, most of the templates in FrontPage come with a lot of extra goodies and cool features already added. For example, they come with navigational links

3

between pages, images that serve as headlines and banners, and color-coordinated pages so that they look similar to the others within your same Web site. To continue the building analogy, when you use a template, your site has the plumbing, elevators, and carpet already installed. You just need to add furniture, create some walls, and hang a painting or two.

The FrontPage 98 Templates and Wizards

FrontPage 98 comes with a half-dozen templates and wizards, which are listed and described in Table 3.1.

Table 3.1. FrontPage 98 templates and wizards.

	FrontPage 98 Wizards
Corporate Presence Wizard	This wizard generates an entire complex site for a small business. It builds pages for multiple products, services, and general news and information about the company. By using this template, you'll immediately be able to make a good-looking site for any business. FrontPage enables you to add as many products and services as you would like and will build each page in your theme-coordinated Web site for you.
Discussion Web Wizard	This wizard lets you add a complete threaded discussion to your Web site. You select the discussion topic, the layout for the page, and then let the wizard do all the work for you. Discussion Webs can be added to any FrontPage Web.
	FrontPage 98 Templates
Customer Support Web	This template creates a set of about 20 pages and is perfect for creating a site to share information with your customers. Separate pages include a Frequently Asked Question (FAQ) site, a simple discussion Web, a product download page, a bug listing, an introduction to the site, and the ability to search the whole Web. This template is geared toward supporting a specific product and would work well when integrated with the Corporate Presence Wizard.

continues

Table 3.1. continued

Empty Web	This template creates a blank FrontPage Web with no pages. All the Web settings remain at their defaults and you can create each page individually.
Learning FrontPage	This default template generates pages that go along with the FrontPage user's manual and is intended to show you some of the basic features FrontPage has to offer. With this book in your hand, you won't need to use this template.
Project Web	This template creates a decent template for managing a small project among a handful of individuals. This template builds pages for archived documents, status reports, and a group discussion.

TIME SAVER

Creating an empty FrontPage Web isn't quite as difficult as starting from scratch. When you create a new page, you can select from 40 different single-page templates within the FrontPage Editor. These default one-page templates give you larger and more effective building blocks when generating the site. You'll learn more about these simple one-page templates in Hour 4, "FrontPage Editor Basics."

When Do You Use a Template?

Although templates are very functional and can save a lot of work, they're useful only when you find a specific one that coordinates with the type of Web site you want to build.

Therefore, if you are trying to create a Web site for your small business or want to add a discussion to your pages, the FrontPage templates come in handy. But if you want to make a personal page for you or your family, create a site dedicated to your favorite band, or build a virtual information booth for a governmental candidate, the FrontPage templates and wizards won't quite fit.

As you continue to learn about FrontPage 98, you'll get a better grasp of when you want to build from a template or wizard, when you must use the single-page templates within the FrontPage Editor, and when you must start from scratch.

Whether or not a specific template meets your exact need, you'll want to explore the ones that come by default with FrontPage 98. They'll show you different types of Web sites that you can build and help you understand some of the advanced features.

Building with a Template

Now that you know the basics behind understanding FrontPage templates, it's time to use one and build an entire site.

This section steps you through building a Customer Support Web site by using the provided template. You'll see how the site is generated and then understand how you can make modifications so that the generic Customer Support site is customized for your needs.

Creating a Customer Support Web Site

Follow these steps to create a new Customer Support Web site by using the included template with FrontPage 98:

1. The first step is to start FrontPage from the Windows Start button. By default, FrontPage appears in the Programs submenu after you click the Start button.

2. When FrontPage starts, you must select whether you are opening an existing Web or creating one from scratch. Figure 3.1 shows the Getting Started dialog box, in which you should choose Create a New FrontPage Web.

Figure 3.1.

You can open an existing Web or build a new Web each time you start FrontPage.

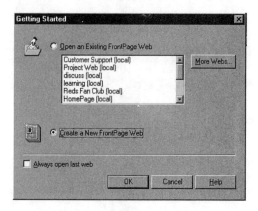

3. In the New FrontPage Web dialog box, select the From Wizard or Template radio button, and then choose the template or wizard to use when generating the Web site. Figure 3.2 shows this dialog box for you.

JUST A MINUTE

Although FrontPage comes with a standard set of templates, Microsoft enables you to create your own customized templates by using the FrontPage Developer's Kit. You can download the kit at http://www.microsoft.com/frontpage/softlib/fs_fp_sdk.htm and learn how to build templates, hotbots, and other customizations for FrontPage.

Figure 3.2.

All registered wizards and templates are available from here.

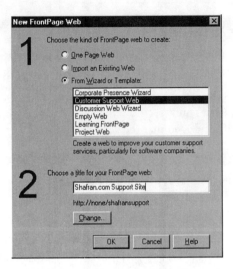

4. For this example, choose the Customer Support Web template and click OK. FrontPage then creates the entire Web site from the template. Figure 3.3 shows the document in the newly created template site.

Figure 3.3.

Quite a few files are built when you use the Customer Support template.

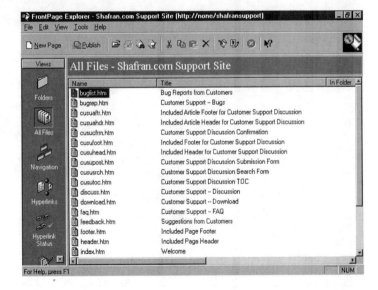

FrontPage actually did quite a bit of work besides creating a few HTML files. In addition, FrontPage built a whole navigation path and relationship between the pages in this FrontPage Web. This navigation path is used to dynamically generate a navigation bar for your Web site. In the FrontPage Explorer, click the Navigation icon in the left icon bar. The navigation scheme is shown in the main FrontPage window (see Figure 3.4).

Figure 3.4.

Although it's a simple navigation scheme, all pages are accessible from the main page.

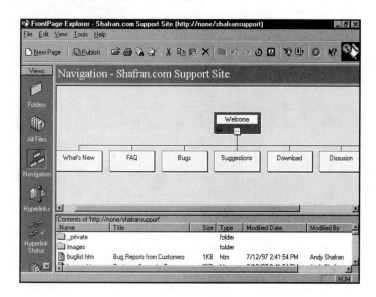

In addition, FrontPage built hyperlinks and relationships between many of the different pages on this Web site. Click the Hyperlinks icon in the FrontPage icon bar and you can see how each page links to others within your Web for a graphical view of the links created. Figure 3.5 shows this graphical relationship.

Modifying the Web Site

After you build the initial site from a template, the next step is customizing it to fit your particular needs. This section makes several modifications to the Customer Support site you just created and suggests several others that might be useful. In general, you must edit each page within your FrontPage Web to make sure it contains accurate information.

Figure 3.5.

FrontPage makes tracking all the Web's hyperlinks easy.

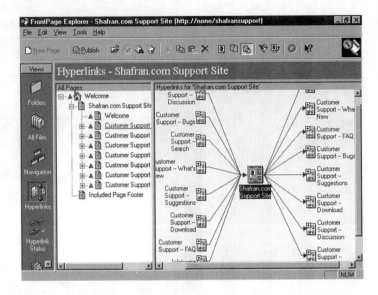

NEW TERM A *theme* is a color- and graphics-coordinated set of controls that makes up your page's appearance. Themes control the color of text, titles, and the background of your Web pages, as well as the icons used for buttons and bullets. Themes are applied to every page within a specific FrontPage Web and are used to ensure a uniform look across the entire site.

Before you actually create any of the pages, first set the theme for the Web site. FrontPage comes with several themes for you to select from within the FrontPage Explorer. Click the Themes icon within Explorer (see Figure 3.6). From here you can select any of a variety of themes, or even turn off the theme option. Themes are great tools to use when building sites and are covered in more depth during Hour 21, "Applying Web Themes."

After you set your theme, the next change you'll want to make is editing the index.htm file. On the Web, index.htm is the default home page for every site. For example, if you visit http://www.shafran.com, you are actually opening up the index.htm file on that Web site. Therefore, this is going to be the first—and consequently the most important—file that everyone will see.

Figure 3.6.

This site will use the Saturday TV Toons theme to add a "fun" component for visitors who stop by.

Edit the `index.htm` file by double-clicking it from within the FrontPage Explorer. The FrontPage Editor starts up and loads `index.htm` ready for you to use. Figure 3.7 shows the Editor editing `index.htm`.

Figure 3.7.

The FrontPage Editor in action.

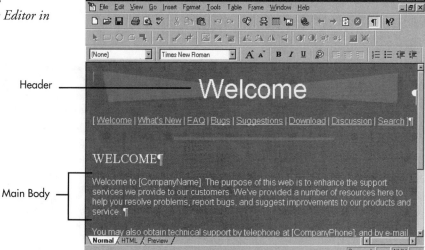

When you look at this screen, you are actually seeing three separate HTML files simultaneously: a header file, a footer file, and the body. The header file—or `header.htm`—is embedded at the top of `index.htm`. Actually, this header is inserted at the top of every page within the Web site and consists of two parts: the title of the current Web page and a navigation bar to other pages. Similarly, the footer file—or `footer.htm`—is at the bottom of this page.

TIME SAVER

> You must make changes to the header and body separately because they are two separate files. To change the header of your site, double-click the `header.htm` file from within the FrontPage Explorer.

Within the FrontPage Editor, update the text of this Web page. FrontPage even helps you by providing sample text. Of course, you must type your company name, phone number, and e-mail address where there are brackets for that information. And, if you scroll to the bottom of the page, you'll see the standard footer (`footer.htm`) that is attached to every page within the site as well.

After you finish typing your changes, make one final change to this page. The header file at the top of the page contains a special FrontPage command that automatically displays this page's title. The header displays the title of the page in which `header.htm` was inserted. To change your title, right-click anywhere within the FrontPage Editor and choose Page Properties from the pop-up box that appears. Figure 3.8 shows the Page Properties dialog box.

Figure 3.8.

Page-wide defaults and preferences are set from here.

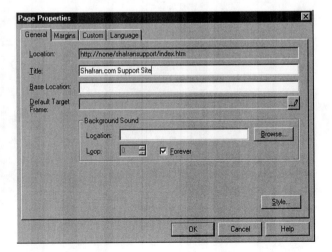

3

In the Title text box, erase the default title (Welcome) and type a better, more descriptive title for this newly created site. When you're finished, click OK. Nothing much happens within the Editor except that the text in the title bar at the top of the screen changes, but not the large title that you wanted to update. That's because you need to press the F5 key to refresh the entire page; that's when FrontPage reloads the header and footer documents again. After pressing F5 or clicking the Refresh button, you'll notice that the large headline of your page changes automatically!

You must get used to using the F5 key to update how your page is rendered, or displayed, onscreen. F5 tells FrontPage to update all the special components such as embedded headers and footers, and dynamic titles.

Finally, save your updated page by choosing File | Save from the menu bar. Now switch back to the FrontPage Explorer, and you'll see that the title of this page has been changed (see Figure 3.9). The FrontPage Editor and Explorer have a dynamic relationship with each other, and they keep in constant communication. When a change is made in one, the other is aware of it and will update itself.

Figure 3.9.

This shows how the FrontPage Editor and Explorer keep in contact with each other.

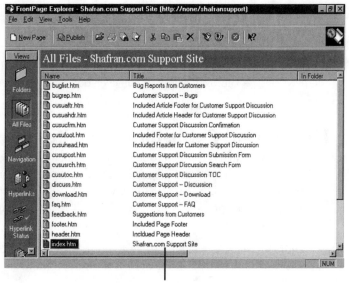

The new title for index.htm

You can make a lot of other changes to this template. You should update each file to add your specific company name and information. Next on your list should be footer.htm so that you can make each page display accurate information on your company or site.

Many Web sites won't need all the pages created with this template. For example, maybe your company doesn't have a list of Frequently Asked Questions. In that case, you can easily wipe out the faq.htm file by selecting it within Explorer and pressing the Delete key. FrontPage removes the file and updates all the links and navigation bars for the entire site, removing FAQ links from every page.

JUST A MINUTE

Making Significant Changes to This Template

As you can imagine, this hour described only several very basic ways to update and control how a template-driven Web works. You can literally change every file as well as the complete inner workings of a whole site—even when it was created by a template.

For example, perhaps you are a Realtor and need a site where people can learn more about you, your houses for sale, and your company. You might consider using the Customer Support site as an example to begin with instead of starting from scratch. Of course, you must make significant changes to each page—renaming it, resetting its title, and adding different information—but much of the hard work required to link pages together, set a common theme, and use standard headers and footers is already done.

Don't be afraid to create a site from a template that is close—but not a perfect match—to the site you need and then make your own specific improvements. You can even add totally new pages to the Web site.

Testing and Publishing the Site

After you've edited this site to your heart's content, take a look at the different pages through the eyes of a Web browser. Remember back to Hour 2, "Installing and Using FrontPage," where you learned how to install FrontPage and configure the Personal Web Server. Start your browser and point to your Personal FrontPage Server. Figure 3.10 shows how this page looks in Netscape.

Explore the entire site and don't be afraid to test all the links. Make sure that there are no problems and that the pages look exactly how you want.

Unfortunately, your site is still on your personal computer and available only to you. The last step in building this sample site is making it available to the millions of people on the WWW.

Figure 3.10.

FrontPage did a pretty nice job of building this site.

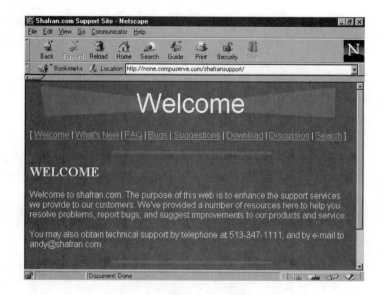

3

This process, called *publishing* or *uploading,* sends each file electronically from your computer to another that is permanently connected to the Internet. Publishing is handled within the FrontPage Explorer. Click the Publish button to start the uploading process.

FrontPage asks you where you want to send your site. You must have a Web account to publish files. This process can be tricky if you aren't careful, and for that reason there is a whole hour dedicated to stepping you through it. Go to Hour 17, "Publishing to the WWW," for more information and a complete description of the entire publishing process.

Visiting a Real-World FrontPage Site

Not surprisingly, many people who create sites with FrontPage use the built-in templates. In general, these templates are very powerful and flexible when building real-world sites. Adding all the customizations and functions that the Customer Support site uses to a blank set of pages would take a long time—and testing it out thoroughly would taken even longer.

To get an idea of what type of site you can create from a FrontPage template, visit http://www.youngsdairy.com. This Web page is the electronic home of a regional dairy that wanted to build an electronic billboard and presence for its techno-savvy customers. Figure 3.11 shows the Young's Dairy home page. If you look at it carefully, you'll notice that it was built from the Corporate Presence Wizard within FrontPage.

Figure 3.11.

Young's Dairy Farm has the best ice cream around!

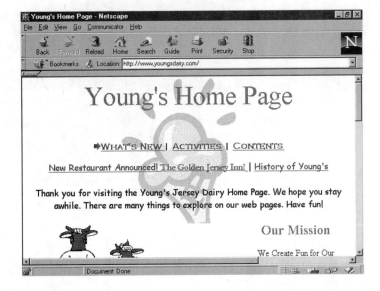

Notice how Young's changed the default title for the page but used the default links to other pages within the site. The company added a few images of its business as well as updated the standard footer (if you scroll to the bottom of the page you'll see it).

Click the Activities hyperlink and see another page within this site (see Figure 3.12). This page describes what you can do when you stop by the farm and restaurant. It follows the same style as the original page, ensuring a consistent look throughout the entire site.

Figure 3.12.

There's a lot to do if you stop by Young's.

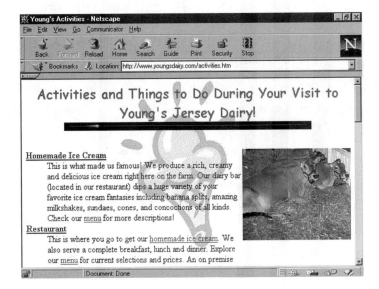

You can explore the rest of this site for yourself. It was created by Dan Young (hence the name Young's Dairy Farm) on his own computer with FrontPage. More than 30 different pages are on this site—pretty large for a single site—and a lot of images and links to related sites. When creating the site, Dan had much of the text (such as the menu) already saved as Word files or in other formats on his computer, and he simply copied and pasted text into FrontPage. Overall, the whole site took between 30 and 40 hours to create, a fraction of the time required to make this site block by block in straight HTML or without the help of a template.

Summary

All in all, creating a site from a template saves you a tremendous amount of work and effort. FrontPage uses its own characteristics to build hyperlinks and a navigation bar, in addition to a standard header and footer for the whole site.

Even if you can't find a particular template that fits your exact needs, it's likely you'll want to start with one that is close and then make your own changes to it. Templates are a great tool and should not be overlooked when making your own new Web site.

Q&A

Q What is the Discussion Web Wizard and how does it work? Can anyone use it?

A The Discussion Web Wizard lets your visitors read and leave messages in a threaded fashion. For example, if you have a site dedicated to pets, you could have one discussion on cats, another on dogs, and so on. Each person who visits can read previous messages, create a new main topic, or reply to an existing message.

Q When I used the Corporate Presence Wizard, FrontPage built several tasks for me to complete. Why were so many tasks generated?

A The Corporate Presence Site is one of the most complicated templates around. The site changes dramatically depending on how you answer the questions FrontPage asks you when you select it. Besides creating a bunch of HTML pages, FrontPage also generates a handful of tasks that it deems important enough for you to accomplish before you can consider the site finished. Tasks are important because they serve as reminders for jobs that must get done within the Web. Therefore, FrontPage created a task that reminds you to update the headers and footers of the site. You would probably remember this on your own, but now you have a log and accountability for accomplishing them. Tasks are very useful for larger Web sites because you can stop working on the Web at any point. When you resume, you simply tackle the next task on the list. Of course, creating these different tasks does take extra time, but in the long run it is well worth it. FrontPage added tasks to this wizard so that you can gain experience using this advanced feature.

Q When I create a site through a template, FrontPage takes 30 to 60 seconds before it seems to build the actual pages. Then when I close and reopen FrontPage, the whole program seems to be running a little slow—and I have a powerful computer with a lot of memory. What can I do to speed it up?

A The only drawback to working with templates is the amount of horsepower they require on your computer. Templates are complex and have a significant amount of complicated actions to calculate. The larger your FrontPage Web, the longer it'll take to load your site and make changes to any page. The best rule is to be patient and realize that the extra five seconds it takes FrontPage to recalculate links saves you a lot of time if you had to do it on your own.

Workshop

The Workshop contains quiz questions and an Activities section to help reinforce what you've learned in this hour. Try not to look at the quiz answers until you've tried to work them out yourself!

Quiz

1. What is the difference between a wizard and a template?
2. Under what situations do you *not* want to use a template or wizard to create your site initially?

Answers

1. Both wizards and templates are automated ways to build complete sites from scratch. All sites created from a template start out looking the same. A template-built site always has the same number of different pieces each time you create it.

   A wizard, on the other hand, goes one step further and customizes your Web site before you start working on it. FrontPage wizards ask you several important questions about the site you want to build and then create the appropriate pages depending on how you answer each question.

2. Templates and wizards are useful, but not always perfect for each individual. You don't want to use them when none come close to matching your specific need for a site—building an interactive online store, for example, or a fan club for your favorite band. Also, when you are very knowledgeable about HTML and FrontPage, templates and wizards can sometimes slow you down and add extra initial work to getting your site up and running.

3

Activities

1. Now that you've finished creating a template-driven site, move on to Hour 5, "Adding Style to Your Text," to learn all about working with colors and cool special effects.

2. Web graphics make a template-built site shine. Read through Hour 9, "Understanding and Using Web Graphics," and Hour 10, "Controlling Images with FrontPage."

3. Make a mental note to carefully read Hour 21, "Applying Web Themes." Themes are very integral to the FrontPage template and wizard processes.

Hour **4**

FrontPage Editor Basics

In Hour 3, "Quickstart: Using the FrontPage Templates," you learned how to quickly create a simple Web site using one of the default FrontPage templates. Templates are useful when you create a new page, but you'll spend most of your time editing and configuring each page inside the FrontPage Editor. The FrontPage Editor is where you actually type in the information for your Web pages and then change the way text and graphics appear within a browser.

Much of this book focuses on using the FrontPage Editor to customize and configure individual Web pages, and this hour is where you learn the initial basics. For the next hour you'll learn how to make simple—but important—changes to a Web page and become more familiar with how the FrontPage Editor works.

Specifically, this hour you'll learn how to

- ☐ Add multiple-sized headlines to your page
- ☐ Include horizontal lines within pages
- ☐ Set simple font attributes such as alignment and indention with the FrontPage Editor
- ☐ Use the FrontPage properties boxes to select your text and font styles and formats

Editing a Web Page

When you start FrontPage from the Windows Start button, it is really the FrontPage Explorer component that comes up. From the Explorer, you can start other components, such as the Editor or Image Composer, as needed. The Explorer is very useful and flexible. You can create new FrontPage Webs and add additional pages from here, but you cannot edit or update them. That's where the Editor becomes essential.

In fact, if you are like most people, you'll spend over three-quarters of your time in the FrontPage Editor. Although the task list and Explorer help you manage the entire site, the Editor helps you decide how an image is to be included or what hyperlinks to build to other sites.

 Within FrontPage, start the Editor by double-clicking any HTML file from the All Files or Folders view. The Editor starts up and automatically lets you begin working on the file you've selected. Figure 4.1 shows the Editor, ready to go.

Figure 4.1.

All HTML editing is accomplished within the Editor.

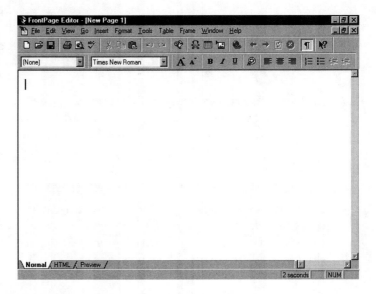

From here, you'll learn how to format and style text and graphics. When you save a file (using the File | Save command), FrontPage stores the file within the Web that is currently open in the Explorer. All files are saved in HTML format—FrontPage translates all the work you do within the Editor into the correct HTML tags for you. Remember, a Web browser reads this HTML file and then decides how to display text within its window.

In general, the FrontPage Editor displays each Web page in the same manner as it will appear within a Web browser. However, because the Editor and browser are separate programs, they occasionally interpret specific HTML tags differently. This is important because various programs might interpret HTML tags differently. You'll always have to test each HTML file within your site to make sure that your page looks good within both the FrontPage Editor and the Netscape and Microsoft browsers.

Conveniently, the FrontPage Editor lets you keep many different files open simultaneously. Use the Window command from the menu bar to see a listing of all the HTML files that are currently open. As you continue to expand your site, you'll often find yourself regularly switching between different HTML files.

FrontPage lets you multitask (that is, work on multiple HTML files simultaneously) only with files from a single Web. Because the Editor is tied to the Explorer, if you try to edit files from two different Webs, FrontPage will try to save files to the current open Web within the Explorer. In general, only use the Editor to make changes to files within one Web at a time.

4

To create a new page within your site, choose File | New Page from the menu bar within the FrontPage Editor. The New dialog box appears (see Figure 4.2). You can create several different types of pages from this dialog box. To create a blank Web page, select Normal Page within the Page tab, and then click OK.

Figure 4.2.

You can create more than 25 different types of Web pages.

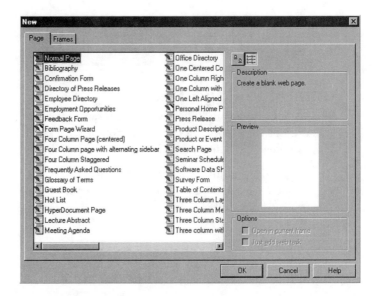

Web Page Basics

Now that you've created a new page, it's time to learn basic Web page editing techniques. This section introduces you to the basic components that you'll use on virtually every Web page: titles, Web headings, horizontal lines, and more.

The First Step: Saving and Naming Your File

Before you start typing information onto your Web page, you first want to save your new Web page. Saving your page lets you name the HTML file on which you are working and identify it more easily within the FrontPage Explorer. Also, saving your page early is good practice. You want to save your Web pages regularly so you don't lose any changes if your computer happens to lock up or turn off accidentally.

To save your page for the first time, choose File | Save from the Editor menu bar. The Windows Save As File dialog box appears (see Figure 4.3). In this window, you name the file. In general, it is a good idea to use a descriptive word or phrase to name each specific file. For example, if this is going to be a Web page about your personal life, name it personal.htm. The more descriptive the filename, the easier it will be to manage your entire site. You can use the .HTM or .HTML file extension.

Figure 4.3.

Each Web page must have its own unique filename.

Setting the Page Title

After you've saved your file, the next step is setting your Web page title. Within a browser, the title of a page appears at the very top of the screen in the title bar. In addition, the title bar also shows up in the FrontPage Explorer to describe each specific page within the Web.

In the FrontPage Editor, you can set the page's title by right-clicking anywhere within the screen and choosing Page Properties from the pop-up box. Figure 4.4 shows the pop-up menu box that appears when you right-click, and Figure 4.5 shows the Page Properties dialog box.

4

Figure 4.4.

Pop-up boxes like this are commonly found throughout FrontPage.

Figure 4.5.

You can modify several important settings within this dialog box.

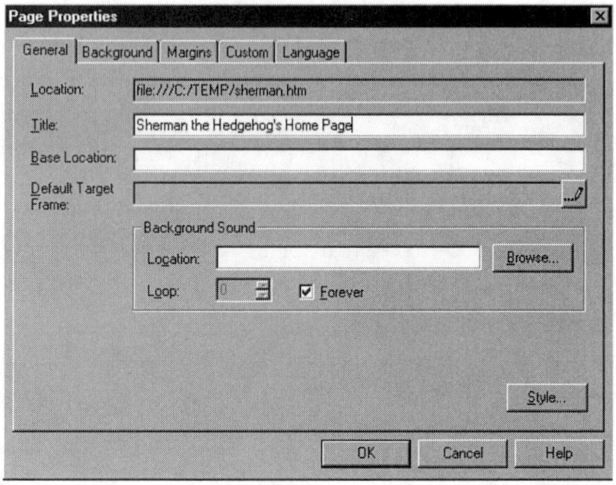

In the Title box, type in the text you want to use to describe this page. Then click OK to save your title.

TIME SAVER

Web page titles should be short, informative, and to the point. They should fit within the Web browser title bar as well as help visitors recognize the page they're looking at.

Here are some good Web page titles:

- ☐ Andy Shafran's Home Page
- ☐ Recruiting News for ACME Company
- ☐ Favorite Cajun Recipes

On the flip side, here are some bad Web page titles:

- ☐ My Site
- ☐ Get a job
- ☐ The perfect page for learning how to make Cajun chicken casserole without using too much guacamole, too many spices, or too much orange juice

Within FrontPage, Web page titles serve more than one purpose, including creating automatic banners at the top of each page. You'll learn more about how FrontPage uses these automated tactics—called *components*—in Hour 21, "Applying Web Themes."

Adding Important Headlines

When you read your local newspaper, each story has a different-sized headline. Sometimes you see huge headlines indicating something very important, whereas other times you notice a smaller, moderately sized headline. Each headline size is important in a newspaper.

Within Web pages, headlines (also called headings) come in six different sizes, numbered from 1 (the largest) to 6 (the smallest). You might use all six sizes on your Web page, depending on how much you need to draw attention to different pieces of the Web page.

Figure 4.6 shows a comparison between the six different-sized headings you can use on a Web page.

Figure 4.6.

You might use each of the six different headline sizes on your Web page.

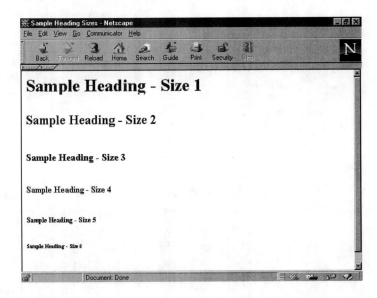

Each of the six headline sizes works the same way. First, you type in your text and then you designate its size within FrontPage. Your text automatically resizes onscreen to the appropriate height, thickness, and size.

To add a headline to your Web page, type a brief word or phrase within your empty Editor window. Then, highlight your text and click the down arrow in the Text Style box at the top of the FrontPage window. Select the heading size you want to use.

Headlines are an excellent way to break up long, boring paragraphs of text to make your page more aesthetically pleasing to read. Figure 4.7 shows a very simple home page that uses a couple of sizes of titles.

Figure 4.7.

The main headline draws the attention of visitors.

Remember that Web pages are written in Hypertext Markup Language (HTML), and that HTML is a tag-based language. Therefore, FrontPage simply creates the proper tags for headlines and titles for you.

When you use the FrontPage Editor, you can check out the actual HTML tags whenever you like by clicking the tab marked HTML, located in the bottom-left corner of your screen. Figure 4.8 shows the HTML tags behind the Web page shown previously in Figure 4.7.

Headlines are one of the most commonly used HTML tags found on Web pages. For your benefit, here's a list of common tips and techniques for using headlines properly in your Web site:

☐ Don't be afraid to use different-sized headlines within your Web page to add variety to the way it is organized and structured. For example, Size 3 headlines are commonly used above paragraphs of text.

☐ In general, Size 1 headlines are used at the top of each Web page so that visitors know what they're looking at.

☐ When using two levels of headlines right after each other, increment or decrement the headline size by only one step at a time. For example, don't place a Size 3 headline underneath a Size 1 headline; use a Size 2 headline instead. Within Web browsers, visitors will notice if you skip headline levels because text naturally flows from one level to another.

Figure 4.8.

Read through this simple screen and you'll realize that HTML isn't too complicated or difficult to understand.

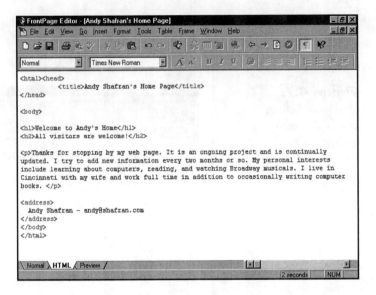

Simply Typing Text

With a headline included on your page, it's now time to start adding some text. You can type as much information as you like within a specific Web page, using the Enter key to separate paragraphs. FrontPage will add special paragraph formatting tags to your HTML file so that your information appears the same in FrontPage as it will in a Web browser.

By default, when you are typing and press Enter, FrontPage assumes you've reached the end of a paragraph. The Editor lets you continue typing and places an empty line between the previous and new paragraphs. Occasionally, you'll want to include a carriage return in your page while typing, but not automatically include a blank line between each paragraph. Instead of pressing Enter, hold down the Shift key and then press Enter. This Shift+Enter combination tells FrontPage you simply want to continue typing on the very next line.

Alignment and Indention

After you have text on your Web page, there are two simple, but important ways you can control its appearance within a browser: alignment and text indention.

HTML gives you three different text alignment options: left, right, and center. As you can guess, left alignment simply aligns each line of text with the left side of the screen. Similarly, right alignment lines up each row of text with the right side of the screen. When you center text, all information in a Web browser appears equidistant from the left and right sides of the computer screen.

4

You'll use all three alignments for different types of information and different types of Web pages. In general, alignment options are most commonly used in conjunction with Web graphics and images as well as formatting text within tables. Figure 4.9 shows a simple paragraph of text formatted for all three alignments.

Figure 4.9.

For this paragraph, left alignment seems to work best.

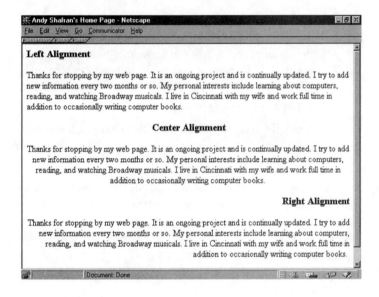

To set your text alignment, place the cursor inside your paragraph (or select multiple paragraphs with the mouse button) and click the appropriate icon from the Editor's icon bar. Table 4.1 shows the three alignment icons you can use.

Table 4.1. Shortcuts for setting text alignment.

Left aligned	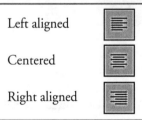
Centered	
Right aligned	

Besides controlling text alignment, you can also set certain paragraphs to be indented when displayed in a browser. By clicking the FrontPage Indent Paragraph icon, you can indent the selected paragraphs of information about a half-inch from the left border of the screen.

> Do you need text deeply indented? Try clicking the Indent Paragraph icon several times. FrontPage lets you continue indenting text as many times as you want.

Horizontal Lines

With headlines and simple text formatting under your belt, the next important element to learn is the horizontal line. You can include various types of horizontal lines that separate and organize your Web page. These lines simply run from left to right on the screen and can be configured in length, color, alignment, and height.

For example, you can add a horizontal line right above your e-mail address at the bottom of your Web page. This logically separates that part of the page from the rest of the information visitors can see.

You can insert a horizontal line into your page by choosing Insert | Horizontal Line from the FrontPage Editor's menu bar. Figure 4.10 shows a Web page with two horizontal lines.

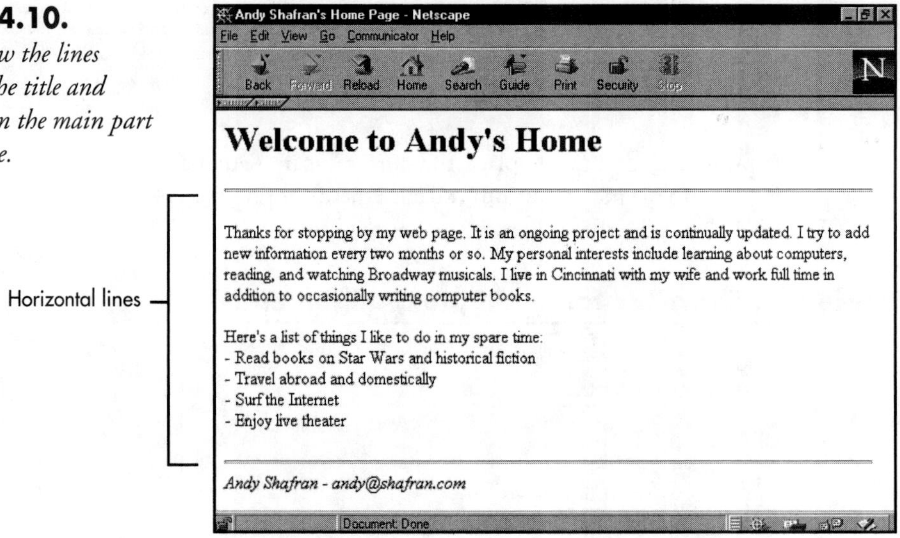

Figure 4.10.

Notice how the lines separate the title and footer from the main part of the page.

Horizontal lines

Andy Shafran's Home Page - Netscape
File Edit View Go Communicator Help
Back Forward Reload Home Search Guide Print Security Stop

Welcome to Andy's Home

Thanks for stopping by my web page. It is an ongoing project and is continually updated. I try to add new information every two months or so. My personal interests include learning about computers, reading, and watching Broadway musicals. I live in Cincinnati with my wife and work full time in addition to occasionally writing computer books.

Here's a list of things I like to do in my spare time:
- Read books on Star Wars and historical fiction
- Travel abroad and domestically
- Surf the Internet
- Enjoy live theater

Andy Shafran - andy@shafran.com

Document Done

The default horizontal line is a thin line that runs across the entire width of the browser's window. Often you will want to customize the way horizontal lines appear by changing the line thickness, length, or even color and alignment.

To customize your horizontal line, double-click it within the FrontPage Editor (or right-click and select Horizontal Line Properties from the pop-up menu). FrontPage brings up the Horizontal Line Properties dialog box (see Figure 4.11).

4

Figure 4.11.

There are many options available when configuring your horizontal lines.

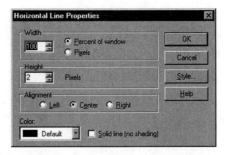

Table 4.2 describes each of the horizontal line properties you can configure.

Table 4.2. Configuration options for horizontal lines.

Option	Description
Width	The Width setting is the most common configuration you'll use with horizontal lines. Change a line's horizontal width when you don't want it to go completely across the screen. Often you'll use a width of 50% and then change the line's alignment to be centered to include a good-looking and nonintrusive line on your screen. You should almost always set the width according to a percentage of the window.
Height	Height controls how tall the horizontal line should be in screen pixels. You can change this setting to anywhere ranging from 1 to 175 pixels. In common practice, common line height (often called *thickness*) settings range from 2 to 15, depending on how noticeable a line you want to build.
Alignment	Alignment works exactly as you would expect it—setting the line up with the left or right borders or directly in the center of the screen. Alignment settings take effect only when you've changed the line's width; otherwise, the line always goes across the screen.
Color	Horizontal lines can be set to virtually any color. To change a line's color from the default black, click the drop-down arrow and select one of 16 named colors ranging from Teal to Red. Read Hour 5, "Adding Style to Your Text," for more information on effectively using different colors within your page.

Experiment with the different horizontal line settings until you feel familiar with the various types of effects you can create. Figure 4.12 shows a sampling of some different horizontal lines you can create with FrontPage.

Figure 4.12.

Here are several different styles and types of lines available to you.

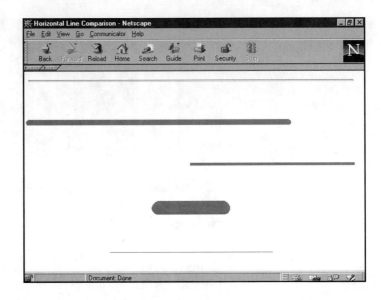

TIME SAVER

See the quiz at the end of this hour to learn the exact dimensions of each horizontal line in Figure 4.12.

Testing Your Page in a Browser

After you've finished creating your basic Web page, your first step is to look at this page with your favorite browser. You can use either Netscape Communicator/Navigator or Microsoft Internet Explorer. It's important to view each of your pages within a browser to make sure they come out exactly as you designed them within the FrontPage Editor. In addition, it's not such a bad idea to use both popular browsers because each of them might render your page slightly differently.

Start your browser and point it to your local FrontPage Personal Web Server. If you're unsure of how to point to your PWS, revisit Hour 2, "Installing and Using FrontPage," where you installed and configured FrontPage. Each computer's Personal Web Server is in a different location. Then point your browser to the FrontPage Web you've created, and you'll see your HTML files appear in the browser.

4

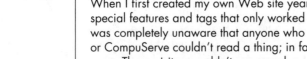

You'll want to check out your Web page often using both the Microsoft and Netscape browsers. Because you probably can't control which browser visitors use, it's worth a few extra seconds of testing to make sure your visitors see what you want them to.

When I first created my own Web site years ago, I used all sorts of special features and tags that only worked with Netscape's browsers. I was completely unaware that anyone who stopped by my site from AOL or CompuServe couldn't read a thing; in fact, they got a really cryptic error. Those visitors couldn't even read my e-mail address to tell me something was wrong—and, because they were just browsing the Web, they weren't very likely to even send me mail. Finally, I fixed my Web site, but it was a rough lesson to learn the hard way.

Summary

In this hour you learned the basics of building simple Web pages. Besides getting acquainted with the FrontPage Editor, you should be comfortable typing text, including headlines, and using horizontal lines on any page you create or edit. These three important building blocks will be constantly used throughout this book as well as the life of your entire site.

When you feel comfortable with the building blocks, you can move on to the next few hours and create some fantastic-looking sites using advanced features such as tables, lists, and Web graphics.

Q&A

Q **You talked about indenting text during this chapter, but what if I need to "outdent" a paragraph or two in my Web page?**

A Right next to the Indent icon, FrontPage supplies you with the Decrease Indent icon. To create an outdented effect, select your entire Web page (Edit | Select All) and click the text Indent icon. Then select the paragraph you would like outdented and click the Decrease Indent icon, and you should be all set.

Q **Why is it important that my Web page title is so perfect? Wouldn't a good headline at the top of the page be just as effective? I'm concerned that people won't even read the title bar.**

A That's a good point. A title isn't always critical for each visitor who stops by your Web page; they aren't even always likely to read them. However, a title is critical for other reasons:

☐ The FrontPage Explorer identifies your individual pages by their title and filename. Often the filename is too short to be useful; therefore, an effective title lets you use the Explorer to build links between pages and to manage your whole site. As your FrontPage Web grows, a title will become increasingly more important. In addition, the automated FrontPage components can build special graphics depending on the title of your page, which you'll learn more about during Hour 16, "Embedding FrontPage Components."

☐ Visit one of the popular Internet search engines—such as AltaVista (`http://altavista.digital.com`). Many search engines have programs that run all the time, indexing all the millions of pages on the Internet. Titles are used to label each page that a search engine indexes. When you search for a word or phrase at AltaVista, a list of matching pages is returned. You pick where you want to visit by reading through the titles of each page. Therefore, it's important that each page is properly titled so you (and others) don't waste time visiting pages of no interest to you.

☐ Finally, sometimes it takes quite a few seconds for your browser to load an entire page. Often, pages have many large Web graphics on them, or perhaps your modem connection isn't a speed demon. In these situations, browsers always load the title of a page first before they display any other information found on that page. That enables your visitors to know whether this page is worth waiting for; otherwise, they can click the Back button to return to the previous screen.

Q Why would I ever set my horizontal line's width in pixel length instead of as a percentage of the browser's screen?

A When placing horizontal lines inside an HTML table, occasionally you'll want to set the line width to be a certain pixel width instead of a screen percentage. This technique is effective only when you have thoroughly tested your Web page with multiple screen resolutions and Web browsers—to make sure it looks okay for all types of visitors. In general, you shouldn't set width in pixel coordinates unless you absolutely need to.

Workshop

The Workshop contains quiz questions and an Activities section to help reinforce what you've learned in this hour. Try not to look at the quiz answers until you've tried to work them out yourself!

4

Quiz

1. In Figure 4.12, there are several different horizontal lines. What are the dimensions of each line (width, height, and alignment)?
2. How do you set the title of your Web page within FrontPage?

Answers

1. Here are the line dimensions from top to bottom:
   a) A standard line from the Insert Horizontal Line command
   b) Width 80% of the screen

      Height 10 pixels

      Alignment set to Left
   c) Width 50% of the screen

      Height 5 pixels

      Alignment set to Right
   d) Width 20% of the screen

      Height 25 pixels

      Alignment set to Center
   e) Width 50% of the screen

      Height 1 pixel

      Alignment set to Center
2. Within the FrontPage Editor, right-click your mouse button and choose Page Properties from the pop-up box that appears. Your page's title can be typed in the box labeled Title within the Page Properties dialog box that comes up.

Activities

1. Explore the raw HTML of the basic pages created during this hour. You don't have to be a programmer or HTML expert to understand them, and they'll go a long way toward increasing your understanding of how pages are built using this flexible markup language. You can learn a bit more about HTML in Hour 20, "Under the Hood with HTML." Alternatively, check out *Creating Your Own Web Pages, Second Edition*, written by Andy Shafran and published by Que.
2. Continue your learning experience with FrontPage 98 by turning to the next hour. You'll see that FrontPage allows tremendous flexibility when configuring the way text appears on a Web page. You won't believe the different sizes, fonts, and special effects you can use!
3. FrontPage lets you include many different types of automatically created graphics and special components within your Web site. These advanced features can be discovered in Hour 21.

PART
II

Web Site Building Blocks

Hour

Hour 5

Adding Style to Your Text

In the first four hours of this book, you were introduced to FrontPage 98 and saw how you can start building your own Web sites. This hour introduces some important techniques for designing the way information appears on your Web page.

By default, all text and information on a Web page appears in a single font and is boring and colorless to look at. This lesson shows you how to add style such as color, text attributes, and different fonts to your Web page.

Specifically, in this hour you'll learn how to:

- ☐ Change how text appears on your Web page from the boring default font, size, and color
- ☐ Make a well-styled and color-coordinated FrontPage Web page
- ☐ Include special characters within your Web pages

Using Multiple Colors

The quickest way to liven up the text on a Web page is by changing its color. By default, every bit of text on your page shows up in black, but text can be any of a full rainbow of colors—16.7 million colors, to be exact. You have complete flexibility over the color for each piece of your Web page, down to each individual character.

Setting your text color is easy, and you must do it when you are using the FrontPage Editor. To do so, follow these steps:

1. First, load the Web page you want to modify into the FrontPage Editor. Then, with your mouse, highlight the text whose color you want to modify, and click your right mouse button.

2. Select Font Properties from the pop-up box to bring up the Font dialog box.

3. Click the drop-down box marked Color. From there, you can change your text's color to one of 16 different named colors or keep your text color at the default setting, which is black.

   Figure 5.1 shows the available colors.

Figure 5.1.

The drop-down list gives the name and an example of each of the 16 colors available, which enables you to pick your favorite hue easily.

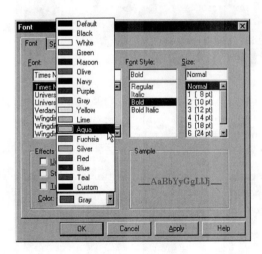

4. If none of these colors are acceptable, choose Custom from the drop-down box, and FrontPage will let you pick from 16.7 million colors in the spectrum by using your mouse. Figure 5.2 shows the Color dialog box.

5

The number of colors you can choose from is dependent on the type of monitor you are using. If your monitor supports 16.7 million colors, then you choose from literally any of them. Some monitors support only 256 different colors onscreen, limiting the different hues you can choose from.

Figure 5.2.

You'll find all the colors in a rainbow and then some when you choose a custom text color.

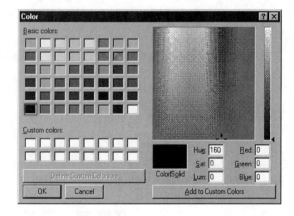

JUST A MINUTE

Look carefully at the 16 named colors that you can use to set text color, because they might be familiar. These 16 colors were the original 16 that Microsoft used when it first developed Windows. Everything on the computer came in one of these 16 colors. Today, most of you have 256 different colors available, if not millions, on your computer.

These original 16 colors have become the default and are even recognized by name in the HTML language. If you were programming in HTML, you could simply tell your text to be Red, Yellow, Teal, or any of the other colors. This common denominator enables you to always know which color you are selecting because you recognize its name. This is easier than trying to set a custom color by using FrontPage.

In most situations, you'll probably find that the 16 named colors are diverse enough to fit your Web needs.

Changing the Default Color

Using the Font dialog box is great for making small, individual changes to your text. You might want to make more wholesale changes in the color of your entire Web page to something other than the default black. Although black is perfectly fine for many situations, current Web site designers might want to color-coordinate their standard text with the rest of their page and site.

Changing the default color for all your text comes in handy in two popular situations, one of which is color coordinating, as I just mentioned. Imagine having a Web page dedicated to love or having a Valentine's Day motif. You'd likely have some type of romantic theme. You can see how red text could fit nicely within the whole page scheme.

Another time you might want to change the default text color is when you use a different background color or image beneath your text. All Web pages show up with a gray or white background by default, but if you change your background color to something dark, such as navy blue or maroon, black text becomes very difficult to read. In that case, you'd set your default text to something bright, such as white or yellow. This technique, called , is commonly used in magazines and news-letters to draw attention to a particular story or page.

Changing the default text color is easy. Simply right-click anywhere within the FrontPage Editor, and choose Page Properties from the pop-up menu. In the Page Properties dialog box, click the tab labeled Background (see Figure 5.3).

Figure 5.3.

This is the starting point for color coordinating your entire Web page.

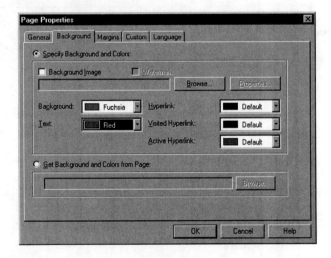

In the Text drop-down box, you can again choose between the default 16 colors or pick one of your own custom concoctions. When you click OK, the text color for the entire page immediately changes, except where you've previously set it by using the Font dialog box. All text, even headings and the text within tables, is affected by this change. In addition, you can change the color of three different other types of text, all relating to hyperlinks. Normally, all hyperlinks appear in blue on a Web page, but sometimes you'll want to update their appearance for the same reasons you'll want to change the way standard text appears. For more information on this issue, see "Updating Link Colors" in Hour 8, "Linking Pages Together."

5

Working with Font Properties

Now that you can set your text color, the next important step is learning how and when to change the default font when standard text appears on your Web page. You'll learn what each option means in the FrontPage Font dialog box and how to configure these settings effectively.

Remember from the last section that the Font dialog box appears when you highlight the text you want to change, click your right mouse button, and select Font Properties from the pop-up menu. Figure 5.4 shows the default Font dialog box.

Figure 5.4.

You can set nearly all your text attributes from here.

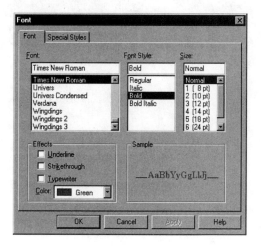

Text Size

NEW TERM   A *point* is a holdover term from common desktop-publishing tools such as Adobe PageMaker. Points are a publisher's terminology for how large a font appears onscreen. An 8-point font is smaller than a 12-point font, which in turn is much smaller than a 24-point font. Traditionally, 1 inch equals about 72 points for both width and height.

There are seven different font settings for how text can appear within a Web page. These seven sizes correspond to different font settings ranging from 8- to 36-point text.

You can change any piece of standard text to be any of these seven settings. The default text size is 3, which is about 12-point text, the standard size for how information appears in most word processors. In the Font dialog box, if you leave the Size setting to the default, everything you type will show up as size 3—or 12 point.

5

Change the text on your home page to one of the other six settings. You'll find yourself often making text larger to draw attention to itself, or smaller to fit in a lot of data. (But size 1 text is very small and is appropriate only for information you don't want people to read easily—much like the teeny-tiny text that appears on your TV when you watch a car sales commercial.)

Figure 5.5 shows how these seven sizes of text compare to one another in a browser.

Figure 5.5.

Each of these seven text sizes has its own use on a Web page.

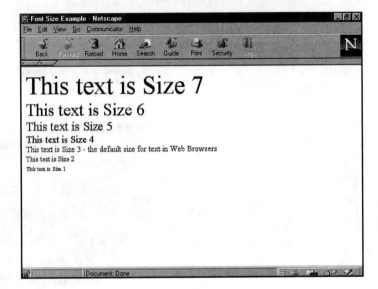

Font Styles and Effects

The next setting in the Font dialog box is Font Style. You have four options: Regular, Italic, Bold, and Bold Italic. The Bold setting simply makes your text slightly thicker and darker onscreen, whereas Italic adds a slant to the text.

You can also indicate whether you want to underline your text, put a strikethrough line across it, or have it appear in a typewriter-like font. These three effects are controlled in the Effects area of the Font dialog box.

Using these styles and effects is very common, and can even be done by using the buttons at the top of the FrontPage Editor instead of by bringing up the Font dialog box. Table 5.1 shows the correlation between these styles and the buttons on the FrontPage toolbar.

5

Table 5.1. Shortcuts for setting font style.

B	Bold
I	Italic
U	Underline

Controlling Your Fonts

Probably the most significant change you can make to your Web text is to use different fonts. If you're like most people, you have literally dozens of different fonts loaded on your computer, each of which can be used for separate occasions. By default, all text on your Web pages shows up in the Times New Roman font.

Different fonts are easy to use and effective at changing the style and meaning of a Web page quickly. You can use any of the different fonts that have been loaded on your computer. Simply choose one from the Font area of the Font box, and your text will automatically be updated.

If you aren't sure which font you want to use, select one from the list and see how it looks in the Sample area. This area lets you see how your font changes will look before you click OK and actually apply them to your text. Figure 5.6 shows a sample Web page that uses several different fonts to add variety.

Figure 5.6.
Audrey's page wouldn't be nearly as exciting in a single font.

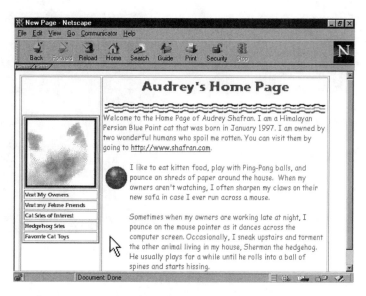

5

CAUTION

You'll want to exercise some caution when using multiple fonts on your Web page because of the way Web browsers use them.

When a visitor stops by, he first downloads the entire Web page to his computer. Then Netscape Navigator or Internet Explorer figures out how to properly display the page. When the browser comes across the command to use a different font, it checks the visitor's computer to see if he has that particular font loaded. If he does, it displays the text properly. But if the visitor doesn't have the specified font, the page just appears in the normal Times New Roman font—not the way you intended him to see your page.

The bottom line is that you should use only very common fonts that the vast majority of people will have, and not any specialty fonts that you might have downloaded or installed on your computer from somewhere else. Here's a list of common fonts you can expect most people to have:

Courier	Arial	Comic Sans MS
Lucida	Wingdings	Times New Roman
Coronet	Century Schoolbook	

Using Special Styles

The final text settings you can control are specialized options that you'll occasionally set when working with certain information on your Web page.

Click the Special Styles tab in the Font dialog box to see the other ways you can control your text (see Figure 5.7).

Figure 5.7.

Although used less often, these options help control the details on your Web site.

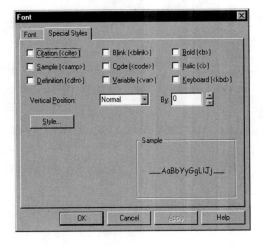

5

Click in the various checkboxes to see how the text appears in the Sample area of the dialog box. You're likely to use these three settings most often: Blink, Subscript, and Superscript.

The Blink checkbox makes text blink intermittently on a Web page. Often, you'll find sites that set some text to be large, red, and blinking—which really draws the visitor's attention. Be careful not to overuse this style, however, because text that is constantly blinking on and off the screen can easily irritate visitors.

The other two settings, Subscript and Superscript, can be found in the Vertical Position drop-down box. Subscript text appears as slightly smaller and lower on the line of text and is used in formulas, such as H_2O. Superscript text appears smaller, but on the top of the line of text and is used for addresses and footnotes, such as 201 West 103rd St.

Using Special Characters

When you type your Web page, you probably will be using a standard 101-key keyboard with letters, numbers, punctuation, and a handful of special characters. You're likely to have trouble adding some other, commonly used special characters on your Web page. Symbols such as the copyright mark (©)—or perhaps a letter from a foreign language, such as the French cedilla if you wanted to correctly include the word Français on your page—are simply not on your keyboard.

Fortunately, FrontPage enables you to include these and dozens of other symbols and characters on your Web page. To include a symbol, choose Insert | Symbol from the FrontPage menu bar, and a listing of 200 available symbols shows up (see Figure 5.8).

Figure 5.8.

Nearly any symbol you can imagine is available from here.

To include a symbol in your Web page, select the one you want to use and click the Insert button.

5

Summary

This chapter covers the basics of controlling and modifying how text appears on your Web page. Just because everything appears in black Times New Roman characters by default doesn't mean that you can't make your own customizations and make your page exciting for visitors to see when they stop by.

You'll want to immediately use these techniques to spice up your Web page and make it easier to read and pay attention to.

Q&A

Q Why would you want to change the default link colors within a Web page rather than leave them the default blue?

A You might want to color-coordinate your entire Web page. For example, if your headlines are red and the body of your text is purple, blue hypertext might disrupt the flow of reading your page. Instead, you could change the link text to be purple, but that would be indistinguishable on your page. Another alternative would be to set the linked text to mauve so that it will stand out from the regular text on your page but still color-coordinate with the rest of the page.

Q I was using the FrontPage icons to increase the size of text on my Web page, and I clicked on the icon 15 times. The text was huge in the FrontPage Editor, but was the same size as size 7 text when I looked at my page in a browser. What happened?

A HTML supports only seven sizes of text. So, even though you added several sizes in FrontPage and it looked bigger there, you are limited by the maximum limits the browser can recognize. You can get around this by creating gigantic text in Image Composer and then saving it as an image and including it on your Web page as a graphic.

Workshop

The Workshop contains quiz questions and an Activities section to help reinforce what you've learned in this hour. Try not to look at the quiz answers until you've tried to work them out yourself!

5

Quiz

1. How would you modify your text so that most of it appears normal, but the first letter in each word is larger, drawing attention to that phrase as a headline?

2. How could you add a fraction to your Web page, such as ¼ or ¾?

3. What are the two ways to change your text color?

Answers

1. With your mouse, select the first character of each word and make it a larger font size, perhaps 5 or 6, while keeping the rest of your page standard. Your text will look like this in a Web browser:

Your Home Page

2. By using the Symbols command, you can include several standard fractions on your Web page. You could also use the Superscript and Subscript settings to emulate an equation.

3. One way is to set the default text color for the entire page in the Page Properties dialog box; the other is to set the color of each word individually by using the Page Properties dialog box.

Activities

1. Read Hours 6–8 to continue learning how to control the way text appears on your Web page. In Hour 9, "Understanding and Using Web Graphics," you will begin to learn how you can use graphics and images on your Web page when controlling your text just doesn't offer enough variety.

2. Create a new page within the FrontPage Editor. Experiment with some of the new font-controlling techniques learned in this chapter. Color-coordinate your page by using your favorite color scheme—don't be afraid of bright colors, either!

3. Add some new symbols to your existing FrontPage Web. Add the copyright symbol to the bottom of all your pages. Make sure that you know how to include these unique symbols that aren't available on your keyboard.

5

Hour 6

Building Lists

Now that you've learned the basics of how to add text and headlines to your Web page with FrontPage, it's time to learn how to organize related pieces of information by using lists. With HTML lists, FrontPage lets you add bulleted and numbered items to a Web page to show step-by-step ordered processes and to group together related information.

NEW TERM A *list* is something that depicts pieces of information in an orderly, step-by-step fashion on an HTML Web page.

Lists are often used to include related pieces of information with your Web page. You'll use lists on a Web page in the same way you'd use them in a Microsoft Word document—to indent and group information that should be displayed together. Lists come in several different flavors: bulleted, numbered, and indented. You might use a numbered list to create a recipe on your Web page, because recipes must be followed in an ordered manner. Or you might take a long, windy paragraph and reduce it to a few simple bullet points that capture the essential meaning of the paragraph in an easy-to-read manner.

Specifically, in this hour you'll learn how to

☐ Understand the three different types of lists available for you to use

☐ Create a simple list with the FrontPage Editor

☐ Configure list properties to change the default way lists appear in a browser

What Lists Let You Do

Before you can start using lists in FrontPage, the first step is to understand when you can make good and effective uses of them. In general, lists come in three different styles, each of which has its own particular advantages when used properly.

This section gives you an overview of when you might want to use a list or lists on your Web site.

Organize Related Information

The most common way to use lists is to itemize information in an organized, easy-to-read format. Unnumbered lists show up as bullets of information and naturally draw attention to themselves when someone looks at your Web page. They are much easier to read than long paragraphs of information and often call attention to the important points on a Web page.

Take the following paragraph as an example. It describes a set of interests and was originally depicted as a simple paragraph on a Web page:

```
Even though I spend my days working full time, I'm still quite busy writing
computer books and learning about topics that interest me. I spend a lot of
my time working with a product called Lotus Notes, which is collaborative
software that people can use to share information with one another.
Additionally, I also love learning about the WWW and finding easier and
more effective ways to build and share Web pages, such as using
Microsoft FrontPage 98. In my spare time, I find myself listening to
Broadway musicals and attending as many Reds baseball games as I can.
```

When this paragraph is included on a Web page (see Figure 6.1), it is somewhat unorganized, making it difficult for the user to identify what is important. Although it could be tightened up and broken into smaller paragraphs, reworking it as a list turns out to be a much more effective way to get the same point across.

Figure 6.2 shows roughly the same information, now called out and organized in a simple bulleted-list format. All the important items have been captured as separate items and are organized in a simpler fashion.

6

Figure 6.1.

This boring paragraph of text might never be read on a Web page.

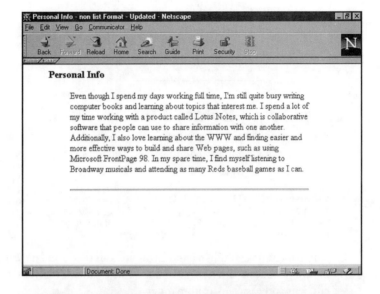

Figure 6.2.

Much easier to read, this list helps organize the Web page.

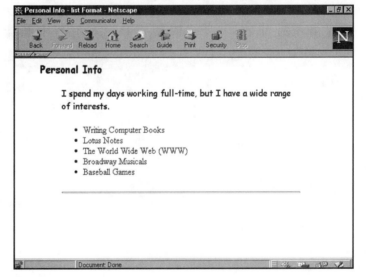

JUST A MINUTE

Actually, organizing a Web page with lists is only the first step in making information more inviting to visitors. FrontPage 98 has a lot of other important and useful features that let you bring the information you want visitors to see immediately to their attention.

For example, you'll want to include vivid Web graphics (Hour 9) and use cool fonts and colors (Hour 5) to really draw attention to important information. You'll also find yourself using tables (Hour 7), imagemaps (Hour 12), and frames (Hour 13) in your quest to make your page enjoyable for readers.

Simplifying Related Information

Another popular time to use lists is to simplify a set of related information that doesn't seem to work well within a paragraph. Take the following example:

```
I really enjoy viewing and listening to Broadway
musicals and live theater. Musicals are enjoyable
because they tell a story line in a pleasant and
fun manner and can be sung along with. Some of my
favorite musicals are Pippin, Sunset Boulevard,
Les Miserables, and Jeckyll and Hyde.
```

This paragraph contains a handful of musicals that could have been better formatted as a list. Figure 6.3 shows the newly formatted list, which gets the same purpose across in a more efficient and easier-to-read manner.

Figure 6.3.

Collections of favorites, such as musicals, make for perfect lists.

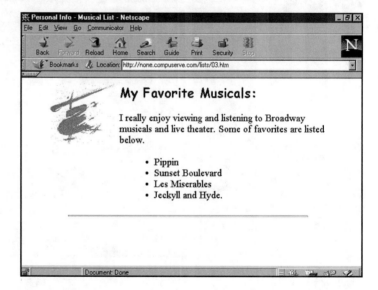

Describe a Step-by-Step Process

Another common use of lists is to describe a step-by-step process, such as instructions or a recipe. Lists can be automatically numbered so that each item in the list appears subsequently. Figure 6.4 shows an example of a list that describes a very important step-by-step process.

6

Figure 6.4.
You'd better follow all these steps if you want to parachute safely!

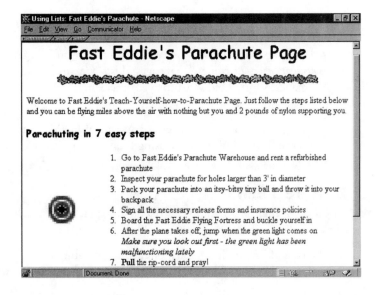

Include Definitions

You can also use lists to create a set of terms and their definitions. This type of list is used to display information that is split into two distinct sections, such as you would find in a dictionary in which you have the original term and then its definition and usage. Figure 6.5 shows a sample definition list in action.

Figure 6.5.
Read these definitions carefully if you're going to fly with Fast Eddie.

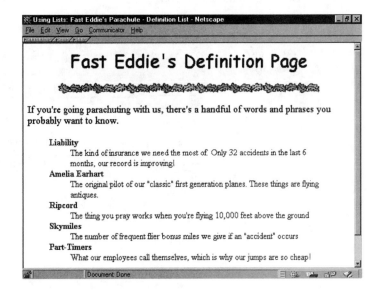

Creating Lists in FrontPage

In FrontPage, lists must be created within the FrontPage Editor, where you edit and customize each of your Web pages. Lists are simply another paragraph style that is automatically formatted and displayed onscreen. Just as you can with headings, you can select a list type from the Style drop-down menu at the top of the FrontPage Editor.

FrontPage lets you build and select any type of HTML-supported list easily. This section shows you how to build lists by using FrontPage and how you can modify them to fit your particular needs.

Bulleted Lists

 A *list item* is an individual element within a list. Each list is comprised of multiple list items that can be controlled individually.

The type of list you'll use most often when you build Web pages is a simple bulleted list. FrontPage lets you create and modify bulleted lists almost entirely with your mouse.

To create a bulleted list, follow these steps:

1. Type one or two items that will make up your list. Press the Enter key between each list item so that each one is on a separate line.

2. Select your list items with your mouse and choose Bulleted List from the drop-down Paragraph Style box on the FrontPage toolbar (see Figure 6.6). You can also click the Bulleted List icon.

Figure 6.6.

Bulleted lists are simply another paragraph style you can use.

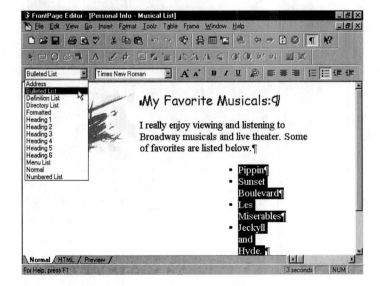

3. As soon as you select Bulleted List, FrontPage automatically indents your text and adds a small, round bullet icon to the left of each of your list items. You can continue typing, adding new elements to your list. FrontPage creates a new item in your list every time you press Enter.

4. You can alter these bullet icons by clicking your left mouse button anywhere within the list. Then click your right mouse button and select List Properties from the pop-up box. A set of options appears, as shown in Figure 6.7.

Figure 6.7.

List icons come in circles and squares, filled and unfilled.

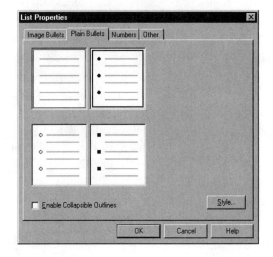

5. You can choose from any of the four default bullet settings for this type of list. Select a different type of icon and click OK. FrontPage will automatically update all your list items. If you're using a FrontPage theme, the icon for bulleted lists will show up instead of the icon indicated. See Hour 21, "Applying Web Themes," for more information on using themes in your Web site.

TIME SAVER

You can also change the icon settings for a single item within a list. First, select the specific list item you want to change, and then click the right mouse button over the item you want to change and choose List Item Properties from the pop-up box. The same List Properties dialog box appears, and you can change the icon setting for just that list item.

Numbered Lists

In a numbered list, FrontPage automatically numbers each subsequent list item rather than add bullets. By default, FrontPage displays standard numeric values for each entry in the list

(1, 2, 3...) but numbered lists come in many shapes and formats, including lettering and roman numerals.

Numbered lists are convenient because you can add or remove steps within a process and the items automatically will be renumbered. Each entry is just considered an item within the list and is numbered as it appears onscreen within the Web browser.

To Do

Creating a numbered list is similar to working with bulleted lists. Here's how:

1. Type one or two items that will make up your list. Press Enter between each list item so that each item is on a separate line.

2. Select your list items with your mouse and choose Numbered List from the drop-down Paragraph Style box on the FrontPage toolbar.

3. As soon as you select Numbered List, FrontPage automatically indents your text and numbers each item in the list. You can continue typing, adding new elements to your list. FrontPage creates a new item in your list every time you press Enter.

4. You can control the numbering system FrontPage uses. Click your left mouse button anywhere within the list; then click your right mouse button and select List Properties from the pop-up box. A set of options appears, as shown in Figure 6.8.

5. Choose any of the six numbering schemes from this dialog box. Click OK, and your change will automatically take effect.

Figure 6.8.

You can use six different numbering schemes interchangeably.

6

By default, all numbered lists will start with 1 (or its equivalent) and continue from there. But you can have numbered lists start with any number by changing the value in the Start At drop-down box in the List Properties dialog box.

Definition Lists

As you might imagine, definition lists work like the other two lists—you must set each list item as a standard paragraph style. But definition lists are different because two types of entries are required for each list item instead of one. That's because of the way definition lists work—first you add the term to be defined, and then you add the definition.

To create a definition list, follow these steps:

1. Type the word or phrase that appears as the term being defined.

2. Select the line you just typed, and choose Defined Term from the drop-down Paragraph Style box.

3. With your cursor at the end of this line, press the Enter key to go to the next line, and then type the phrase that serves as the term's definition.

4. Select that second line and choose Definition from the drop-down Paragraph Style box.

5. Repeat the first four steps until you have added all your terms and definitions.

Of course, you don't have to use definition lists just to define certain words or phrases, but it's easy to keep that metaphor in mind when you use them on your Web page.

Summary

This chapter focuses on using lists to organize and format your Web pages. Lists are powerful and flexible tools that let you condense a large amount of information into short snippets that visitors will be able to read easily. By moving information from long paragraphs into one of the different types of lists, you usually end up with a page that is more inviting to look at and easier to get the important points from.

Lists are just the beginning when it comes to advanced formatting techniques for information on your Web page, however. Next on your agenda is understanding how tables operate. Tables offer a row-and-column organization that can be used with lists to create really well-organized and exciting Web pages.

6

Q&A

Q Do bullets look the same in every Web browser?

A No. Just like all HTML tags, lists are subject to interpretation by every Web browser. For example, older browsers once displayed different icons for the first level of lists—some used squares, others used circles. In general, most lists look the same across browsers, but there always will be subtle differences in the amount of indentation and the way icons appear.

Q When would I ever use definition lists except to define words on my Web page—which I don't do very often?

A Definition lists come in handy because they tie together two pieces of information. For example, you could create a Frequently Asked Question page (FAQ) where the term was the question and the definition was the answer, because browsers always indent the answer right below each question. In general, definition lists are used less often than others.

Q In the FrontPage List Properties box, there are two other types of lists: *directory* and *menu*. You didn't mention them, and FrontPage barely even has a help entry on them. What are they, and when should they be used?

A Directory and menu lists are remnants from the older versions of HTML. Originally, directory lists were intended to list many short, simple items, and menu lists were similar to definition lists but were also meant for shorter items. These two types of lists are rarely used and not well supported. To understand why they were included in the HTML standards, imagine how the U.S. Congress passes a bill. Someone might introduce a bill that creates a law governing a general set of conditions. But some specialized members of Congress might make a few small and unnoticed changes to the bill, which eventually gets passed. These loopholes exist, but are rarely used or exploited and shouldn't be worried about. The end result? You won't use menu or directory lists at all when creating Web pages.

Q Can I embed lists within other lists?

A Yes. You can create recursively embedded lists within one another. By working around a limitation within FrontPage, you can embed multiple lists within one another. After typing a list item, press Enter and type the next list item.

Then click the Increase Indent icon from the FrontPage menu bar.

Finally, click the bulleted or numbered list icon, and voilà—an embedded list is created.

Workshop

The Workshop contains quiz questions and activities to help reinforce what you've learned in the chapter. Try to work through them before looking at the quiz answers or going on to the next hour's lesson.

Quiz

1. What are the three different types of lists you'll commonly use within FrontPage?

2. How can you create a list within your Web page?

Answers

1. The three list types are numbered, unnumbered (bulleted), and definition lists.

2. Lists can be created one of two ways. You can create the list first and then type your information, or type your information onto separate lines and then switch it from multiple paragraphs into list format. Either way, you activate bulleted and numbered lists from their respective icons in the FrontPage Editor's icon bar. Definition lists must be selected from the drop-down paragraph style list, also found within the FrontPage icon bar.

Activities

1. Rather than make you always use bullets for your lists, FrontPage lets you use all sorts of icons instead. Icons are readily available when you use FrontPage themes, and can also be set in the List Properties dialog box. Try using a colorful or animated icon instead of a bullet and see how much spice that adds to your site. Check out Hour 21, "Applying Web Themes," for more information on using icons and themes in your Web site.

2. Create a bulleted list within your Web page. Try converting some type of paragraph into a smaller and easier-to-read list.

3. Create a new empty page and add a recipe to the screen. When making the recipe, use both definition and numbered lists. Use a definition list for all ingredients, describing each ingredient required, and then add a numbered list identifying all the step-by-step instructions for creating your masterpiece dish.

Hour **7**

Constructing Tables

Creating lists of information for your Web page is great, but sometimes you need better layout and formatting control over the appearance of the information on your Web page. By using tables, FrontPage 98 enables you to organize information and images in the common column-and-row format. You'll use tables to display information, to provide navigational tools, and even to enhance the layout of your site.

NEW TERM A *table* provides a way to organize information on a Web page by using columns and rows. You can type information within each row and column.

Tables can be used for a variety of reasons on a Web page. You'll use tables to structure large amounts of information, as tools to place Web graphics and organize a complex page, and as navigational tools to guide visitors through your site. Tables are commonly found on many Web sites today because of the flexibility they offer.

In this hour, you'll learn how to

☐ Create simple tables with the FrontPage Table Editor

☐ Resize and edit your table graphically with your mouse

☐ Use tables to compare and contrast information in your site

☐ Configure several advanced table options

Recognizing Tables

Web page tables come in all shapes, sorts, and sizes. They range from the standard column-row format, which looks similar to a spreadsheet, to advanced ways of placing images and text in certain areas of the screen.

Look at Figures 7.1 and 7.2. Both of these Web pages use tables, but in remarkably different ways. Tables are extremely flexible because, although they start out as simple row-column tools, you can customize each row and column, even build a table within another table, and control colors to amazing precision.

Figure 7.1.

This Web site uses a table in a relatively standard fashion.

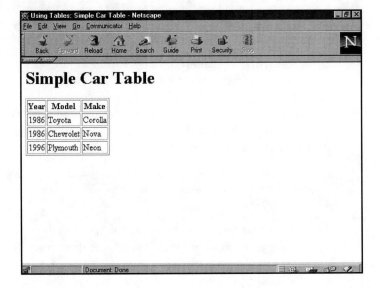

7

Figure 7.2.

You can't even tell that tables are used here, but that's how the organization of the page is structured.

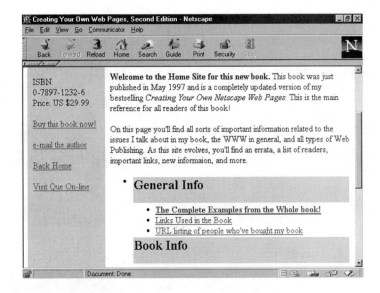

Making a New Table from Scratch

Of course, FrontPage 98 lets you build and customize tables to your heart's content. In this hour, you'll see how to add a simple table to your Web page and then tweak different table options within FrontPage. You can control the color, border, alignment, spacing, and content of each cell within the table.

Before FrontPage, tables were primarily built by inserting one row or column at a time and then working with each cell individually. FrontPage 98 changes this process for the better. Now you can insert a complete table and make changes to columns and rows as you go. By using the table drawing tools, you draw a new row if you need one. If you have an extra column, click the erase tool and, poof, it's gone. In fact, you'll find tables are a breeze to work with, whereas your predecessors—HTML gurus—dreaded managing the dozens of tags required to make a single, small table.

You must build tables within the FrontPage Editor because they are a piece of the entire page. Start the FP Editor and create a new, blank page.

To add a table to this page, choose Table | Insert Table from the menu bar. This brings up the Insert Table dialog box shown in Figure 7.3.

7

Figure 7.3.

You can set your table size and layout from here.

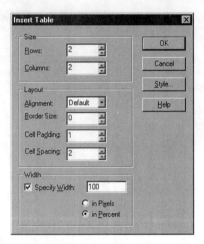

Here's where you can choose from several basic options for your new table. Most important, you can choose the number of columns and rows that belong in the table. In the Size section of the Insert Table dialog box, you enter the number of rows and columns that your table should contain.

You can also control several important layout features that will affect your entire table. Table 7.1 describes the four layout options available.

NEW TERM   A *pixel* is a unit of measurement for computer monitors that relates to the number of dots that make up the screen. A VGA monitor is 640 pixels wide and 480 pixels high. Each pixel corresponds to one of the dots on your computer screen that make up the complete image.

Table 7.1. Options for table layout within FrontPage 98.

Layout Options	Choices
Alignment	Determines how the entire table is aligned on your Web page. *Left* aligns the table to the left side of the screen, and *Right* aligns it along the right side of the screen. *Center* automatically places the table horizontally in the middle of the screen. The default setting, (default), aligns the table according to alignment already set for this area of the Web page.

Layout Options	Choices
Border	By default, the lines that separate each cell from one another are invisible. The border can be set from 0 to 100 pixels thick when appearing within a Web browser. Whether or not you select a border thickness, the FrontPage Editor draws dotted lines between each cell of information so that you can determine which cell you're working within.
Cell Padding	*Cell padding* is the number of pixels between the border of the table and the contents of a specific cell. By default, this setting is one pixel and shouldn't change unless you need extra padding space to keep the contents farther away from the table border.
Cell Spacing	Similar to cell padding, *cell spacing* is the number of pixels between cells in a table. By default, the cell spacing is set to two pixels and isn't likely to change unless you must separate the cells of your table from one another.

Normally, when you create a table, FrontPage automatically creates each row and column dynamically—depending on what you type in each specific cell. This dynamic sizing ensures that your table is only as big as the contents it holds.

Sometimes, you'll want to predetermine the table width to make sure that it covers the entire screen. In this situation, you'll want to change the Width setting in the Insert Table dialog box. Width can be set by percentage across the screen, or by choosing a specific pixel width. Most likely, you'll want to specify width by percentage so that the table can dynamically resize itself depending on the monitor size of each particular visitor.

TIME SAVER

When using pixels to set a table width, always stay smaller than 640 pixels. The minimum default screen width that most people have is 640 pixels wide. If you use larger tables, some visitors to your Web site might have to scroll off to the right to see the complete table. Also be aware that visitors browsing your site with a WebTV have a screen width of only 540 pixels.

After you set the table options, click OK, and FrontPage automatically generates the table according to your specifications. FrontPage shows an outline of the entire table so that you can see the size and shape of every cell when editing your Web page. Figure 7.4 shows three separate tables in FrontPage, all with different attributes:

7

☐ Table 1: 2×2, border set to 0, aligned left

☐ Table 2: 8×2, border set to 4, aligned center, width set to 50%

☐ Table 3: 3×5, border set to 30, aligned right, width set to 180 pixels

Figure 7.4.

These three tables give you an idea of the flexibility FrontPage allows when generating tables.

Table 1

Table 2

Table 3

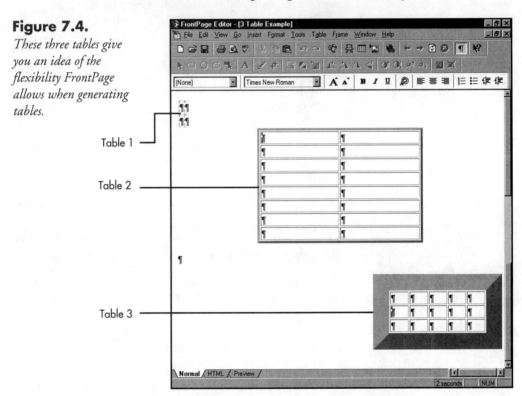

Using the Insert Table Icon

Like most actions in FrontPage, there are two ways to create simple tables. You just learned how to build a simple table with all the options, but you can also create one by using the Insert Table icon found in the FrontPage icon bar.

 Click and hold your left mouse button on the Insert Table icon. FrontPage lets you drag your mouse to create the size of table you need. Figure 7.5 shows a 4×4 table being created by using the mouse.

When you've sized the table you want, let go of your mouse button, and your table appears immediately. Of course, you can set any of the table options that the Insert Table dialog box allows. Click your right mouse button inside your new table, and choose Table Properties from the pop-up box. From here you can set the table width, borders, and alignment easily.

Figure 7.5.

You can graphically create tables of any size with your mouse.

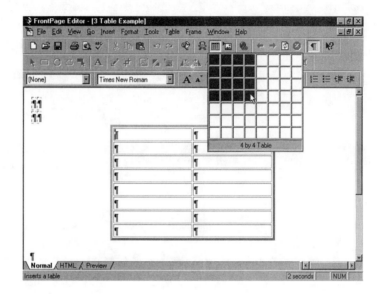

Filling Out Your Table

After you create your table, you can include images and text in any cell. Click your mouse in any cell and start typing. You can use all the special text characteristics described in Hour 5, "Adding Style to Your Text," such as changing text attributes, using a different font, modifying text color, and more. Any way that you can modify text on a Web page, you can use to control text within a table.

FrontPage 98 lets you select paragraphs of text from a Web browser, Microsoft Word, or any other Windows application and drag it directly into a cell within your table. Or, you can use the Windows Clipboard to copy and paste text from other sources into your Web page.

Similarly, you can also include Web graphics in your table's cells. See Hour 9, "Understanding and Using Web Graphics," for more information on using FrontPage to include images on your Web page.

Figure 7.6 shows a simple table that's used to organize a lot of information into a few rows and columns.

Don't forget to save your new page as part of your FrontPage Web.

7

Figure 7.6.
This baseball table compares some of the best pitchers to one another.

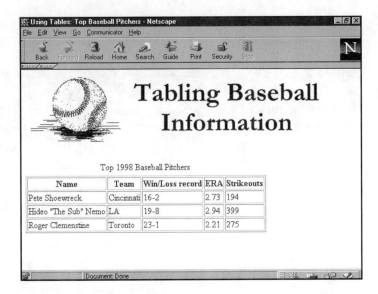

Modifying Your Table Attributes

After you create your table, you can always set and change the default table properties by right-clicking and selecting Table Properties from the pop-up box. Figure 7.7 shows the Table Properties dialog box, which looks similar (but not identical) to the Insert Table dialog box you used to build your table originally.

Figure 7.7.
Your table's border, width, and spacing can always be changed from here.

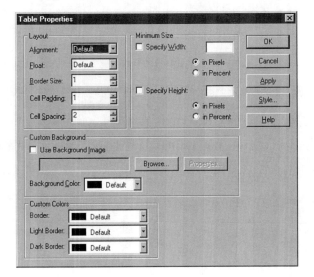

7

Modifying Your Individual Cell Attributes

Besides making changes to the entire table, FrontPage also lets you modify each specific cell individually. To customize a particular cell, click in the cell you want to change, and then right-click and choose Cell Properties from the pop-up box.

Figure 7.8 shows the Cell Properties dialog box. Although this dialog box contains options that are similar to the ones you can choose in the Table Properties dialog box, these options affect only the cell your cursor is currently in.

Figure 7.8.

This is "cell central" for controlling how each square in your table appears.

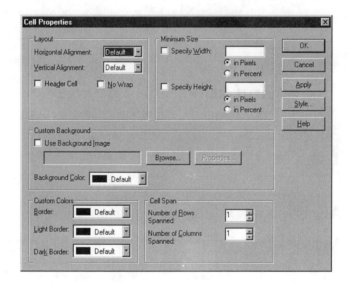

Adding New Rows and Columns

After you've built your table, you might find yourself needing an extra row or column to add some additional information. Adding rows and columns to an existing table is easy because you are always looking at your table graphically within FrontPage.

To add another row or column to your table, follow these steps:

1. Click in a cell near where your new row or column is to be added.
2. Choose Table | Insert Rows or Columns from the FrontPage menu bar. The Insert Rows or Columns dialog box pops up, as shown in Figure 7.9.

To Do

7

Figure 7.9.
Add as many rows or columns as you like from this dialog box.

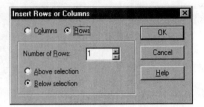

3. From here, you can choose whether you need to add a row or column, how many to add, and whether the row should be above or below your cell (or to the left or right of your cell if you are adding a column). When you click OK, FrontPage automatically adds the new row(s) or column(s), and you can start filling in the cells.

Removing Rows and Columns

Getting rid of rows and columns in your table is just as easy as adding them. Follow these steps:

1. Click in a cell within the row or column you want to delete.

2. Choose Table | Select Row or Table | Select Column from the menu bar to highlight the row or column you want to remove.

3. Press the Delete button on your keyboard, and your highlighted area is gone!

JUST A MINUTE

If you accidentally make a mistake and delete the wrong row or column, choose Edit | Undo Clear from the FrontPage menu bar, and your mistake is rectified.

TIME SAVER

Want to delete the entire table instead of a single row or column? Click in any cell of the table and choose Table | Select Table from the menu bar; then press the Delete key on your keyboard.

Resizing Rows and Columns

FrontPage will dynamically size your table depending on what material you type within each cell. Often, you'll want to have more explicit control over the row and column sizing. By using your mouse, you can drag any of the borders within the table to make a particular cell larger or smaller. After you resize the table, FrontPage will automatically reposition all the text within the affected cells.

7

To start resizing, simply move your mouse over the row or column border you want to change until the mouse pointer changes from a pointer to a double-edged arrow. Then, click and drag the table border to the new row height or column width. Figure 7.10 shows a row within a table being resized to be slightly smaller.

Figure 7.10.

Resizing tables is a breeze because you control their style and how they appear within your Web page.

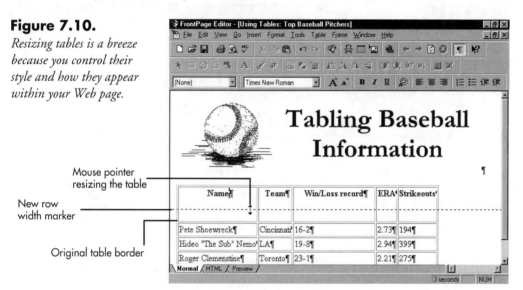

Mouse pointer resizing the table

New row width marker

Original table border

Working with Advanced Table Features

As you can see, building and including simple tables on your Web pages is relatively easy. Tables are an integral part of HTML and are often used by many Web developers. So far, you've hit only the tip of the iceberg when it comes to using FrontPage to customize and control exactly how tables should appear. This section guides you through using several powerful, advanced table features to enhance the way your tables appear.

You can control these advanced table features by using the Cell Properties or Table Properties dialog boxes. Remember, these option-setting dialog boxes appear when you right-click anywhere within the table.

Spanning Multiple Rows

As you continue to use tables, you'll quickly find that sometimes you must break out of the standard row-and-column structure. Occasionally, you might want a cell that spans across multiple rows or columns. FrontPage lets you easily control cell spanning graphically and in a straightforward manner.

In the Cell Span section of the Cell Properties dialog box, you can select how many rows a particular cell should span. A cell can span only as many rows as there are in the table. Figure 7.11 shows the baseball table with a cell that spans multiple rows.

Figure 7.11.

Now Cincinnati has two top 1998 pitchers.

A cell spanning two rows ——

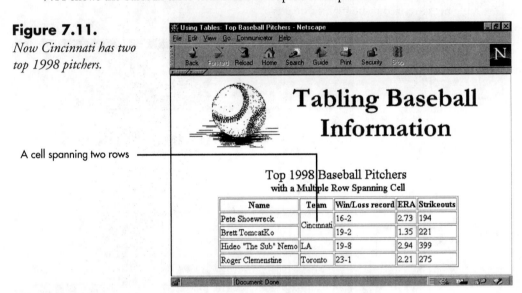

Spanning Multiple Columns

You can also have cells within a table that span multiple columns. Spanning columns is almost identical to spanning rows. Select the cell you want to span, and then bring up the Cell Properties dialog box. Next, change the number of columns spanned to be greater than 1. Again, you can span only the number of columns a table contains.

Figure 7.12 shows the same baseball table with a new row that spans multiple columns.

Cell Alignment

Text and image alignment within your table's cells can be controlled in two ways: horizontally and vertically.

Horizontal alignment controls how text appears in comparison with the left and right borders of the cell. You can set text and images within a cell to be left aligned, right aligned, or centered.

7

Figure 7.12.

Spanning multiple columns helps you organize tables logically and thoughtfully.

Rows spanning two and three columns

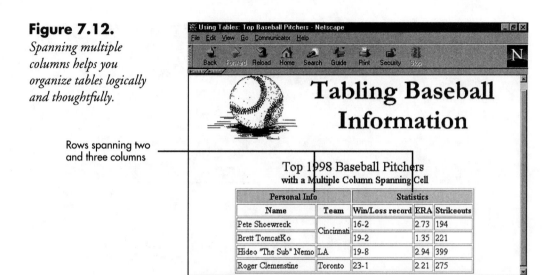

Similarly, *vertical* alignment sets the distance of text and images within a cell from the top and bottom borders. Vertical alignment also comes in three flavors: top, middle, and bottom.

You'll want to use both types of alignment when you add images and longer pieces of text to cells within a table. Each cell can be given a different type of alignment, which comes in handy when you want to organize how a complex table appears in your Web page.

Both horizontal and vertical alignment are controlled in the Layout section of the Cell Properties dialog box.

Lists Inside Tables

Last hour, you saw how lists can also be used to organize multiple pieces of information in a logical manner. This hour has shown you how tables can accomplish similar but different goals. As you can imagine, you'll often need to use lists and tables together, taking advantage of the best features of both techniques.

FrontPage lets you easily place lists inside any table cell. Figure 7.13 shows the baseball table containing a new column with an unnumbered list inside it.

7

Figure 7.13.

Using embedded lists enables you to include larger quantities of information within a single table cell.

Embedded list ————

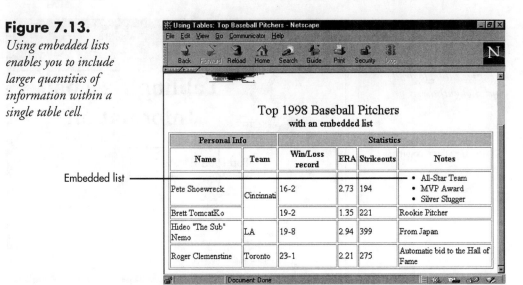

Controlling Table Colors

Finally, FrontPage lets you control all the colors relating to a table, including border colors and background colors. You can set table-wide color defaults or set each cell to appear differently. Controlling table colors works just like controlling text color. You can choose one of the 16 named colors, or you can select from the 16.7 million available colors (or the maximum available on your computer).

Colors are controlled table wide from the Table Properties dialog box (or for the individual cell from the Cell Properties dialog box). You can control two different sets of colors within a table: the background color and the border color.

TIME SAVER

When setting the color of table borders, there are two suboptions. Table borders are actually made up of two lines—an outside table border and an inside table border. By default, when you set the border in the Cell Properties or Table Properties dialog box, you are controlling both the outside and inside lines of the table.

However, you can also set the two different border lines individually to give a three-dimensional look to your table. The Light Color option represents the inside border color, whereas the Dark Color option sets the color for the outside line in the border.

Try experimenting with this cool option and see if you can create a three-dimensional table in FrontPage.

7

Within browsers, the color scheme you set for a particular cell always takes precedence over a table-wide setting. Therefore, if your table background is set to blue, you can set a few individual cells to have a red background by working with the specific cell properties.

Summary

Tables are an essential ingredient to building a FrontPage Web. By creating multiple columns and rows, you can compare and contrast a significant amount of information within a small area of a Web page.

You'll find yourself using tables regularly within your Web site. Whether comparing information or adding a cool design to your site, tables are easy to work with and fun to include. FrontPage even includes top-notch table support, letting you drag your table borders to fit your specific needs and page requirements. You'll want to immediately use the following techniques to spice up your Web page.

Q&A

Q Sometimes when I browse other sites on the Web, I come across areas where the tables scroll off the right side of the screen. This makes it difficult to read and browse the site. Am I browsing incorrectly, or is there a problem with the way tables are used?

A Table width is set according to either number of pixels or percentage of screen width. Often when tables are created, their default width is set according to pixels, which makes the table look different depending on your monitor's resolution. To avoid this problem, make sure that all your tables are sized according to a screen percentage. This ensures that they dynamically resize themselves. As for sites that don't use this technique, you must be patient and scroll to the right to see their entire table.

Q FrontPage seems to support both tables and frames. What are the differences between these two items?

A Frames enable you to split up your browser window and load multiple HTML files into each separate window. Therefore, when you click a link within a frame, the new page is loaded only in that frame, leaving the other parts of the browser screen intact. Tables, on the other hand, are all part of a single Web page.

7

Workshop

The Workshop contains quiz questions and an Activities section to help reinforce what you've learned in this hour. Try not to look at the quiz answers until you've tried to work them out yourself!

Quiz

1. How can you emulate a newspaper feel on your Web page by having multiple columns of information?

2. How could you place four separate images within different cells in a table but make them appear as if they are one single image?

Answers

1. Set up a table with only one row but with two or three columns. Within the table, set Cell Padding to be 5 to 10 and the borders to be 0. Then you can type all the way down each column within the table, but the information stays in the same cell. Because you can add headings and images as well as colored text, you are only a few steps away from a newspaper-like feel.

2. First set your Cell Padding and Cell Spacing properties to be 0, so there is no extra empty space within the various cells of your table. Then set the Horizontal and Vertical Alignment of your four individual cells to the following:

	Column 1	*Column 2*
Row 1	Right, Bottom	Left, Bottom
Row 2	Right, Top	Left, Top

Activities

1. The next level of controlling how your Web page appears means learning about frames. FrontPage supports all sorts of frames and even has a built-in Frame Wizard. Experiment with the FrontPage Explorer to learn how frames work as compared to tables. Hour 13, "Framing Your Web Page," covers frames in more detail.

2. Read Hour 10, "Controlling Images with FrontPage," to learn all about using background images on your Web site. Then review the properties of the tables you create and explore how to use background images for your tables rather than simply set colors for the cells.

3. Add a two-column table to your Web site and experiment with configuring the cell properties and changing the table borders with your mouse. Make sure that you can set table-wide and cell-wide properties.

7

Hour 8

Linking Pages Together

Probably the most important reason the World Wide Web has become popular is the concept of *linking*. Linking enables you to point to any other page on the entire Internet from within your Web page, literally any of the millions of HTML files. In this hour, you're going to learn how FrontPage lets you build hypertext links so that you can spin your own intertwined section of the WWW.

Hypertext links are the lifeblood of the Web as well as FrontPage 98. You should already be familiar with using links; that is, clicking underlined text and being whisked away to a new Web site.

Before you can create links to other HTML pages, you must know where you want to connect your Web page. You can create links to pages within your Web site and across the world.

Specifically, in this chapter you'll learn how to

☐ Understand how hyperlinks work when connecting two pages to one another

☐ Create a hyperlink to other Web pages in your current Web

☐ Create hyperlinks to other pages and sites across the world

☐ Configure how your hyperlinks appear within your Web pages

Building Hyperlinks Within FrontPage

The easiest and most common type of link you'll build connects the various pages within your FrontPage Web site. Through the past few hours, you've learned how to build several types of different HTML pages and how FrontPage lets you keep track of them all using the FrontPage Explorer. Unless you used a FrontPage template or wizard, none of your Web pages are interlinked to each other, meaning you can't get from one page to another when you use your Web browser.

Almost always, you must build hypertext links between related pages in your Web site. FrontPage lets you easily build links between HTML pages using simple dialog boxes. You can even accomplish this by dragging and dropping pages on top of each other using the Explorer and FrontPage Editor.

The most common type of hyperlink you'll build in FrontPage connects pages within the same Web site. You'll quickly find that you have multiple pages in your site, because everything you want to say rarely fits on a single page.

Hyperlinks must be built within the FrontPage Editor, but they can be tracked and watched using the FrontPage Explorer. You'll understand more about this interrelationship between the Explorer and Editor as you continue in this section.

First, type a word or phrase on your Web page that will serve as the text that links this page to another. In Web lingo, this text is called "hot," because it directly links one page to another when viewed using a Web browser.

Picking a useful word or phrase is important, because you always want to give your visitors descriptive clues as to their destination before they click a link. For example, suppose you were building a link to Microsoft's home page at http://www.microsoft.com. When you type your link (or hot text), you want to use something like "Microsoft" or "Microsoft's Home Page." Similarly, you wouldn't want to use "A software company in Washington" or some obscure term.

TIME SAVER

> One important phrase that should never serve as your linked text is "Click here." You can assume that visitors to your home page know that they should click a hyperlink to visit another page; therefore, using "Click here" as your linked text isn't descriptive (that is, it doesn't tell your visitors where they're going to go).

8

After you've typed your hot text, select it with your mouse and choose Insert | Hyperlink from the FrontPage menu bar or click the Add/Edit Hyperlink icon from the FrontPage icon bar. Figure 8.1 shows the Create Hyperlink dialog box.

Figure 8.1.

From here, you can connect this Web page to another within your FrontPage Web site.

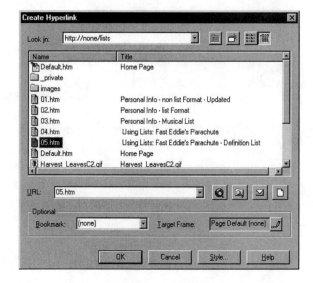

FrontPage lets you select the Web page to which you want to link. You can also link to a graphic or an image instead of another HTML page. By default, only the pages (and images) within your current FrontPage Web page appear.

Besides linking your page to another HTML file in the same FrontPage Web site, you also have several other linking options available to you. Remember that links require you to know the full URL of the linked page, which can be literally anywhere on the Web. FrontPage doesn't care whether the file to which you link is on your computer or on a computer in New York City or Singapore—it all looks the same because of URLs.

TIME SAVER

For a more in-depth description on URLs, see Hour 1, "Welcome to Web Publishing."

There are four special icons that appear within the Create Hyperlink dialog box that enable you to create a link to other spots on the Web. Table 8.1 describes how to use these four icons when you build a hyperlink.

Table 8.1. Linking outside your FrontPage Web page.

Icon	Description
	FrontPage has a close working relationship with your Web browser. This icon lets you browse anywhere on the WWW, and then FrontPage picks up the current URL you are visiting and saves it as the hyperlink. This is a great tool, and it's often used when building lists of favorite sites.
	On your computer, not all links will be made within the current FrontPage Web page. Sometimes you might want to link to an HTML file or image located elsewhere on your hard drive. Click this icon to browse your computer and select the file to which you want to link. FrontPage will copy that file into the currently open Web page.
	Another popular type of hyperlink lets you send e-mail instead of visiting another Web page. Click this icon, and you are prompted for an e-mail address instead of a standard hyperlink.
	This final button lets you create a new page to hyperlink to. FrontPage then adds this new page to your To-Do list and lets you build it in the future. This is a great strategy for expanding your site; you can finish working on your current page before moving to the next one.

After you've selected a file or URL to which to link, click OK. FrontPage reformats your hot text so that it appears underlined and in blue—the default appearance of hypertext on the Web.

You can change the URL for this specific link any time in the future by right-clicking the hot text and choosing Hyperlink Properties from the pop-up box that appears. When you are updating a hyperlink, you have the same options available as you did when you built one from scratch.

After you initially build your hyperlinks, switch back to the FrontPage Explorer. Click the hyperlink icon and you can see the dynamic relationships you've created between pages.

Figure 8.2 shows a single page that is linked to a half dozen others. Notice how there is a graphical relationship that shows you how the pages are connected to each other; also note that the page title appears, to help you recognize each page.

You can create as many hyperlinks on your Web page as you want. Feel free to mix and match links between your Web page, your e-mail, and Web pages across the world, because they all look the same within a browser. In addition, you don't even have to type hot text before you create the hyperlink. In this situation, FrontPage simply displays the linked file's name as the hot text when your link is created.

Figure 8.2.
FrontPage shows you how all your pages are linked together.

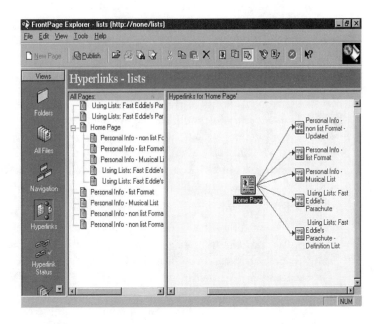

Updating the Linking Text

At any point, you can make several different types of changes to your hot, hyperlinked text. Just like standard text on your Web page, you can retype, erase, or modify hot text simply by using your mouse and keyboard.

CAUTION

Remember to be careful when you change text that links pages. You *always* want hypertext links that lead to other pages to be thoughtful and descriptive. Your visitors should always know exactly what page they're visiting before they click a link. The goal is to always make your linking text vivid and descriptive.

Updating Link Colors

As previously mentioned, every link you build with FrontPage will automatically appear underlined and in blue when viewed through a Web browser. However, there are several subtleties to the colors of hyperlinked text—it isn't always blue. In a browser, click a link and notice how the hypertext momentarily turns red, indicating that you've *activated* the link. Then click on your browser's Back button. The link you just followed is now purple instead of the original blue, indicating that it is a *previously followed* link. These color changes help visitors (and you) keep track of sites you've visited on the Web and let you know which link has been activated when you click your mouse.

NEW TERM   *Hyperlink text* is the text on a Web page that is programmatically linked to another page or site on the Internet. Hyperlinked text used to always appear underlined and in bright blue so that it stood out on a Web page. In fact, until very recently, HTML didn't support underlining of any text on a page, except for hyperlinked text so that visitors wouldn't be confused.

NEW TERM   *Active hyperlink text* is defined as the piece of hyperlinked text on a Web page that has just been clicked. Active hyperlinked text is colored differently so that you, as an individual who browses the Web, know which link was clicked. Imagine a large Web page with lots and lots of links. You'll always know which link you clicked because it appears in red (by default) momentarily. It is a subtle distinction, but one that all the major browsers adhere to.

NEW TERM   *Visited hyperlink text* lets you know when you've already visited a particular link. Visited links are stored within your Web browser's cache, which is purged periodically. Therefore, even if you visited a link a month ago, your Web browser might have forgotten and could show the link as standard hyperlink text. Visited hyperlink text is useful because it saves you from following the same link time and time again. You can control your browser's cache by editing the default preferences and settings.

To Do   Now that you understand what the different types of hypertext are and how they appear in a browser, it's time to learn how you can customize their appearance. Keep in mind that you can change the default color settings for all three types of hypertext on a Web page and that your changes affect the entire page. Follow these steps:

1. Anywhere within your Web page, right-click and choose Page Properties from the pop-up selection box that appears. The FrontPage Page Properties dialog box then appears.

2. From this dialog box, click the Background tab. Figure 8.3 shows the dialog box with the background properties of the page available for customization.

3. You can change the default color in which hyperlink text, active hyperlink text, and visited hyperlink text appear by selecting a color from the drop-down menu bar. There are 16 named colors from which you can choose. If none of these fits, choose Custom from the drop-down menu bar, and you have literally 16.7 million colors from which to choose—all the colors of the rainbow and then some! Figure 8.4 shows the Color dialog box, in which you can pick any color from the Color spectrum field.

4. When you've set your hypertext colors, click OK; FrontPage will return you to the Editor.

8

Figure 8.3.

*The properties in
this dialog box
affect the entire
page, so be aware
of the changes you
make.*

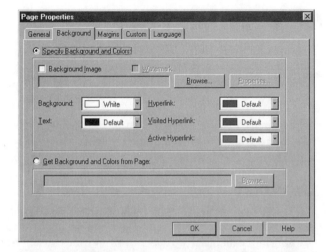

Figure 8.4.

*Custom colors are
difficult to identify
from this color
spectrum, but you
have tremendous
variety here.*

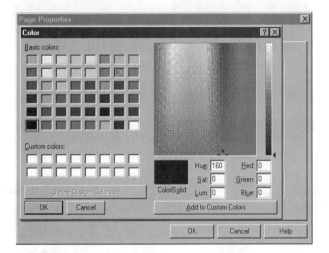

The changes you've made affect all hypertext for your entire page. If you must make a specific
color change for a single link, you can always select that link's text and change it by using the
font properties described in Hour 5, "Adding Style to Your Text." These font options take
precedence over the default hypertext color settings.

Useful Linking Tips

Knowing how to add WWW links to your Web page contributes greatly to your FrontPage expertise. Along with increased power and flexibility, however, comes the opportunity to make your Web page much more confusing and difficult to use for people who stop by for a visit.

Here's a list of some important issues to remember when adding links to your home page. Some are common sense, but others might seem more obscure. By following this set of tips, you won't have to worry about making your Web page more confusing when you add links.

Organize Your Links with Lists

Now that you've started using links in your Web page, it's important to keep them orderly so that they're understandable and simple to use. It's easy to let your links become disorganized and fall into disarray. Every time you add new information to your Web page, you must make sure that the page remains organized and easy to read.

One popular method for keeping links organized is using a list. As explained in Hour 6, "Building Lists," lists can present many different pieces of information in a crisp, bulleted format. Lists work perfectly when you want to include a bunch of links on your home page. For example, almost everyone has a compilation of neat Web pages, favorite places to visit, or pages related to their own. These types of links can usually be best organized using lists.

 Creating a list of links is the same process as building a list from scratch. Simply type each link on a separate line, select all the items, and then click the Bulleted List icon in FrontPage. Figure 8.5 shows a neat and simple bulleted list that organizes five links.

Figure 8.5.

Lists of links help keep Web pages looking ship-shape.

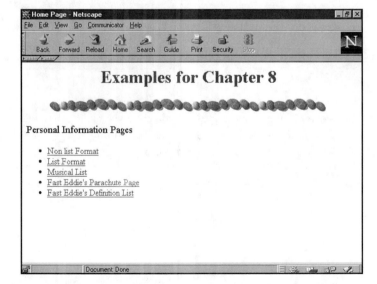

Don't Over-Link

Nothing is more confusing than stopping by a Web page with 200 words of text, where 180 of them are linked to different spots on the Web. Figure 8.6 shows a page that contains too many links. Because linked text appears underlined and in blue, having too many links in a paragraph (or page) makes it completely unreadable, as well as difficult for visitors to enjoy stopping by.

Visiting various Web pages is a lot like window shopping. If you see a store that has a hideous, cluttered front window, you're probably less inclined to go in and shop. Keep this in mind when you are adding links to your Web pages. If you want to include many different links, consider adding a simple (but organized) list at the bottom of your page.

Figure 8.6.

You probably get a headache just looking at this page.

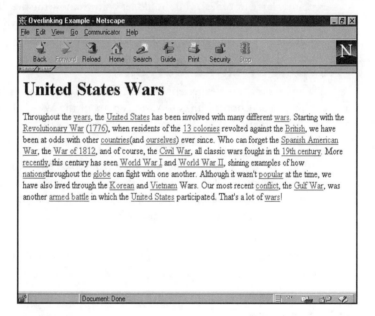

Link Specific, Descriptive Words

Although the Web relies on links that connect pieces of information with each other, try to make your links transparent. Here's an example (the links are in bold). The following paragraph includes a link that is *not* transparent:

Barney's Circus is a barrel full of fun. Individuals and families of all ages and backgrounds can come to the circus and enjoy themselves. **Click on Barney's Circus** to see a picture of what the big-top tent looks like. The tent is world famous as the tallest tent in use today.

Here's similar text with a transparent link:

> Barney's Circus is a barrel full of fun. Individuals and families of all ages and back-grounds can come to the circus and enjoy themselves. You won't want to miss the **big-top tent**, the world's tallest tent still in use today.

Your links shouldn't interrupt the flow of text, as the link in the first example did by using the words "Click on." You can assume readers know that clicking underlined text brings them to a related area.

Describe Large Links

Whenever you link your Web page to large graphics, files, audio bites, or video clips (even extremely large text files), you should let visitors know the file size before they click the link. They deserve fair warning, because large files can take a while to download. Hour 14, "Multimedia and Animation," discusses this in more detail.

Keep Your Links Current

As you become more experienced and continue to build your home page, you are likely to compile a collection of links to various parts of the Web. Occasionally, these links might become obsolete. A Web page you reference might be deleted or might move to another site. Whatever the reason, it's likely that some of your links will be lost every few months.

Visitors who stop by and see a neat link in your Web page will try to use that link, and they will be disappointed if they find that the page no longer exists. If you're going to have links on your Web page, you should periodically check to make sure that they all work. Otherwise, you shouldn't include them on your Web page.

In addition, FrontPage even has an automated tool that checks your links for you. Click the Hyperlink Status view from the FrontPage Explorer and you'll see the current status of all the links within this current Web.

Summary

Hypertext links are the main reason why the Web is so popular. The capability of connecting related pieces of information through a simple link is attractive, and it depicts how the WWW got its name—from building a web of hyperlinks back and forth across the globe.

You should feel comfortable building and using hyperlinks within your Web page and across the world using FrontPage. In addition, this hour you learned several important techniques for maintaining your links' appearance and usability after you create them.

Q&A

Q How do browsers interpret and use hyperlinks?

A When you see a link on a Web page, your browser has simply indicated that a particular phrase will whisk you to another corner of the Web. The fun stuff happens after you click the link. Your browser reads the full URL of the file you want to retrieve and sends a request to the computer hosting that file, asking to see the HTML page and all embedded graphics. The Web server then interprets that request and sends back the specific files to your browser, which in turn constructs the page for you. All that work happens in the background without you worrying about it!

Q Most links I use end with `.COM` or `.EDU`, but some only end in two characters, such as `.FR` or `.IL`. What's the difference between these types of links?

A These URLs are different only in their *domain name*, or the last few characters of the URL. By default, every country in the world has its own two-character domain name: the United States' is `.US`, whereas `.FR` is for France and `.IL` is for Israel. However, these two-character domain names are really secondary to the main domain names, which help identify the type of Web site to which you are connecting. Several domain names don't necessarily indicate the country in which the server is physically located. These domain names—`.COM`, `.EDU`, `.GOV`, `.ORG`, `.NET`, and a couple of others—tend to be much more popular for Internet addresses from the U.S. because they were around before the two-letter country codes. From your point of view, the different domain names just help you identify where the server is located, that's it. Browsers treat all URLs the same.

Q Why would you want to change the default link colors within a Web page, instead of leaving them the default blue?

A You might want to color coordinate your entire Web page. For example, if your headlines are red and the body of your text is purple, blue hypertext might disrupt the flow of reading your page. Instead, you could change the link text so that it appears purple and is indistinguishable on a page. Another alternative would be to set linked text to be mauve, so that it stands out from the regular text on your page but still color coordinates with the entire page.

Workshop

The Workshop contains quiz questions and an Activities section to help reinforce what you've learned in this hour. Try not to look at the quiz answers until you've tried to work them out yourself!

Quiz

1. How can you build a link to another page within your current FrontPage Web?

2. How can you build a hyperlink to a page that's elsewhere on the WWW, somewhere across the world?

3. What are the three different types of hyperlink text and when does text change from one type to another?

Answers

1. Linking to a page in the same Web you are in is easy. First, type the hyperlink text that will appear "hot" in your browser. Then select the text and click the Add/Edit Hyperlink icon from the FrontPage icon bar to bring up the Create Hyperlink dialog box. Then select the file to which you want to link, and click OK.

2. Basically, you'll follow the same steps as before except you must type a valid URL instead of selecting the file to which you want to link. You have several options here. The easiest is you can use a browser to find the page to which you want to build a link, and then create your hyperlink from FrontPage while browsing that site. FrontPage will pick up the current URL for you automatically. Or, you can copy and paste the URL into the Create Hyperlink dialog box or manually type the URL yourself.

3. The three different types of hyperlink text are hyperlink text, visited hyperlink text, and active hyperlink text. Hyperlink text normally appears on your pages (in the default color of blue) until you activate a link. For the few seconds your browser is looking for the new page, the hot text becomes active hyperlink text. Finally, after you've visited a site and found a new link to the same spot, the text becomes visited hyperlink text, enabling you to tell which sites you've been to already.

Activities

1. Read Hour 22, "Site Design Tips," to learn more about generating automatic navigation bars between pages in your FrontPage Web. These navigation bars are advanced features that dynamically change, depending on the number of files in your current Web.

2. Build a hypertext link to http://www.shafran.com or to another external site across the Web. Make sure you feel comfortable linking to any URL, because you'll use this tactic often when you create Web pages.

PART
III

FrontPage and Web Graphics

Hour

Hour 9

Understanding and Using Web Graphics

So far, you've learned all about how to set text appearance and add information to your Web page. This new section teaches you how to add colorful, exciting graphics and images to your FrontPage Web page.

Graphics make the Web exciting, and virtually all Web pages use them in some fashion. Graphics can be photographs, icons, buttons, and more. In this hour you'll learn the basics of including and displaying graphics on your Web page. You'll see how FrontPage lets you customize your graphics as well as how they appear.

Specifically, in this hour you'll learn how to

- ☐ Find cool Web graphics to use for your Web pages
- ☐ Include clip art and pictures interchangeably within your FrontPage Web
- ☐ Learn how to build your own Web graphics from scratch

NEW TERM *Web graphics* are digitized images that are saved electronically. Your computer saves them as bits and bytes, but it knows how to display them with all the colors and fanfare required. Web graphics are computer images that are saved explicitly for use on the Web and take advantage of certain features to enhance the way they appear in a Web browser.

Using Web Graphics

Virtually every Web page you'll ever explore and visit will use graphics in some fashion. That's because graphics are the lifeblood of the Web—the spark that entices millions of users to get online and browse from work and home.

You'll find everything from business logos, famous paintings, and city maps on the Web. In fact, you'd be hard pressed to imagine virtually any site without some sort of attractive graphic. Imagine visiting the Louvre online (`http://www.louvre.fr`) without graphics. Reading a description of Venus de Milo isn't the same as seeing the famous statue for yourself.

You can find another good example of how graphics enhance a site by visiting the Microsoft home page at `http://www.microsoft.com/sitebuilder/` (see Figure 9.1). Microsoft blends a nice array of graphics with its Web page.

Figure 9.1.
Without graphics, this page would be excruciatingly boring.

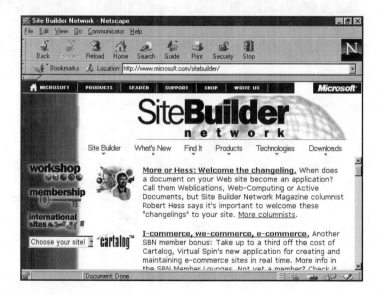

Types of Graphics You Can Use

In general, all graphics on the Web come in one of two popular formats: GIF and JPEG.

GIF is short for the Graphical Interchange Format and was originally developed to be an efficient and flexible way for people around the world to send computer graphics to one another. It was pioneered by CompuServe and became the first graphical file type supported by the WWW. Today, there are millions of images available in GIF format. GIF images allow only 256 different colors to be used. This limitation helps keep file size down for small graphics, but it doesn't work very well for large images and photographs, in particular.

JPEG, or the Joint Photographic Experts Group format, was designed specifically for photographs and images with millions of colors. The JPEG format has proved to be significantly more efficient in compressing large photographs electronically and is now supported by virtually every graphical Web browser. In general, JPEG images handle colors and image details better than GIF images do.

You'll find yourself using both these formats interchangeably when it makes better sense to take advantage of their respective features. In general, you'll use GIFs for icons, buttons, bars, and backgrounds; JPEGs are more commonly used in photographs, complex logos, and maps. FrontPage handles both formats smoothly, so you don't have to worry about the nitty-gritty details of counting colors or changing formats.

JUST A MINUTE

Recently, a new type of image has gained in popularity. Billed as the replacement for GIFs, Portable Network Graphics (PNG, pronounced *ping*) images are supported by FrontPage 98 and are slowly being accepted by the leading browsers.

PNG graphics are very similar to GIFs, but they are more efficient and can better handle a vast array of colors. Soon, GIF images will probably be phased out and PNG images will be used instead. PNG graphics can be displayed as transparent images, and you can choose to save them in interlaced or non-interlaced format.

For more information on the PNG graphics type, visit my favorite PNG information center at http://quest.jpl.nasa.gov/PNG/. It's good to know that FrontPage supports this innovative graphics type and that it enables you to include them on your Web page (if that's what you want).

Rather than bore you with all the details, I'll quickly summarize why PNG exists. Several years ago, CompuServe (an online services company) created GIF as its international image standard, and many people adopted it as their standard as well.

A few years ago, Unisys realized that CompuServe had used some of its patented computer code when developing the GIF format, and it decided to enforce the patent. Not wanting to be dependent on another company's patent, CompuServe (along with other developers on the Internet) introduced PNG to be the communitywide graphics format standard. PNG has started to become more popular because of its advantages over the GIF file format—such as not having to tussle with Unisys over who owns the format.

As you can imagine, not all the computer graphics you'll want to use come in one of these recognizable formats. That's fine, because FrontPage has a built-in set of filters that automatically convert images of all types into GIF and JPEG. Images are saved as GIFs if they use only 256 different colors, and they are saved as JPEGs if they use more. FrontPage automatically translates TIFF, PCX, BMP, and several other formats whenever you use one of them on your Web page. This fantastic feature will save you hours of worry and headaches.

Finding Good Graphics

Now that you understand the importance of the different types of Web graphics, the next step is to learn how to locate several to use yourself.

There are several ways you can get Web graphics to use for your own Web site. This section shows you several methods with which you can find and use graphics for yourself.

Using the FrontPage 98 Graphics

FrontPage 98 comes with a whole slew of graphics you can use on your Web page. There are over 400 icons, bars, buttons, and bullets that can be inserted or customized for your Web page. The rest of this lesson describes how you can use these built-in icons.

In fact, FrontPage goes one step further by providing you with *themes* for building Web sites. These themes come with an entire set of graphics and icons. See Hour 21, "Applying Web Themes," for more information on using the built-in FrontPage themes. Figure 9.2 shows the sample graphics that come with building a Web page using the "Arcs" theme.

Figure 9.2.

All the banners, buttons, icons, and bars are built for you when you select a theme in FrontPage.

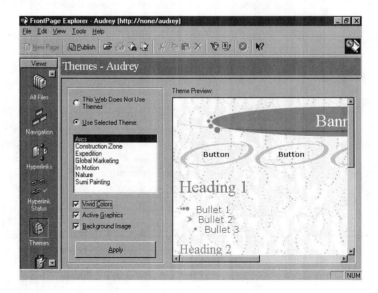

As if the other graphics in FrontPage weren't enough, if you have Microsoft Office 95 or 97, you have all the MS clip art available at your fingertips. When you insert images from

FrontPage, you can also browse through the shared clip art available to the entire suite of programs in MS Office.

Finding Images on the Web

There are millions of Web graphics available for you to download and use when building your FrontPage Web page. In fact, any Web graphic you can see can be saved for your own personal use by using Netscape or Internet Explorer.

Your best bet is to visit one of the many online warehouses of free images for your Web page. Here are a couple that are comprehensive, and they allow you to use their images freely:

The Rainbow Collection

`http://www.geocities.com/SiliconValley/Heights/1272/rainbow.html`

GraphX Kingdom

`http://www.efni.com/~haven/graphx/index.html`

You can browse through these and other collections on the Web until you find the image you want to use. Then you can download it and add it your Web page.

Here's an example of how to download and save images to your computer:

1. Start your favorite Web browser and go to `http://www.shafran.com`.

2. Move your mouse so that it hovers over the photograph on the left side of the page. Next, right-click to bring up the Browser pop-up box.

3. If you're using Internet Explorer, choose Save Picture As from the pop-up box. In Netscape, the command is called Save Image As. Figure 9.3 shows this image being saved in Netscape.

Figure 9.3.

Saving images from other Web sites is easy and straightforward, but make sure you have the owner's permission to use them.

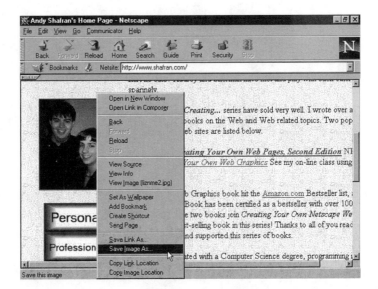

4. The Save As dialog box appears and lets you pick where on your computer you want to place the Web graphic. The filename is already filled in for you. Choose where you want to save your image, and click the Save button. Your browser automatically downloads the image you've selected so that you can use it in FrontPage.

TIME SAVER

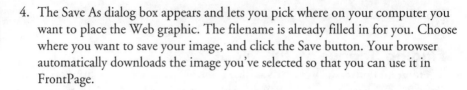

FrontPage has an even easier way to use images directly off the Web without downloading them to your computer. You can have FrontPage copy the image directly from your Web browser if that's the only item you're looking at. For this example, FrontPage wouldn't know which image you wanted to use unless you right-clicked the image and selected View Image. With the image in your Web browser, FrontPage enables you to import it just as if you were including the image from your personal computer.

CAUTION

Be aware that images you see when browsing the Web might be protected under copyright laws. Even though you can easily save images with a browser, you must have permission to use borrowed images on your own home page.

Although many individuals on the Web don't mind if you borrow icons and images from their Web pages, businesses and corporations often have a different point of view. Their images usually are custom developed, and they (as well as the court system) view saving copies of their images as stealing. So be careful when you take images from sites around the Web. Many images and graphics are copyrighted, and the owners can—and sometimes do—take legal action against people who infringe upon their copyrights.

One good example that makes the point is browsing cartoons on the Web. Dilbert, one of the world's most popular cartoon strips, can be found at http://www.unitedmedia.com/comics/dilbert/. Every day a new cartoon is online, displayed as an image. This cartoon, however, is copyrighted and you are not allowed to save or use it on your Web site in any fashion, no matter how fitting it is or funny it might be.

Always read through the copyright notices at a site from which you want to save an image. Many image collections indicate that their graphics can be used freely on personal Web pages, whereas others might have certain rules or restrictions. If you are ever unsure whether an image is copyrighted, send an e-mail to the person in charge of the Web page and ask.

9

This issue is being examined in-depth by copyright and patent organiza-
tions around the world and is particularly difficult to manage because of
the variety of copyright laws in different countries.

Making Your Own Images from Scratch

Although FrontPage comes with hundreds of graphics (and you can find thousands more on
the Web), most likely you'll find yourself acting like Picasso or Rembrandt at least a few times
when building a Web site. Building or modifying your own Web graphics has become very
common, and it is simple to do with Microsoft Image Composer (which comes with
FrontPage 98).

Figure 9.4 shows the Image Composer in action. Image Composer is an excellent program
because it comes with several automated tools for building images, and it works perfectly with
FrontPage 98. You learn all about how you can use Image Composer in Hour 11, "Working
with Image Composer."

Figure 9.4.

*Microsoft Image Com-
poser edits, creates, fixes,
and modifies any type of
graphic for your Web
page.*

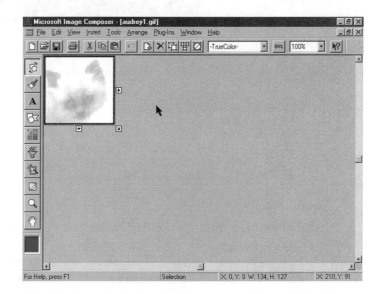

Although Image Composer is an excellent tool, another popular product you can use to build
Web graphics is Paint Shop Pro. Developed by Jasc software, you can download Paint Shop
Pro at http://www.jasc.com. Paint Shop Pro is shareware, which means you can download
and test it before you decide whether it's worth the purchase. You'll find Paint Shop Pro to
be a robust and all-encompassing tool that enables you to create and modify professional-
caliber images for your Web page.

Figure 9.5 shows Paint Shop Pro working on another image.

Figure 9.5.

Paint Shop Pro is the standard tool that Web developers have in their arsenal when building comprehensive graphics for their Web sites.

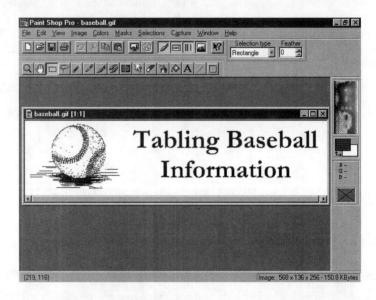

TIME SAVER

Both Image Composer and Paint Shop Pro are great programs because they offer a tremendous amount of flexibility. There are books available on these programs. For more information on Image Composer and the ins and outs of using it, see *Wild Web Graphics with Image Composer*, by David Karlins, and for more on Paint Shop Pro, pick up *Creating Your Own Web Graphics with Paint Shop Pro*, by Andy Shafran and Dick Oliver. Both books are published by Que, and they give you your fill of information on building custom graphics for your Web page.

Scanning Graphics and Photos

NEW TERM   A *scanner* is a separate piece of computer equipment that takes pages and photographs and stores them electronically on your computer. The scanner must be physically connected and configured to your computer to work properly. Scanners come in all shapes and sizes, and they work with a variety of computers.

When you want to include personal pictures and drawings on your Web page, sometimes the only way is to use a digital scanner. Scanners come in all different price ranges, and they vary in quality. You can find an affordable black-and-white scanner for $79, but high-end color scanners can run $999 or more, depending on the quality you are looking for.

9

Scanners are rated according to *resolution*. Resolution is the number of itsy-bitsy dots that a scanner observes when digitizing your photographs and drawings. Resolution is important because the better the resolution your scanner uses, the more detailed your digitized images appear.

When you are looking for a scanner, you should get at least a 300×300 dpi resolution. This means that for every inch scanned, 90,000 dots are picked up by the scanner. That might sound like a lot, but a standard fax machine uses 200×200 dpi resolution—and you're probably familiar with how blurry faxes can sometimes be. Often, a scanner comes with software that enhances the resolution of scanned images significantly.

High-resolution scanners often cost a premium, and they can be overkill if you are simply scanning pictures in for your Web page. Often, 300×300 dpi or 600×600 dpi is enough resolution for the casual user.

To put personal images on your home page, you must scan them directly into your computer. FrontPage 98 interfaces directly with most scanners while building your Web site.

COFFEE BREAK

Personally, I use a Logitech PageScan color scanner. For about $250, I got a 400×600 dpi resolution scanner that comes with all the necessary software to scan color as well as black-and-white images, and it can even make photocopies and send faxes. All the photographs at http://www.shafran.com were scanned at this level. This will help give you a good idea of the type of resolution you might want when buying a scanner.

TIME SAVER

Initially, if you can't afford your own scanner or aren't sure you need one, head down to your local Kinko's or other copy store. These types of stores usually have scanning equipment available to rent for just a few dollars. You can scan in a half-dozen images, save them to a disk, and print them out in full color for under $20. Along the same lines, many local public libraries also have multimedia equipment as well—and they are free!

Adding Graphics with FrontPage

Of course, FrontPage lets you add and manipulate all sorts of graphics when building your Web page. You can use FrontPage-supplied images, import your own, and even drag and drop Web graphics with your mouse.

Adding FrontPage and MS Office Clip Art

You must add graphics within the FrontPage Editor while you are building a specific Web page. To add one of the built-in FrontPage Web graphics, choose Insert | Clipart from the FrontPage menu bar. The Microsoft Clip Gallery dialog box appears, as shown in Figure 9.6.

Figure 9.6.

You can browse hundreds of FrontPage and MS Office images through this gallery.

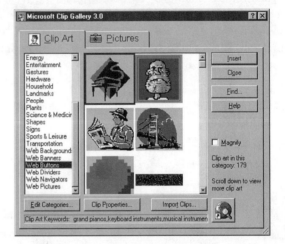

There are tabs for Clip Art and Pictures, both of which you can include on your Web page. Browse through the FrontPage Web graphics by clicking on the Clip Art tab and scrolling to the bottom. There are several categories of Web icons, buttons, pictures, and dividers. Similarly, you can browse the rest of the Clip Art categories to use any regular MS Office clip art.

To insert an image in your Web page, select the graphic you want to use, and click the Insert button. FrontPage automatically makes a copy of the image you selected and places it in the same directory as your HTML files. Then, FrontPage adds the image to your Web page so that you can see it side by side with the text, lists, and tables also on the screen.

Figure 9.7 shows a sample Web page with two newly added FrontPage clip art images. Notice how the bar is used to separate a headline from the rest of the page. This type of icon is commonly used in Web sites instead of the horizontal line because of its additional colors and character.

Figure 9.7.

The little ball is an icon that comes with FrontPage and is added as a standard piece of clip art.

The FrontPage bar

The FrontPage icon

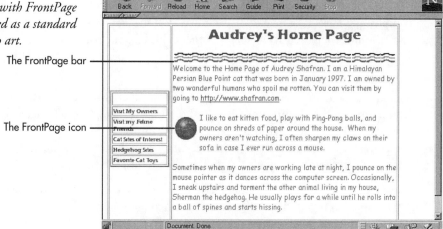

Including Other Web Graphics

 Similar to working with clip art, adding non-FrontPage and Office clip art images is a breeze. To include a graphic on any page, choose Insert | Image from the FrontPage menu bar to bring up the Image dialog box (see Figure 9.8).

Figure 9.8.

This is center stage for adding images to your FrontPage Web page.

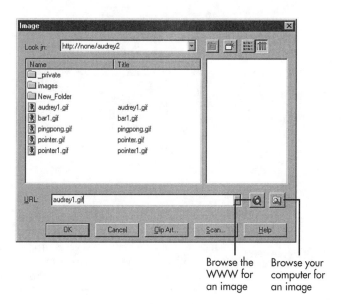

Browse the WWW for an image

Browse your computer for an image

Using your mouse, you can select an image from anywhere within your existing FrontPage Web page. If you need to browse your computer's hard drive to find your Web graphic, click the Browse icon located in the bottom-right corner of the Image dialog box. Browse your computer and select the image you want to add. If the graphic is a GIF or JPEG, FrontPage copies it into your Web's directory and then adds it to the page the Editor is working on. FrontPage will automatically convert other image types into GIF or JPEG format, if necessary.

You can also add images while browsing Web sites. To do this, click the Browse the WWW icon located in the bottom-right corner of the Image dialog box. This icon activates your default Web browser and lets you explore the Web until you're looking at the image you want to use. When you've found the right image, click OK in the Image dialog box, and FrontPage downloads the graphic you selected and displays it on your page.

Figure 9.9 shows the same Web page used in this chapter with two more images: a custom-built graphic of the mouse pointer, and a scanned photograph.

Figure 9.9.

This page uses FrontPage clip art, a scanned photo, and a from-scratch image to show you how they all work together.

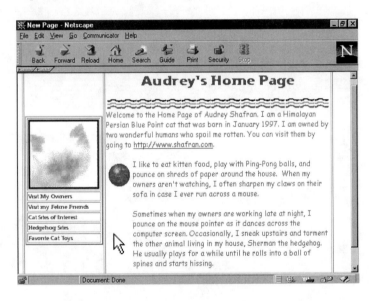

TIME SAVER

Besides using the Insert I Image command, you can also drag and drop graphics from Windows Explorer onto the FrontPage Editor. This is a great tactic if you want to add several graphics to a page quickly. You can select as many images as you like; then drag them to the FrontPage Explorer and release the mouse button. FrontPage copies each of the images into the current FrontPage Web page and adds them to the current page.

9

Moving Your Images

After you've added images, you can drag and drop them to different locations on your page. In addition, you can double-click any image and FrontPage starts Image Composer, enabling you to make modifications to that specific image.

Summary

During this hour you learned all about Web graphics. There are several popular image formats, and FrontPage lets you use them when creating a site. In addition, you should feel comfortable finding and including images in your FrontPage Web page. Finding cool Web graphics can be difficult unless you know where to look. By using FrontPage images, collections on the Web, and tools to create images yourself, Web graphics should be easy for you to come by, and even easier to include on your pages.

Q&A

Q How is GIF pronounced? Like the peanut butter, or the word *gift* without the *t*?

A Always the debate of countless Web denizens and artists, *GIF* is properly pronounced with a hard "G" sound, so that it rhymes with the word *whiff*.

Q Do I have to worry about some sort of GIF tax on my images because of that dispute between CompuServe and Unisys?

A Unisys settled the GIF patent issue with CompuServe and began enforcing its patent on companies that let you build and edit GIFs. Companies such as Microsoft (for Image Composer) and Jasc (for Paint Shop Pro) pay Unisys royalties to let you build images on your own. You, as an end user, don't have to worry about this royalty because it was covered by the author of the software you use.

Q When I try to add images to my Web page, nothing shows up when I want to use clip art from Office 97. Do I have to do something special to get FrontPage to recognize and use this clip art?

A FrontPage automatically recognizes all clip art from Office 95 and up. Sometimes, clip art is not installed when you put Office on your machine. To correct this, insert your Microsoft Office CD-ROM into your computer and step through the installation process again. Make sure you select Custom Installation, where you can pick and choose the components you want to add. Select only the MS Office Clip art. When the installation is complete, FrontPage will be able to recognize and use all the clip art from Office. In addition, Microsoft has many new clip art images on its Web site at http://www.microsoft.com/clipgallerylive/.

9

Workshop

The Workshop contains quiz questions and an Activities section to help reinforce what you've learned in this hour. Try not to look at the quiz answers until you've tried to work them out yourself!

Quiz

1. When should you use a GIF instead of a JPEG, and vice versa?

2. Why can't you just download and use any image you find on the Web?

3. What's the easiest way to add over 20 images to a Web page at one time?

Answers

1. GIF images should be used for all graphics that use 256 colors or less. In addition, the GIF format is optimized for all graphics that are small (such as icons and buttons) for Web pages.

   The JPEG format should be used for all photographs and pieces of photographs, as well as for images that are much larger and take up the entire screen.

2. The answer is copyright laws. By default, all images (and text) are protected by copyright laws, meaning that you need explicit protection from their owner before you can use them on your Web site.

3. Start up the Windows Explorer and FrontPage Editor. Select all the images from Explorer and drag them, using your mouse, into the Editor. FrontPage will add all the images for you at once.

Activities

1. Experiment with all the clip art that comes with FrontPage and MS Office. Make sure you understand what graphics are readily available to you before you start trolling the Internet or try to create some for yourself.

2. Explore several collections of Web graphics on the Web. Download and use several images in one of your Web sites. Bookmark the sites you enjoy the most so that you can return there later when you need more exciting and innovative graphics.

3. Check out the next hour to learn how you can use some more advanced image techniques when including graphics on your Web page. You can place and wrap text around graphics by setting special image properties, and you can also use some graphics in the background of your page.

4. Fortunately, FrontPage and Microsoft Office come with a vast array of clip art, icons, and images you can use. For a wider selection of graphics, visit http://www.shafran.com/frontpage98 for a detailed listing of popular graphics sites on the Web.

9

Hour 10

Controlling Images with FrontPage

Including images in your Web page is just the tip of the iceberg when it comes to working with graphics inside FrontPage 98. Because Web graphics are so vital to a great-looking site, spending extra time learning how to make them appear great in a browser is worth it. There are many different ways you can control and customize how all sorts of images appear.

In this hour you will learn how to get the most out of including graphics within a particular page. You'll understand each of the different FrontPage image properties and then how images can even serve as hypertext links.

Specifically, in this hour you'll

☐ Control image alignment and appearance within FrontPage and your Web browser

☐ Understand some advanced features that improve the speed, performance, and appearance of images

☐ Place a patterned image in the background of your page

☐ Use graphics to create hyperlinks that point to other sites with your Web graphics

Setting Image Properties

As you learned in Hour 9, "Understanding and Using Web Graphics," adding an image to your Web page is relatively easy. You simply insert it, and the image appears right beside your text. It's also easy to drag the image back and forth across your Web page until you've placed it precisely where you want it to appear.

In addition to these techniques, FrontPage enables you to set several other important and useful properties for each image you place on your Web page. You must be in the FrontPage Editor to see and set your image properties. Once there, click your right mouse button over any image on your page and choose Image Properties from the pop-up dialog box that appears. FrontPage brings up the Image Properties dialog box (see Figure 10.1).

Figure 10.1.

There are over a dozen different properties at your fingertips from this dialog box.

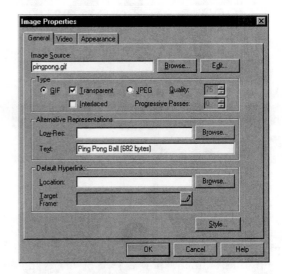

This section covers the image properties available under the General and Appearance tabs in the Image Properties dialog box. You'll learn about the Video tab in Hour 14, "Multimedia and Animation."

General Tab: Image Source

The first piece of information in the General tab is the Image Source box, which contains the filename of the image. There are two buttons you can click: Browse and Edit.

The Browse button lets you search for a different image to include instead of the one that is currently there.

The Edit button starts up Image Composer and lets you edit and make changes directly to your Web graphic. You'll learn more about the Image Composer in Hour 11, "Working with Image Composer." Figure 10.2 shows Image Composer editing the ping pong ball image.

Figure 10.2.

Within Image Composer, you can completely modify the appearance of your Web graphic.

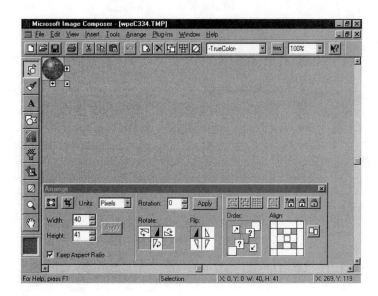

General Tab: Type

The next section of the Image Properties dialog box lets you set the information about the file format your graphic is saved as. On the WWW and within FrontPage, there are two common graphics file formats you'll run across: GIF and JPEG.

You learned about these two formats in detail in Hour 9, in the section labeled "Types of Graphics You Can Use." Both the GIF and JPEG file formats have useful traits that make them attractive to use within a Web site.

Depending on the extension of your Web graphic, FrontPage automatically marks your image type as either a GIF or a JPEG. Table 10.1 describes the two GIF options available, and Table 10.2 describes the two JPEG options you can select.

Table 10.1. GIF image type options.

Option	Description
Transparent	Image Transparency is one of the most popular reasons for using GIFs. When this box is selected, FrontPage automatically makes the background of your image see-through. This lets the color or background of the Web page be seen through the Web graphic. You'll almost always check this box unless you are using a photograph. Figure 10.3 shows an example of transparent and non-transparent images. The cat head is a non-transparent image—that's why the white shows up in the background of the image. The ping pong ball and arrow images are transparent, meaning you can see the background color through the unimportant pieces of the graphic.
Interlaced	This option is usually used for images that are large and can take a while to download. Browsers display interlaced images in multiple passes, with each pass becoming clearer and clearer. Think of your optometrist's office, where things start out blurry but become clearer with each successive pass. Interlaced images let visitors see the image in less detail quicker than waiting for the entire graphic to be downloaded and then shown onscreen.

Figure 10.3.

Both transparent and non-transparent images can be useful on a Web page.

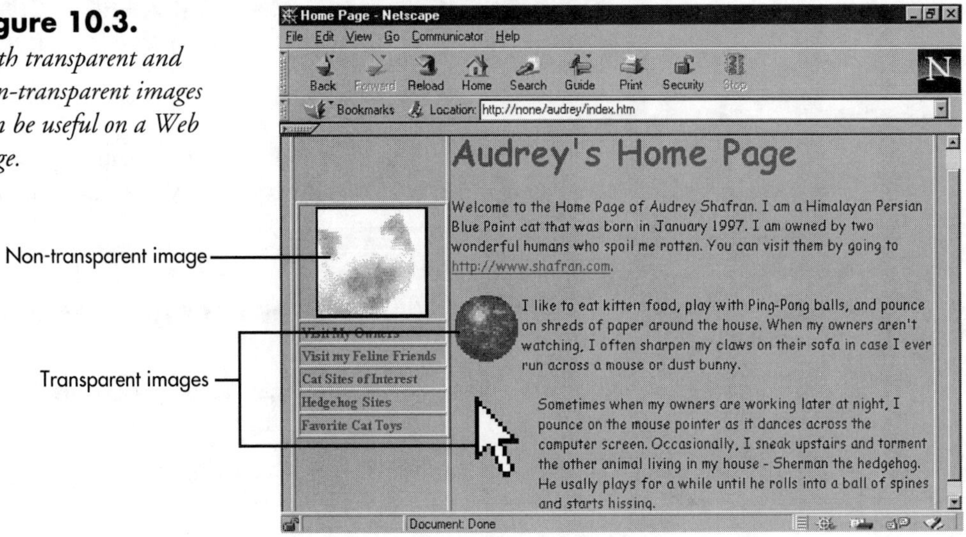

Non-transparent image

Transparent images

Table 10.2. JPEG image type options.

Option	Description
Quality	JPEG images can be compressed and then displayed in a browser to speed up the time it takes to download an image. The default compression quality is 75, which balances out the detail of an image with an optimal file size. You can improve the image appearance to provide a better-looking JPEG by increasing the image's quality. Similarly, if you need to speed up the amount of time an image takes to download, you can lower the JPEG quality, but your image will show up with less details.
Progressive Passes	Much like the interlaced option for GIFs, progressive JPEG images load in multiple passes, each becoming clearer. With JPEG images, you can set the number of passes it takes for an image to be seen in full detail. The default is four passes.

General Tab: Alternative Representations

The Alternative Representations section of the Image Properties dialog box lets you control two settings for how images load and appear within a Web browser.

As you've probably experienced, using very bright and colorful images on a Web page is common. Unfortunately, that often significantly increases the time it takes for an image to load. To solve this problem, FrontPage lets you set a low-resolution image, which then becomes overlayed by the main graphic you intend to use. Here's how it works: The Web browser notices that there is an image to load on this page. First it downloads the image specified in the Low-Res box. Then it starts downloading the larger, full-color image.

Usually a low-res image is in black-and-white, blurrier, and significantly smaller than the main image. Its sole purpose is to give visitors an idea of the larger image that takes a while to download. Visit the Cover Girl Web site (`http://www.covergirl.com`) to see a low-res image in action. First the less detailed black-and-white image appears, then a prettier full-color image overlays on top of it. Figure 10.4 shows this "easy breezy" site.

The other setting in the Alternative Representations tab is the Text box. This box controls what text shows up on Web pages if visitors have image loading automatically turned off. Occasionally, visitors will browse the WWW and tell their browsers not to load images because they take so long to download, or because the user has a very old browser that doesn't support images very well. In these cases, browsers display bits of text in place of the image. Figure 10.5 shows Netscape with image loading turned off and how it displays a piece of text about the image instead of the Web graphic.

10

Figure 10.4.

The hip Cover Girl site uses all the latest HTML techniques.

Figure 10.5.

The info you type in the Image Properties's Text box shows up directly on many Web pages.

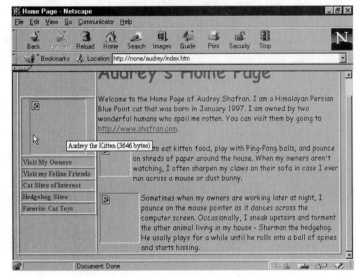

JUST A MINUTE

In general, at least 95 percent of users browse the Web with image loading turned on.

In Netscape you can change this setting by choosing Edit | Preferences from the menu bar. Click the category labeled Advanced and turn off the check box labeled Automatically Load Images.

To turn off automatic image loading in Microsoft Internet Explorer 3.0, choose View | Options from the menu bar to bring up the Options dialog box. In the General tab, check off the box marked Show Pictures. In Internet Explorer 4.0, choose View | Options | Advanced from the menu bar and under Multimedia, uncheck the box labeled Show Pictures.

General Tab: Default Hyperlink

The final setting in the General tab of the Image Properties dialog box lets you link your graphic to another page elsewhere on the Web. Creating a hyperlinked image is the exact same process as creating a standard hyperlink on your Web page. The only difference is that you must include the linked URL inside the Location box of the Image Properties dialog box.

In the Location box, type the filename or URL of where you want this specific image to link visitors. You can also pick up the URL from the current open page with your Web browser by clicking the Browse button.

For a more detailed description of how to build hyperlinks, check out Hour 8, "Linking Pages Together."

Appearance Tab: Layout

When you finish with the General tab in the Image Properties dialog box, click the Appearance tab. You'll see another handful of important characteristics you can set for each graphic on your Web page. Figure 10.6 shows the Appearance tab.

Figure 10.6.

These image characteristics are more commonly used when controlling how images appear beside text within Web pages.

There are two sections to this dialog box, Layout and Size. The Layout section is the most common set of image characteristics you'll use. Table 10.3 describes each of the four properties you can set.

Table 10.3. Image layout options.

Option	Description
Alignment	By default, an image appears wherever you've inserted it in a Web page. If you want an image to appear beside text, you'll probably want to set its alignment. You can choose from 10 different alignment options, and each controls exactly how text flows around your Web graphic. The most common alignment settings are Left and Right. Left alignment places an image to the left of a paragraph of text, and Right alignment does just the opposite.
Border Thickness	Border Thickness lets you add a thin line around your image to set it apart from the rest of your Web page. The FrontPage default border thickness is set to 0, but you can make it anything you'd like. Borders are often nice because they act as a frame around an image. Common border thicknesses range from 1 to 5.
Horizontal Spacing	Horizontal Spacing lets you add a certain number of pixels between the left and right borders of an image and text that you place next to it. Horizontal spacing is measured in pixels. Often the Horizontal Spacing setting is used in conjunction with the Alignment setting and is commonly set to 5 or 10, if used at all.
Vertical Spacing	Similar to Horizontal Spacing, Vertical Spacing adds a few extra pixels to the top and bottom of an image to separate it from other pieces of a Web page. It is rarely used. Vertical Spacing is also measured in pixels.

Appearance Tab: Size

The final image properties you can set directly affect the size of an image on a Web page. Image height and width are measured in pixels, or small dots that run the length and height of the screen.

By default, FrontPage automatically sizes an image according to the file's height and width. You can change the size of an image within Web browsers by changing the pixel Height and Width dimensions. To ensure that your image keeps the same proportions when you resize it, click the Keep Aspect Ratio checkbox within this tab.

CAUTION

> Remember that standard VGA screens are 640 pixels wide and 480 pixels high, so don't resize your image so large that it monopolizes your page.

Quick Image Fixes with the Image Toolbar

Controlling image properties isn't the only technique at your fingertips when working with the FrontPage Editor. Microsoft has also built in a whole suite of simple image editing tools that can quickly modify or change the standard appearance of an image within your page. This Image toolbar (select View | Image Toolbar from the FrontPage menu bar) appears only after you've single-clicked a graphic already added to your Web page.

Table 10.4 shows the icons in the Image toolbar and gives you a brief description of what happens when you select them.

Table 10.4. The Image toolbar icons.

Option	Description
▢ ◯ ⬠ ▥	These icons are used to create imagemaps and are described thoroughly in Hour 12, "Imagemap Education."
A	Adds pieces of text on top of your image. Very useful when adding a button from the FrontPage clipart to your Web page, and then you can place text on top of the graphic.
✎	Identifies the color of a GIF image that appears transparent when set in the Image Properties dialog box.
⌗	Crops part of an image to display only a certain section of it in a Web page.

continues

Table 10.4. continued

Option	Description
	Changes the graphic to look older and faded out.
	Transforms a color image into black-and-white format. Useful in creating the low-res version of an image.
	Removes all the changes you make to the image's appearance and restores it to the last saved edition.
	Rotates an image 90 degrees counterclockwise.
	Rotates an image 90 degrees clockwise.
	Creates a horizontally reversed mirror image of the graphic.
	Creates a vertically flipped image of the graphic.
	Darkens the image by adding additional contrast.
	Lightens an image by removing contrast.
	Applies an image-brightening filter on top of the graphic.
	Applies an image-darkening filter on top of the graphic.
	Adds beveled edges around the image to make a graphic look more like a clickable button.
	Resamples the image to add additional detail if you resize the image.

This handful of commands gives you significant flexibility when you are editing and including images on your Web pages. You'll use these quick filters and image changes all the time to add a button, brighten a photo, flip an image, and more.

10

Web Page Background

After you've gotten through the rigors of understanding and setting each image property, you must learn a new technique for using graphics on a Web site. In Hour 5, "Adding Style to Your Text," you saw how to control the color of text on your Web page. You also have the same flexibility by changing the background color and texture of your Web page. FrontPage lets you set any color to be in the background of a particular page, or you can use an image instead. Background images tile on top of each other so that they appear to add texture to your home page, instead of appearing as a single solitary color.

You set background colors and graphics by clicking your right mouse button anywhere within the FrontPage Editor and choosing Page Properties from the pop-up box. Then click the Background tab to see Figure 10.7.

Figure 10.7.

Background colors and graphics are controlled from this tab in the Page Properties dialog box.

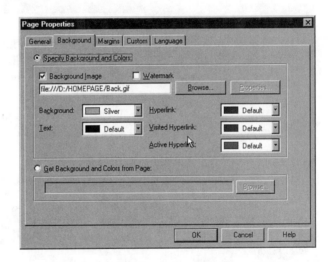

There are two ways you can control how your background appears: using a color or using a background image. Setting your background to be a solid color is easy. Simply click the drop-down Background box and select from the 16 named colors available. If none of those fits your page, you can select Custom and then choose from over 16.7 million colors. A color cube appears and lets you select with your mouse the color you want.

Using a background image instead is just slightly more difficult:

1. First, click the checkbox labeled Background Image.
2. Then click the Browse button to search for the image you want to use in your background. The Select Background Image dialog box appears (see Figure 10.8).

Figure 10.8.
You can select any image you'd like to use in your page's background.

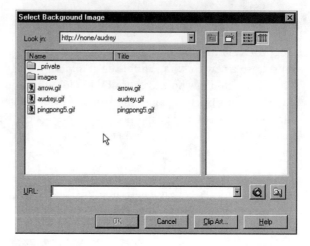

3. You can browse through FrontPage clipart, your hard drive, or sites on the Internet to find a background image to use. You'll find a listing and collection of several hundred background images at `http://www.shafran.com/frontpage98`, this book's official Web site.

4. After you select your image, FrontPage redisplays the page with the new image appearing "behind" the text. Figure 10.9 shows a sample page using a background image.

Figure 10.9.
Notice how the background of the text is no longer plain white.

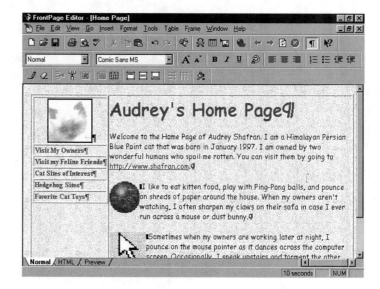

10

TIME SAVER

> Besides setting background images and colors for the entire page, you can also set backgrounds for a table, or even a specific cell within a table. Click your right mouse button anywhere within the table and choose Table Properties from the pop-up box. Similarly, click the right mouse button and choose Cell Properties if you want to change the background of a single cell.
>
> When displayed in a browser, any background settings you give to a table take precedence over the default page background color or graphic.

Summary

This chapter showed you how to use several of the more important and advanced techniques of including images within a FrontPage Web. Images are such a vital part of the Web, and there are literally dozens of customizations and characteristics you can control to achieve a specific effect within a single page.

You should now be familiar with all the settings within the Image Properties dialog box and the Image toolbar. These two sets of tools enable you to build amazingly flexible pages and to customize the precise appearance of each image.

Q&A

Q Why do I lose the quality of my graphic if I change the default Quality settings for JPEG images?

A Remember from Hour 9 that the JPEG format is a *lossy image file type*. This means that when your computer saves a JPEG, it automatically loses some detail in order to compress the file size so it can be downloaded quicker. The lower the quality setting in the Image Properties dialog box, the smaller the file size. This small file size comes at the price of a less detailed image. Similarly, if you increase your JPEG quality, your image will be significantly more detailed, but also much larger; consequently, it will take longer to download. Always leave your image quality at the optimal 75 setting unless you can achieve a similar effect with lower-quality graphics. Regardless, make sure you check out the image within your Web browser to be sure it meets the standards for your Web page.

Q Why is it important to include an image's height and width properties within FrontPage?

A Image height and width are important because of the way browsers load pages. When a Web browser reads a page of HTML, it generates a list of all the images for the entire page. Then it builds the whole page for the visitor but must wait for each image to download before it can display each piece of text. By specifying an image's height and width, you are telling the browser how much screen space to allocate for that image. Therefore, the browser can display the text of the entire page but leave a correctly sized space for each Web graphic. This significantly decreases the amount of time it takes for visitors to start reading and enjoying your page.

Workshop

The Workshop contains quiz questions and an Activities section to help reinforce what you've learned in this hour. Try not to look at the quiz answers until you've tried to work them out yourself!

Quiz

1. How can you include the same image twice on your page, with one displayed only half the size of the other?

2. What are the techniques you should use to improve the speed it takes for large images to appear within a page?

3. Suppose you have a page background color set to red, a table background color set to blue, and a specific cell background color set to blue. Which color appears within that cell and why?

Answers

1. Use the Image Height and Width properties. First add the normally sized image to your page. Then add it a second time but immediately go to the Image Properties dialog box. Take the pixel settings for Height and Width and cut them in half. Browsers will download this image only once, but will see it in two completely different formats on a page.

2. Start out by ensuring that FrontPage 98 includes the height and width of the graphic in the Image Properties dialog box. If it is a GIF file, make sure it is marked as interlaced (or progressive for JPEGs) so it loads in several passes instead of as one large image. For truly large images, use a low-res alternative image that can be a simple base image your larger one can overlay.

3. That cell will appear as blue and the rest of the table will appear in blue. The order of precedence is as follows: a cell background color or graphic is always the most important, then come the color settings within your entire table, and finally the settings you chose for the entire page.

10

Activities

1. Explore how to thoroughly use the icons in the Image toolbar. Insert several types of images into your Web page—an icon, a photograph, a button, and more—and then practice each technique. Learn how fading affects GIF and JPEG images differently, while changing the contrast sometimes helps but doesn't always improve your image's appearance. You should feel comfortable with all the icons on this toolbar.

2. Check out Hour 12, "Imagemap Education," to learn more about putting your graphics to work for you. Imagemaps let you designate different pieces of a single image to serve as hyperlinks to different pages. Using imagemaps is a common way to enhance an entire Web site.

3. Read Hour 21, "Applying Web Themes," to see how FrontPage tries to automate simple image properties and graphics for you. Web themes are collections of related banners, buttons, backgrounds, and color settings that affect an entire site.

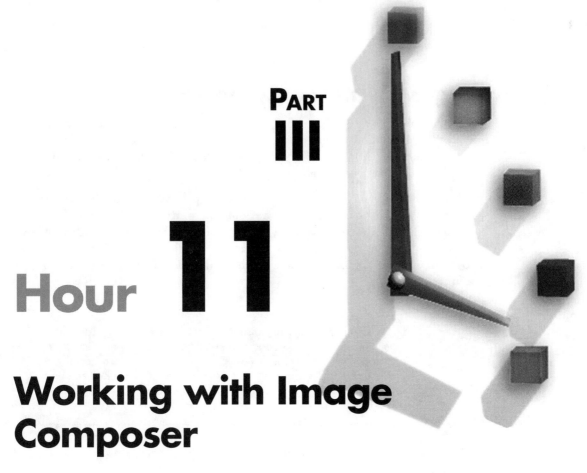

Hour 11

Working with Image Composer

One of the most important components of FrontPage is Image Composer. Image Composer is a full-fledged graphics tool that is optimized toward creating and enhancing graphics for Web pages.

This hour focuses on using Image Composer to edit and create cool-looking graphics from scratch. You'll learn how Image Composer integrates with the FrontPage Editor and how it is probably the best—and only—graphics tool you'll need to generate your own custom Web graphics.

Specifically, in this hour you'll learn how to

☐ Edit and customize graphics included in your Web pages

☐ Create innovative Web graphics from scratch

☐ Use the Image Composer special effects to quickly customize your images

Editing with Image Composer

Image Composer is a separate component of FrontPage that lets you edit and manipulate graphics and focuses on getting them ready to use on Web pages. You can use Image Composer on nearly any type of graphic and create anything from logos and icons to advanced pictures and illustrations.

 The easiest way to use Image Composer is to edit graphics you've already included within a FrontPage Web. You can trigger Image Composer from both the FrontPage Editor and Explorer simply by double-clicking on any GIF or JPEG image. Image Composer automatically starts and loads into the workspace the specific image you indicated. You can also start the Microsoft Image Composer by choosing Tools | Show Image Editor from the menu bar.

JUST A MINUTE

> Image Composer is actually a separate product that is integrated with FrontPage. You can download and install Image Composer without FrontPage from the Microsoft Web page at http://www.microsoft.com. Image Composer is an excellent stand-alone graphics tool and can be used to build any type of computer graphics, not just those built for Web pages.

Figure 11.1 shows Image Composer ready to go, editing an image loaded from an existing FrontPage Web.

Figure 11.1.

Image Composer automatically loads images from the FrontPage Explorer and Editor.

11

When you save your image and close Image Composer, the graphic in FrontPage Explorer/ Editor will automatically be updated.

 Besides editing images from a FrontPage Web, you can also open any graphic on your computer's hard drive. Simply choose File | Open from the Image Composer menu and scour your hard drive for the image you want to load and edit.

Saving Your Images

After you've finished making changes to your Web Graphic, don't forget to save it.

Creating a New Image from Scratch

Image Composer also lets you build completely new graphics in addition to editing existing ones. When you're ready to save your Web graphic, choose File | Save As from the Image Composer menu to bring up the Save As dialog box (see Figure 11.2).

Figure 11.2.
*Give your Web graphic
any filename you choose.*

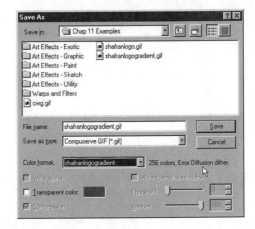

Image Composer lets you give your image a filename and graphics format. Make sure you save your Web graphics only in GIF or JPEG format so they can be seen by all visitors to your Web site.

COFFEE BREAK

One of the graphic format types you can select for your image is Microsoft Image Composer. This special image type is meant for graphics that will be used only within a FrontPage Web and placed on a Web site that uses a special FrontPage server. You'll learn more about using a FrontPage server in Hour 17, "Publishing to the WWW."

This format lets you save special-effect information about your graphic, such as cool enhancements or special warps and filters that can drastically change how it looks within a Web page. In general, you want to stay away from this file format and all others—besides GIF and JPEG—because they are not universally accepted by Web browsers across the world.

Arranging Image Appearance

After you've loaded a graphic into Image Composer, there are many ways you can change and customize it to fit your specific needs. You'll become intimately familiar with the Image Composer toolbox that runs down the left side of the screen.

Each icon in the toolbox represents a different set of actions and tools that let you create and modify your image's appearance. You'll spend most of your time in Image Composer using one of the main four image toolboxes listed in this section. They enable you to draw, reshape, and add text to a new or existing Web graphic.

To switch between the different toolboxes, click the corresponding icon that scrolls down the left side of the Image Composer screen.

 The Arrange toolbox is the first, and most important, set of basic image controls you'll want to become familiar with. Shown in Figure 11.3, this toolbox lets you resize, crop, rotate, and flip your graphic.

Figure 11.3.

The Arrange toolbox in Image Composer.

The next toolbox is the Cutout toolbox (see Figure 11.4). This toolbox lets you select and cut away certain parts of the image. You can cut out sections based on the shape or color of an image.

Figure 11.4.

The Cutout toolbox within Image ComposerV.

 The Text toolbox is also important to recognize and use (see Figure 11.5). This toolbox lets you include words and phrases on your Web graphic. From here, you can select any font, style, and size for text to include in your Web graphic.

Figure 11.5.

The Text toolbox in Image Composer.

The Shapes toolbox, the fourth important basic toolbox you'll use, lets you draw shapes and geometric figures. Much like drawing and painting lines, Image Composer lets you create any size rectangle, oval, or polygon within your Web graphic. After you create your shape, you can fill it in with a solid color or create a pattern inside it. Figure 11.6 shows this toolbox ready to edit your Image Composer graphic.

Figure 11.6.

The Shapes toolbox in Image Composer.

The next toolbox is the Paint toolbox (see Figure 11.7). From here, you can add and draw all sorts of lines and colors to your Web graphic. This toolbox is commonly used when creating a new image from scratch. You'll use it to paint new lines and drawings on the image and to change basic imagewide features such as the brightness and contrast of the entire graphic.

11

Figure 11.7.

The Paint toolbox in Image Composer.

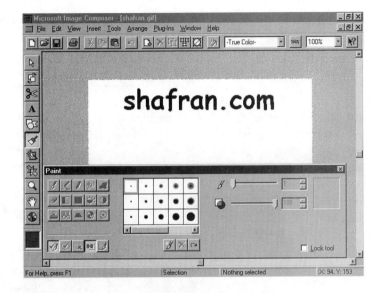

Cool Image Composer Techniques

Now that you're familiar with the Image Composer basics, it is time to learn some of the advanced ways Image Composer can modify graphics to look great on a Web page.

Image Composer comes with a built-in set of over 100 different special effects that transform simple-looking graphics into attractive and complex graphics. These special effects add texture and personality to an image, change the way graphics and text appear, and even use three-dimensional techniques. For example, you can run the Blur special effect over your image, and the entire graphic becomes slightly blurred together, with only a single command. Normally, you'd have to redraw your entire graphic from scratch to achieve this type of special effect.

The best way to use these advanced techniques is to start with a simple image or photo. Figure 11.8 shows a basic image that has only a small phrase on it. This section will show you over 60 different ways Image Composer can change this simple image at the touch of a button.

Figure 11.8.

FrontPage will turn this simple logo into something fantastic.

To run your graphics through the built-in special effects, click the Effects button from the Image Composer toolbar. Figure 11.9 shows the Effects toolbar.

Figure 11.9.

Here's where effects are selected for your Web graphics.

There are 11 different categories of special effects, all of which are described in Table 11.1.

Table 11.1. Categories of Image Composer special effects.

Special Effect	Description
Arts and Crafts	Adds artsy effects to your graphics, such as stained glass or torn paper effects.
Color Enhancement	Takes the colors within your graphic and makes them more vibrant or visible.
Distort	Deforms and reshapes your images. M.C. Esher would love this special effect.
Gradient	Adds a gradient level of colors to your graphics.
Outlines	Selects only the outline or main edges of your image and enhances just those pieces.

11

Special Effect	Description
Paint	Runs your image through a special effect named after painting techniques such as Fresco or Spatter.
Patterns	Adds static patterns such as stripes or a checkerboard on top of your image.
Photographics	Uses special effects that are reminiscent of photographic techniques.
Popular	A collection of popular and common effects from the other categories listed.
Sketch	Changes your images to look like they were sketched, but using a different type of drawing tool, such as a colored pencil or piece of charcoal.
Surface	Deforms your image slightly by changing its appearance without affecting the colors or shapes of the graphic.

Within each category of special effects, you'll find a handful of different ways you can distort and customize each graphic. Each method analyzes your graphic pixel by pixel and then applies some innovative way to deform it.

Each of these special effects work differently on different types of images. Some surface effects make dynamic transformations of photographs, while others might make the photo too blurry and difficult to see. Imagine owning a very expensive camera system with lots of different lenses and gadgets. You could take a picture of a flower with each different lens and get dramatically different results. For example, some photos might be crisp and clear, while others might be out of focus and blurry. Still other lenses might make the same photo look dark. Different special effects simply take the same image and shift the appearance of that graphic by whichever method you select.

In the drop-down menu of the Effects dialog box, you can select from the 11 different categories of special effects. Each category organizes the type of special effect you can expect to find. To apply a special effect, simply choose the one you want to use and click the Apply button. Image Composer recalculates the image, and the resulting graphic replaces the original.

TIME SAVER

If you run an effect you don't like the results of, you can always choose Edit | Undo from the Image Composer menu to return to the original graphic.

Each effect has a handful of characteristics that you can customize. For example, choose the Mesa effect from the Distort category. Then click on the tab marked Details within the Effect toolbar. The Mesa effect lets you change the radius factor and warp direction that will transform the image. Figure 11.10 shows the details you can change for the Mesa effect.

Figure 11.10.

The Mesa effect works very differently when you change these detailed settings.

JUST A MINUTE

In general, you'll want to use the default settings for each effect. Feel free to change and customize any setting you encounter to see how the resulting image might look, but Image Composer sets each effect at the optimal settings by default. If you change the effect's options, you can always click the Use Default button to return to the original values.

Instead of describing every different effect you can use, Figure 11.11 shows you an art gallery of 51 different effects all run across the same image (see Figure 11.8). This is not a demonstration of all the different effects, but should give you a fair sampling of what you can expect to run across using Image Composer.

11

Figure 11.11.
51 images, all with different effects.

shafran.com
Arts-and-Crafts effect: Torn Edges

shafran.com
Arts-and-Crafts effect: Stamp

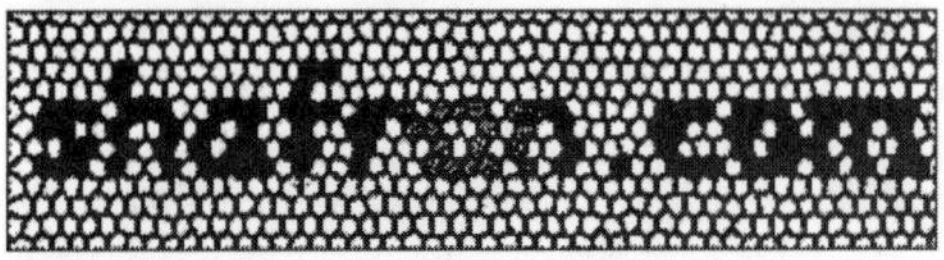

shafran.com
Arts-and-Crafts effect: Stained Glass

shafran.com
Arts-and-Crafts effect: Poster Edge

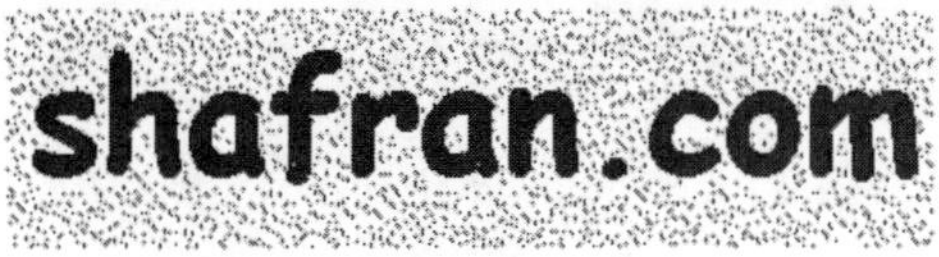

shafran.com
Arts-and-Crafts effect: Notepaper

shafran.com
Arts-and-Crafts effect: Mosaic

shafran.com
Arts-and-Crafts effect: Cutout

shafran.com
Color Enhancement effect: Tint

shafran.com
Color Enhancement effect: Wash

Distort effect: Spoke Inversion

shafran.com
Distort effect: Rectangular

shafran.com
Distort effect: Bulge Out

11

shafran.com

Distort effect: Bulge In

shafran.com

Distort effect: Wave

shafran.com

Paint effect: Dark Strokes

shafran.com

Paint effect: Accented Edges

shafran.com

Paint effect: Watercolor

shafran.com

Paint effect: Underpainting

shafran.com

Paint effect: Sumi-e

shafran.com

Paint effect: Sprayed Strokes

shafran.com

Paint effect: Sponge

shafran.com

Paint effect: Spatter

shafran.com

Paint effect: Palette Knife

shafran.com

Paint effect: Paint Daubs

shafran.com

Paint effect: Fresco

shafran.com

Paint effect: Dry Brush

shafran.com

Paint effect: Waterpaper

shafran.com

Photographic effect: Halftone Screen

11

Photographic effect: Grain

Photographic effect: Film Grain

Photographic effect: Diffuse Glow

Photographic effect: Blur

Photographic effect: Neon Glow

Sketch effect: Rough Pastels

Sketch effect: Ink Outlines

Sketch effect: Graphic Pen

Sketch effect: Cross Hatch

Sketch effect: Conte Crayon

Sketch effect: Colored Pencil

Sketch effect: Charcoal

Sketch effect: Chalk and Charcoal

Sketch effect: Angled Strokes

11

Sketch effect: Smudge Stick

Surface effect: Plaster

Surface effect: Glowing Edges

Surface effect: Glass

Surface effect: Emboss

Surface effect: Chrome

Surface effect: Bas Relief

Surface effect: Ripple

Surface effect: Plastic Wrap

Summary

This chapter just introduced you to some of the very basics of using Image Composer to create and edit graphics for your Web page. Image Composer is an easy-to-use and fun tool that lets you quickly transform mundane graphics into exciting and vivid images.

You should feel comfortable using Image Composer to make simple modifications to graphics included in your FrontPage Webs. In addition, you are now familiar with the crown jewels of Image Composer, the automatic special effects. Using these tools, you have literally an arsenal at your fingertips to create thousands of different and unique images.

Q&A

Q **Image Composer seems to be a useful and fun tool. However, I've heard of some other graphics tools that seem to be popular: Paint Shop Pro and Photoshop. What are the differences between these tools and Image Composer, and what do I need to know about them?**

A Image Composer is certainly not the only tool out there to build and modify graphics on your computer. You pointed out two of the best tools out there. Paint Shop Pro is shareware software written by Jasc (`http://www.jasc.com`), and you can download and evaluate it free and purchase it for $69. Paint Shop Pro is a robust tool for all things graphical on your computer. In functionality and usefulness, Paint Shop Pro is higher on the food chain than Image Composer.

Photoshop is the granddaddy of all image programs. Written and released by Adobe (`http://www.adobe.com`), Photoshop costs hundreds of dollars but is a fabulous program. Virtually all professional artists and graphics creators use Photoshop (or sometimes Paint Shop Pro). There is nothing you can't do to an image with Photoshop. Accompanying this advanced functionality is increased complexity. There have been several 1000+ page books written about the ins and outs of using this gigantic package. You'll want to stick with Image Composer or Paint Shop Pro unless building graphics is your profession. Regardless, all three of these tools can create phenomenal GIF and JPEG images, but due to its usefulness and integration with FrontPage 98, Image Composer is your best bet.

Workshop

The Workshop contains quiz questions and an Activities section to help reinforce what you've learned in this hour. Try not to look at the quiz answers until you've tried to work them out yourself!

Quiz

1. Is Image Composer part of FrontPage?
2. What are the two main file formats in which you must save your images?
3. How can you quickly and completely change an image at the touch of a few buttons using Image Composer?

Answers

1. Yes and no. Image Composer is a separate graphics editing and creation program but is completely integrated with FrontPage 98. It can be installed along with FrontPage or independently.

2. The two main graphics formats for Web pages are GIF and JPEG. GIF images are commonly used for logos, icons, and buttons, and JPEGs are usually reserved for photos.

3. Load the image into Image Composer. Then click on the Effects icon and run the image through one of the embedded special effects. Turn your image into something fancy with these innovative and easy-to-use techniques.

Activities

1. Want some more advanced information on using Image Composer? Head to your local bookstore and pick up *Wild Web Graphics with Image Composer*, published by Que. It is a complete look at all the different features and pieces of Image Composer that make it a great graphics creation and editing program.

2. One of the most useful ways to take advantage of images on a Web page is to turn a graphic into an imagemap. Read Hour 12, "Imagemap Education," for more information on these innovative and interactive graphics.

Hour **12**

Imagemap Education

During Hour 9, "Understanding and Using Web Graphics," you learned how graphics work as the glue for the World Wide Web and make pages exciting and interesting to explore. In this hour, you'll learn how to take your images one step further and put them to work for you. These enhanced Web graphics, called imagemaps, are easy to use; they are quickly becoming a popular tool among Web page creators all over the world.

NEW TERM   With *imagemaps*, you can link different areas of a single image to different HTML files, or URLs. This lets visitors to your Web page navigate from page to page by using their mouse to select different areas of an image instead of clicking an individual link. Imagemaps are inherently easier to use than regular text links because there's no need to explain what the link does. A person doesn't have to read where a link might take him or her; he or she just sees it.

You might think that imagemaps should be used everywhere, but that's not the case. There are some things you should consider before you use them. You must make sure that placing imagemaps where you want them makes sense.

In this chapter you'll learn all of the basics behind adding imagemaps to your site. Specifically, you'll learn how to

☐ Understand how imagemaps work and the differences between them and standard hyperlinks

☐ Re-evaluate how you use images and links on your Web page to explore where using imagemaps might make sense

☐ Build several different types of hyperlink shapes on your imagemap

☐ Optimize your imagemap to work well within your FrontPage Web

How Do Imagemaps Work?

You are already familiar with using FrontPage to add graphics to Web pages. By embedding clip art, photos, and graphics, you've made your page more exciting and relevant to visitors. In fact, you even know how to make those images serve as links to other pages by setting link properties for each image in your FrontPage Web page.

Figure 12.1 shows a simple Web page that includes an image linked to another site. When visitors click the image, the browser automatically loads the file ROME.HTML.

Figure 12.1.

Linking an image to another page within your Web site or across the Web is easy to do.

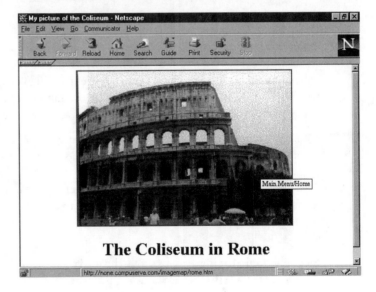

No matter where on the picture you click, you always link to ROME.HTML. This is where an imagemap could come into play. Using an imagemap, you can link different areas of an image to different spots on the Web, based on what section of the image is clicked.

This is an extremely useful technique because it lets visitors who see this Web page become accustomed to a single image and allows them to navigate from page to page by clicking different sections of that image.

Go to the Magnavox home page (http://www.magnavox.com) for an excellent example of an imagemap (see Figure 12.2). Here, the developers have included a picture of a remote control with several buttons drawn on it. Each section of the image takes you to a different spot on the Magnavox Web site. For example, clicking Company Info in the image brings up information about Magnavox, and you can easily imagine what kind of stuff appears when you click Fun & Games.

Figure 12.2.

Magnavox's imagemap is smart, very smart.

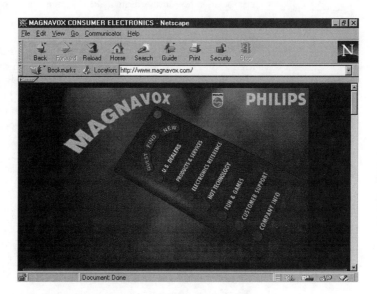

There are many good uses for imagemaps. For example, Italy might place a virtual map online. Using your mouse, you would click whichever region or city of Italy you wanted to learn more about. Clicking Rome might bring up the Coliseum, and Venice could link to a black canal boat. Or perhaps Boeing might place a picture of its new 777 plane on the Web. Visitors could click different parts of the cockpit to learn how the plane operates.

Virtually any image can become an imagemap—and easy to create with FrontPage 98—with all the tools built right in.

COFFEE BREAK

Clickable imagemaps have been around for a long time. You have always been able to add one to your Web page if you knew the right steps to follow. But, adding them to Web pages became a lot easier in 1996 with a new imagemap standard called *client-side imagemaps*.

Previously, to add a clickable imagemap to your Web page, you were dependent on your Web server software. Your server software controls all access to Web pages at a particular Internet site. To add an imagemap to your page, you had to find the right image, decide how each part of the image would link to a different HTML file, and then set up and customize your server properly. This was quite a hassle, even for those people who could understand every step—and some Web servers don't permit imagemaps to run on them. Therefore, using imagemaps on Web pages was effectively limited to professional Web developers and larger companies; few individuals used imagemaps on personal Web pages.

Here's how a server-side imagemap works. When visiting a Web page, you might see a large image that has several different sections on it that are clearly delineated. When each section is clicked, it looks like it will take you to a different Web page. After looking at the image for a while, you click one area (such as one of the buttons on the Magnavox remote control in Figure 12.2), presumably to take you to a corresponding page. Web browsers store the coordinates you clicked as an X,Y pair (the measurement is in pixels) and then send that information to the Web server. The server takes these coordinates and runs a separate Common Gateway Interface (CGI) program that translates the coordinates into a URL—the filename of the linked area that was clicked. Then the Web server sends that filename back to the browser, which loads the correct file.

As you can probably gather, server-side imagemaps aren't extremely efficient and can be difficult to use for several reasons.

Fortunately, client-side imagemaps (called CSIM for short) took the Web by storm, and they are universally used when new imagemaps are built today. With CSIMs, instead of exchanging information with the Web server, Web browsers automatically know which HTML file to link to, and they take you there automatically. This process is significantly quicker to process (you don't have to wait for the Web server) and easier for the browser to interpret. Each region in the image has its pixel coordinates defined within the same HTML file as the rest of the Web page—some sort of interaction with the Web server is not required for this to work.

You always can tell whether you are using a server-side imagemap or a client-side one. Look at the status bar at the bottom of the screen while you move your mouse over an imagemap. If you see scrolling numbers, then you know it's a server-side imagemap (those pixel coordinates are sent to the server when you click). If you see a filename instead of coordinates, then you're using a client-side imagemap.

Creating an Imagemap

This section shows you how to create an actual imagemap from start to finish using FrontPage. You'll learn how to select the right kinds of images, link the different areas to separate HTML files, and set your imagemap properties.

The first important lesson to learn is the terminology. In FrontPage, Microsoft refers to the different areas within an imagemap as *hotspots*. Therefore, one image might have different hotspots, each one linking to a different page.

Finding a Good Image

When you are creating imagemaps, the first step is to select a good image to use. You want to make sure that visitors who see the image understand that there are several different areas on the picture that they can select that are linked to different items. You must select definitive images that have different regions easily delineated onscreen (and that make sense to visitors).

Figure 12.3 shows a sample image that will make an excellent imagemap for the ACME Block Company.

Figure 12.3.

The big blocks make it easy for users to identify the different regions of the imagemap.

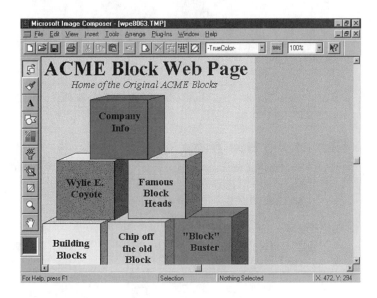

You can create imagemaps from virtually any graphic that you can add to your Web page. Icons, buttons, bars, and pictures, as well as graphics of all types can be sectioned out and presented as an imagemap for visitors—but be careful, not all images make sense for use as imagemaps.

In general, photographs become difficult imagemaps because they often lack clearly defined areas for the user to click. Recall the picture of the Coliseum earlier in this hour (see Figure 12.1)—this image wouldn't be a good imagemap because there aren't any well-defined areas other than the large image of the Coliseum. But, by reworking the same theme with other types of graphics, you can create another image that works well as an imagemap. Figure 12.4 shows a different Italian image that works as an imagemap. (The Italy and world maps are compliments of http://www.graphicmaps.com.)

Figure 12.4.

This image lets you link each city to a different Web page.

Planning the Map

After you've selected an image, the next step is to logically divide it into different regions and define how you want the imagemap to work. Figure 12.5 shows the block image with a plan for where each block will lead off to.

When you have a good idea of how to divide your imagemap, you're ready to move to the next step: adding the necessary HTML tags to your Web page.

CAUTION

Make sure that each HTML file to which your image links exists, or use the FrontPage To-Do editor to remind you to build that page. Otherwise, it's easy to forget to create one or more of the HTML files, and then the imagemap won't work properly.

12

Figure 12.5.

*Planning each link from
your imagemap is an
important step.*

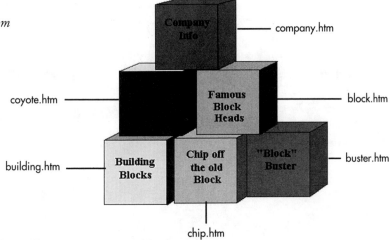

coyote.htm ——————

company.htm

block.htm

building.htm ——————

buster.htm

chip.htm

Adding the Image to Your Web Page

After you've chosen a good image to work with, you'll want to add it to your Web page just
like any other Web graphic. Choose Insert | Image from the FrontPage menu bar. Hour 9,
"Understanding and Using Web Graphics," deals with how to add your image in FrontPage
(if you have any problems).

Mapping Your Image

With the image embedded in your Web page, the next step is to define each region on the
image graphically. Using a set of drawing tools, you'll be able to select different areas of the
Web graphic and then build a hypertext link from that hotspot. Follow these steps:

1. Within the FrontPage Editor, select the graphic that will serve as the imagemap.
   The Image toolbar at the top of the screen is highlighted and available to use.

2. Select the Rectangle icon if you want to draw a square or rectangular hotspot on
   your image; select the Circle icon to create a circular hotspot. The third hotspot
   icon enables you to draw multisided polygon hotspots.

3. Using your mouse, draw the hotspot on your image. Rectangular hotspots make
   you specify opposite corners, whereas circular hotspots start from the center and
   then let you indicate a radius with your mouse.

4. When you are finished drawing the hotspot, the Create Hyperlink dialog box
   appears (see Figure 12.6). It asks you to choose where this hotspot will take your
   visitors.

   Creating a hyperlinked hotspot is the exact same as building a simple hyperlink.
   You can specify a file within your current FrontPage Web page or browse the

12

WWW and choose a different page from around the world. You can even tell FrontPage to link your hotspot to a file that hasn't even been created yet (a file that you can build later).

Figure 12.6.

FrontPage builds hotspot hyperlinks in the same fashion as typical hyperlinks.

5. Repeat steps 2 through 4 until you have created all the hotspots. If you have trouble finding the hotspots on top of your image, click the Highlight Hotspots icon from the Image toolbar. Figure 12.7 shows the Hotspots highlighted without the image displayed.

6. Save your file and look at it through your Web browser. Figure 12.8 shows the imagemap as it appears in Netscape.

You can change where your hotspots point at any time. Move your mouse over the hotspot area within the FrontPage Editor, and then right-click. Select Image Hotspot Properties; the Edit Hyperlink dialog box appears.

Creating a Default Link

Normally, when you create an imagemap, only the areas you specify as hotspots will take visitors to a particular Web page. You can also create a default, or standard, link that activates whenever someone clicks outside a hotspot but still within the graphic. You create this default hyperlink by right-clicking anywhere within the graphic and selecting Image Properties from the pop-up box (see Figure 12.9).

Figure 12.7.

Highlighting hotspots lets you keep track of all the different hyperlinked areas within your graphic.

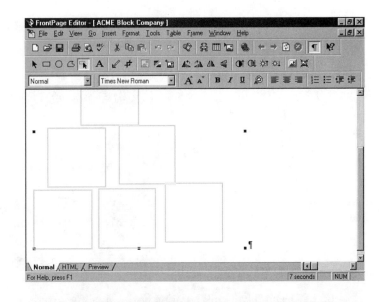

Figure 12.8.

In the Netscape message bar at the bottom of the screen, you're told which file you'll see if you click a particular hotspot.

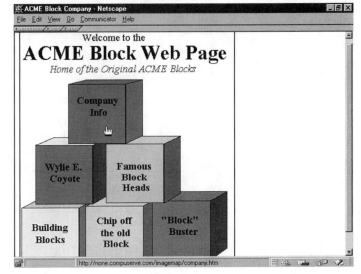

Figure 12.9.

The default link for your imagemap can be anywhere on the Web.

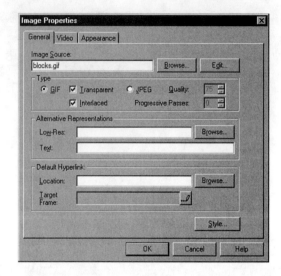

In the Default Hyperlink Location box, you can type (or browse for) the filename or URL of where you want this image to link visitors to when they click outside a hotspot. Hotspot links always take precedence over the default link you type in this dialog box.

Testing the Imagemap with a Browser

When you're finished creating the imagemap, make sure you test it thoroughly with either Netscape or Internet Explorer (or both). Test every region, one at a time, to make sure that your links have been created properly. Many people overlook this step, assuming that there won't be any mistakes as long as they have followed the previous steps exactly; however, typos, incorrect filenames, and other mistakes can easily create flaws in your imagemap.

FrontPage lets you graphically see which pages your imagemap is linked to by using the FrontPage Explorer. Click the Hyperlinks button within Explorer, and FrontPage builds a graphical relationship between the page containing the imagemap and all the linked pages (see Figure 12.10).

12

Figure 12.10.

*The FrontPage Explorer
comes in handy when you
want to see all the pages
to which your imagemap
points.*

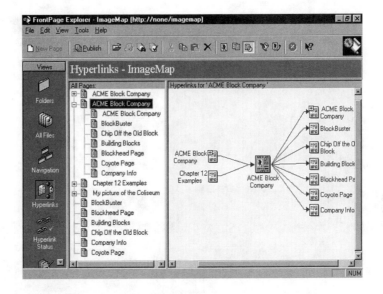

Providing a Textual Alternative

Although virtually all new Web browsers support imagemaps, providing some type of textual
alternative is always a good idea. This accommodates visitors to your page who are using a
browser that doesn't read imagemaps, or visitors who don't want to wait for the entire image
to download before selecting a region on the imagemap. Often, imagemap graphics are large
and can take a few minutes to download into a Web browser. By providing a text alternative,
you enable impatient visitors to immediately continue exploring your site.

Figure 12.11 shows how the ACME Block home page can be updated to have textual links
as well as graphical ones. This page balances Web graphics and text very well by using a two-
column table; the left column displays the main imagemap, and the right column shows a
simple list of links.

12

Figure 12.11.

This simple table provides an alternative to using ACME's imagemap.

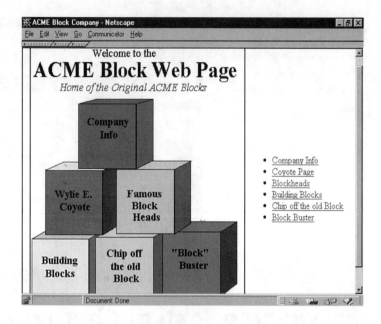

Summary

Using imagemaps is a useful and effective way to put your Web graphics to work and create exciting hyperlinks for your Web site. You'll find yourself using imagemaps often because FrontPage makes working with them very easy. Don't be afraid to create multiple-shape hotspots for all types of images and graphics at your site.

Make sure you select a good, easily discernible image to use, and clearly draw the hotspots so that visitors always know where they're going before clicking anywhere on your imagemap.

Q&A

Q You mentioned another type of imagemap in the beginning of the chapter. Will I ever need to use it?

A Server-side imagemaps were the *de facto* standard before HTML 2.0 was agreed upon. Since then, client-side imagemaps have become supported by all the major browsers. Server-side imagemaps will be around for quite a while, for two reasons. First, with millions of Web pages out there, no one rushed out to migrate all the existing pages to the new imagemap standard, so these older pages will stay as they are until updated. Second, some advanced Web sites dynamically build complex maps and Web graphics for each user as they stop by. These dynamic graphics use server-side imagemaps to make it easier for the Web site to be managed. As a Web developer, you'll always use client-side imagemaps for all your sites.

12

Q **What happens when I create multiple hotspots that overlap one another on the image? Does it break FrontPage or the browser? Where do I go when I click one of the overlapped areas?**

A Overlapping hotspots cause no problems to FrontPage or browsers. In fact, it is common to have hotspots overlap slightly to make sure there are no dead spaces between areas on a graphic. When clicked, an overlapping area takes you to the hotspot that was most recently created within FrontPage.

Q **I want to define a polygon hotspot with a lot of sides. Is there any limit to the number of sides my polygon hotspot can have?**

A Yes, Web browsers recognize only 64 separate sides of a polygon hotspot. If you need to have a more detailed hotspot, you can always draw multiple hotspots right next to each other and have them all pointing to the same location.

Workshop

The Workshop contains quiz questions and an Activities section to help reinforce what you've learned in this hour. Try not to look at the quiz answers until you've tried to work them out yourself!

Quiz

1. What's the order of precedence for an imagemap that has two overlapping hotspots and a default hyperlink for the entire image?

2. What are the traits of a Web graphic that could become a good imagemap?

Answers

1. Whichever hotspot was created last is the link that is activated. Next would come the second hotspot, and the third link is the default image link.

2. Good imagemap graphics are reasonable in file size (so they don't take forever to see), have multiple areas that are clearly discernible from one another, and let the visitor know where they're going before they click.

   Bad imagemap graphics tend to be photographs, such as pictures of people or pets.

Activities

1. Try building a hotspot from a map of your home state or country. Visit http://www.graphicmaps.com and download the map of your choice; then build an imagemap from it. This will give you practice using differently shaped hotspots on an image that has clearly defined areas.

2. Rework your original FrontPage Web page so that you use an imagemap to link to all your subpages. Create separate buttons as part of a single image within Image Composer.

12

PART

IV

Cool Web Page Enhancements

Hour

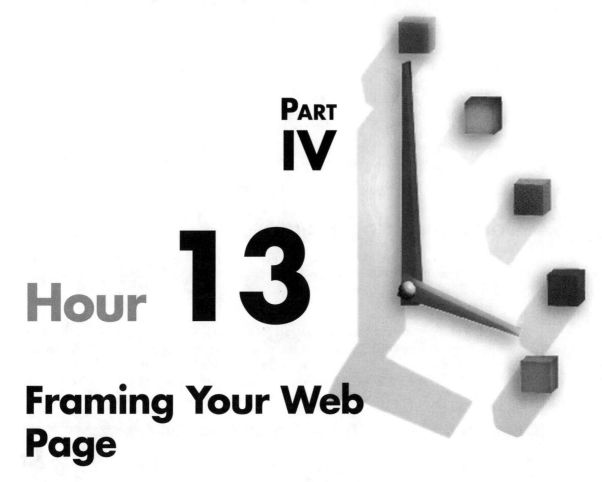

Hour 13

Framing Your Web Page

If you are like most people, you can do several things at the same time. Some people can type while speaking on the phone, while almost everyone can drive and listen to the radio simultaneously. Computers let you multitask, or run several programs, such as Microsoft Word and Excel, at one time. Even televisions have picture-in-picture features that let you check out multiple channels simultaneously.

On the World Wide Web, browsers support a feature called *frames*, which lets you load multiple HTML files at one time into separate areas of the screen. This concept lets you organize Web sites, display two related sites on the same screen, and create an entirely different experience for your visitors rather than a single, sometimes boring page.

FrontPage 98 lets you build and create great-looking Web sites using frames. This hour introduces you to frames and shows you how and when you'll want to use them on your site.

Specifically, in this chapter you'll learn how to

☐ Understand what frames are and how they work

☐ Use FrontPage to automatically build your framed sites

☐ Organize your Web site using the right combination of frames

☐ Recognize when to use and when not to use frames for your site

Understanding Frames

Frames give you significant control over how your Web pages appear to visitors. You can create multiple independent frames that each load a different HTML page. The different frames can interact with one another or be entirely separate. In fact, frames can even load pages from several different Web sites around the world.

Point your browser to http://www.gerrard.org/billnpam/ (see Figure 13.1). This Web site uses a set of four different frames to make up the single screen within the Web browser. There's the navigation frame on the left side, the Title frame at the top of the page, the copyright frame at the bottom, and the main frame in the center. All the information from this site loads in this main center frame while the other three always remain the same.

Figure 13.1.

Bill and Pam's place uses frames efficiently and effectively.

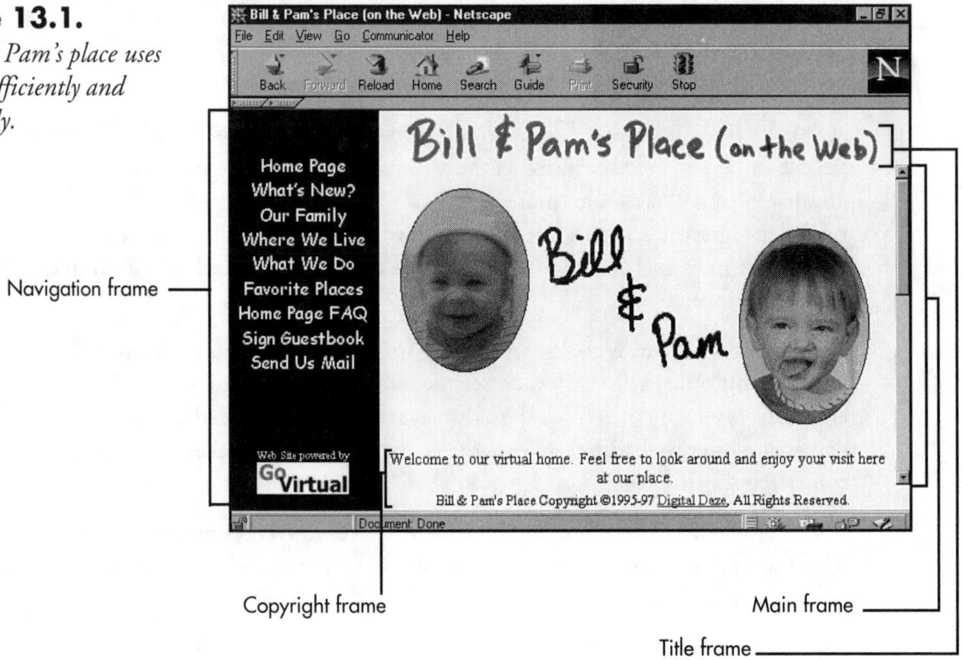

Navigation frame ———

Copyright frame ————

Main frame ————

Title frame ————

Each of the four different frames points to a separate HTML document. When you click on a hypertext link from the navigation frame, only the main frame changes. You always see the same information in the remaining frames when you are browsing through the entire site.

Bill and Pam keep a consistent interface to their entire site and only have to worry about including the title, copyright information, and hyperlinks on one page instead of including that info on every page within the site. This makes it much easier for them to manage the entire set of Web pages that make up their site.

Frames as Navigational Tools

For another idea of how frames are used, stop by http://www.vsat.net/jamboree/. This well-designed site uses a handful of frames to assist visitors exploring the site (see Figure 13.2).

Figure 13.2.

The Boy Scouts make it easy to earn a Computer Merit Badge.

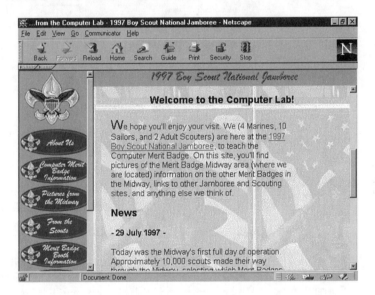

A set of icons scrolls down the left side of the page and serves as another navigational toolbar through the site. This is useful because you never get lost, no matter how many different links you follow. At any moment, you can always click the home icon and return to the main Web page. Also, notice how the different frames use different graphical backgrounds—another implicit benefit of using frames, because each separate HTML file can have its own color and background graphics traits.

13

Uniquely Frames—Playing Tic-Tac-Toe

Figure 13.3 shows a rather different use of frames within a Web browser: playing tic-tac-toe. You can find this sample page on this book's Web site at http://www.shafran.com/frontpage98. It uses frames in a different way than as navigational or organizational aids. In this example, each of the nine different frames show the same HTML file, so you are looking at the same file nine separate times. However, you can click on an X or an O and display different information in each frame.

Figure 13.3.

Who's going to win this intense match?

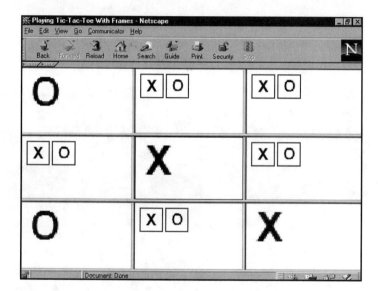

COFFEE BREAK

To understand how your browser can look at the same page simultaneously nine times, it's good to understand exactly how frames work.

To build a framed Web site, you must first create an HTML file that dictates the shape, size, and contents of each frame. This HTML file is called the *frameset* because it contains the definition for the entire set of all the frames. Then you must create each frame's HTML file separately. Therefore, a page that has two frames requires three separate HTML files, one for each frame, and then one that defines the frameset.

FrontPage 98 helps you step through building each frame individually, but you'll always have one more page of HTML than you might normally expect. For the tic-tac-toe game, the browser first loaded the frame definition page. That page told it to create nine evenly sized frames and then, for each frame, to load a file called choose.htm. So the browser requested the choose.htm file nine times from the Web server and placed each one in a different frame.

13

Creating Framed Pages

FrontPage 98 is a fantastic tool for creating and managing framed Webs. FrontPage includes a Frame-Building wizard that will dynamically generate each page of HTML for you and step you through modifying them all.

JUST A MINUTE

Before tools like FrontPage existed, building framed sites was difficult. You had to be an HTML expert, understand a lot of confusing and complex tags and codes, and manage a lot of different files individually. That's one of the reasons why frames are used only sparingly on today's WWW; no one wanted to bother with the complexity. In the future, you'll see frames all around the world in personal and professional sites because they have become much easier to work with (because of FrontPage and related tools).

You must build frames within the FrontPage Editor. After you create each page, you can use the FrontPage Explorer to manage them all, but it is the Editor that has all the frame-building wizards and tools.

This section takes you through the entire frame creation process from scratch, shows you what options FrontPage gives you, and how to quickly use them when building your own Web.

Choosing the Frame Type

After you load the FrontPage Editor, Choose File | New from the menu to bring up the New dialog box. Click the tab labeled Frames and you'll see Figure 13.4.

In the left side of this dialog box is a list of 10 different frame templates FrontPage lets you build. FrontPage shows you in the right side of the box a graphical preview of how each of these 10 templates will look. Select the frame template you want to use and click OK to continue. The example for this chapter uses the Header, Footer, and Contents frame template, which is a set of four different frames (it looks like the same type of site Bill and Pam designed in Figure 13.1).

13

Figure 13.4.

*FrontPage gives you 10
different frame templates
to work with.*

Types of framed sites
you can create

Graphical picture of how
the frames are organized

Frame-building options

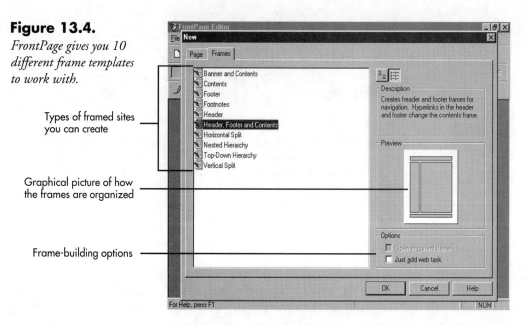

After you click OK, FrontPage builds all the corresponding frames for you and adds buttons
to each frame window, prompting you to create or edit each frame individually, as shown in
Figure 13.5.

Figure 13.5.

*Each FrontPage frame is
ready to edit.*

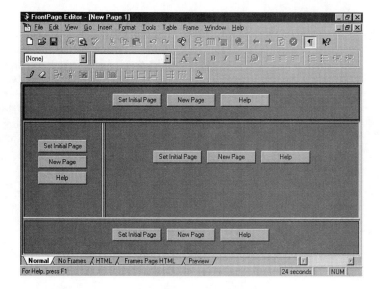

13

JUST A MINUTE

There were two options that you could select when using the FrontPage frame templates. The first option, Open in Current Frame, lets you create nested sets of frames within one another; this is an option you won't use very often.

The second option, Just Add Web Task, lets you create the different frames initially but edit them later by using the FrontPage Task Manager/ To Do list.

Setting Up the Individual Frames

After you create the set of frames, the next step is to customize each one individually. There are three buttons within each frame, as shown in Table 13.1.

Table 13.1. Options for filling in each frame.

Button	Description
Set Initial Page	Lets you set an existing file to appear within this frame. You can select a file within your local FrontPage Web, your hard drive, or somewhere on the Internet to be this initial page.
New Page	Create a new HTML page from scratch that should appear in this frame.
Help	Brings up the FrontPage frame Help information to step you through some of the complexities of creating framed sites.

When you build a new site from scratch, you likely must build a whole set of HTML pages, one for each frame. However, you might want to automatically load your current home page in the larger main content window, so point that window to your home page.

In the top frame, click the New Page button and watch FrontPage transform that frame into a standard blank page. In this frame you can now type text, add images, and include all the information you normally would when making a new page. Figure 13.6 shows this new frame filled in.

13

Figure 13.6.

The top frame is now finished.

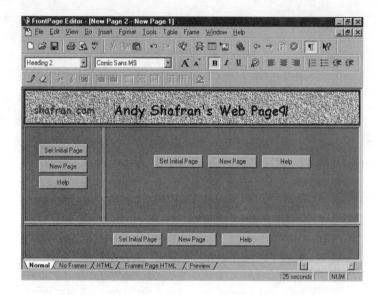

Now go through and edit each frame in your site. Figure 13.7 shows the new and improved set of framed pages. Don't be afraid if your page doesn't look perfect in FrontPage; it is likely to look different within your browser.

Figure 13.7.

All four frames now have something in them.

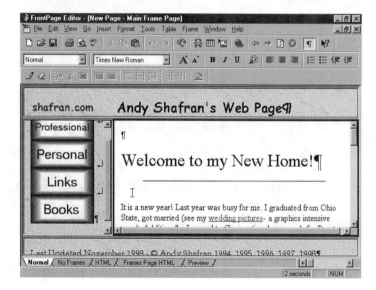

13

When you are finished with your initial creation, choose File | Save from the Editor's menu. FrontPage prompts you with a separate Save dialog box for each frame, and then one for the main page that describes how all the frames are organized. Figure 13.8 shows a frame Save As dialog box. Notice how in the preview section FrontPage highlights the specific frame you are saving so that you can give it an appropriate name, such as header.htm or footer.htm for the top and bottom frames.

Figure 13.8.

Each frame must be saved as a separate HTML file.

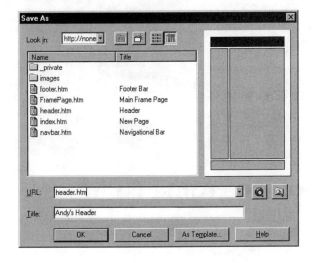

Finally, after you have saved all four frames, FrontPage prompts you with the Save As dialog box one more time. This last box is where you save the frame definition file, the one that tells browsers exactly how to display each frame within their windows. To see the entire set of frames, your visitors will load this file within their browsers. After it is loaded, each of the four other files is then displayed in a specific frame. This final file is often called the *frameset* file because it is just the blueprints for how all the individual frames should appear. Give this file an important name, such as index.htm or another distinctive name, so that it is the default file that opens within your FrontPage Web.

When you are finished saving each frame, start your Web browser and point it toward the FrontPage Personal Web Server. Open the main frame definition file, and you can see how all the different frames will look to visitors. Figure 13.9 shows this sample site so far.

13

Figure 13.9.

Netscape does a nice job of organizing each frame.

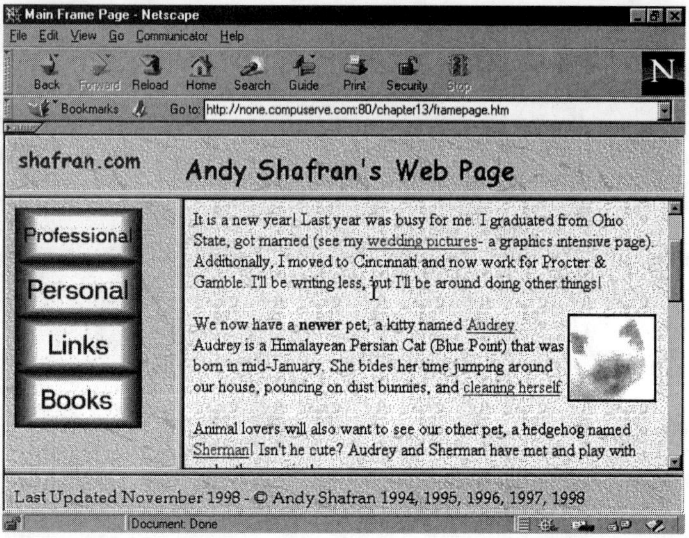

Making Frame Changes

After you've created your initial framed Web site, there are several ways that you can customize and modify each page or the entire set of pages. This section takes you through how to set some basic frame properties with FrontPage.

Resizing Your Frames

By default, FrontPage automatically sizes your set of frames according to the template you used to create them. For the Header, Footer, and Contents frame, FrontPage had to split the page into different horizontal and vertical sections. You shouldn't feel limited by these default frame sizings. Using your mouse, you can drag and drop any and all of the frame borders, resizing each specific section, even adding a new frame to your site!

Resizing your frame windows is easy. Simply click your mouse on the border you want to move and drag it to its new location. Figure 13.10 shows the frame resizing in action.

TIME SAVER

If you want to create a new frame instead of resizing it, hold down the Ctrl button when resizing, and FrontPage generates a completely new frame for you. With this new frame, you can create a new HTML page or point to an existing file.

Figure 13.10.

You can only resize a frame horizontally or vertically at one time.

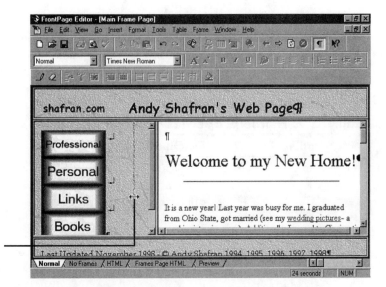

The mouse pointer resizing this set of frames

Configuring Frame Properties

As with everything else inside FrontPage, you can configure several properties that relate specifically to using and displaying frames. Bring up the Frame Properties dialog box by clicking your right mouse button within any frame in the FrontPage Editor, and choose Frame Properties from the pop-up dialog box (see Figure 13.11).

Figure 13.11.

Set your default frame properties here.

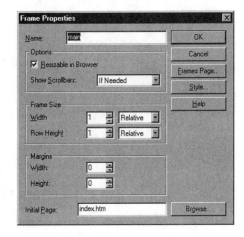

Table 13.2 gives a brief description of all the options from which you can choose within the Frame Properties dialog box. In general, you won't make too many modifications to your frame properties. Unless you must change the frame borders or add margins between different frames, you'll probably stick to resizing the different frames within the FrontPage Editor.

Table 13.2. Frame properties you can modify.

Option	Description
Name	This name enables you to build hyperlinks that appear within a different frame. So if you include a hyperlink in the footer, you can have it appear in the frame named Header instead of in the footer frame. This name is useful for creating navigation bars on the left side of the screen. You can create buttons that link to different HTML pages, but make them appear in the main Contents window.
Resizable in Browser	Sometimes you want to let your visitors resize the borders for each frame. This might occur when a visitor using a smaller screen resolution stops by, or when a visitor wants to expand a frame to see a large image. With this checkbox marked, all visitors can drag and drop all frame borders from within their Web browsers.
Show Scrollbars	You have three options for when scrollbars should appear for each frame: Always, Never, or If Needed. You'll almost always want to display scrollbars only if needed. This lets the browser determine whether information scrolls off the screen, requiring the browser to provide a scrollbar for your visitors.
Frame Size	You can control the frame's height and width by typing numerical values. Resizing frames is much easier, and more effective, by dragging and dropping the frame borders from within the Editor. You can size frames by pixels or the percentage of the screen.
Margins	Measured in pixels, you can add a certain margin space horizontally and vertically between frames.
Initial Page	The name of the HTML file that appears in this frameset.

13

All the characteristics within the Frame Properties dialog box affect only the specific frame you have selected. You can also make frame-wide changes by clicking the Frames Page button inside the Image Properties dialog box. The page properties for the entire frame definition page appears.

This Page Properties box is nearly the same for every page you create within FrontPage. There are two important properties you'll want to learn how to use here:

☐ The title that appears in this dialog box is the default information that appears in the browser's title bar when this whole set of framed pages is loaded.

☐ If you click the Frames tab (see Figure 13.12) you can set two frame-wide proper-ties. You can make the frame borders not appear within a Web browser and set frame-wide margins (measured in pixels). Turning the frame borders off is some-times helpful and sometimes a hindrance. When they are off, the frame borders don't waste valuable screen space and run the various frames right up to one another. Remember Figure 13.1 in the beginning of the chapter? It had its frame borders turned off. However, when they are turned off, visitors no longer can resize the individual frames because the borders they use to drag and drop them aren't there any more.

Figure 13.12.

There are only two frameset-wide properties you can set; all the others are specific to individual frames.

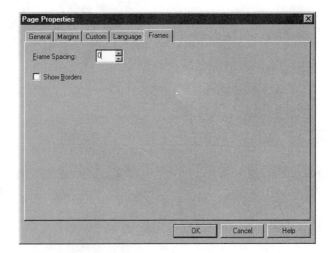

Linking Between Frames

In Hour 8, "Linking Pages Together," you learned how to create hyperlinks to other pages across the WWW and at your local site. It was relatively easy: You type your text (or use an image) and then point it to a new page. When a visitor loads your page and clicks on a link, the whole page reloads to that new site.

Frames change the linking paradigm slightly. There is one more option you can use when building hyperlinks: which frame to load the new page within.

 To see this new hyperlinking process in action, highlight some text within your header or footer frame and choose Insert | Hyperlink from the Editor menu bar. The Create Hyperlink dialog box appears (see Figure 13.13)

Figure 13.13.

You should recognize this dialog box from Hour 8.

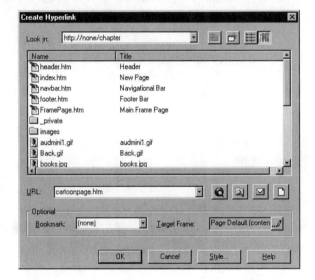

Create your hyperlink as you normally would by typing a URL or selecting a file to which to link the text. Before you click OK, notice the Target Frame option at the bottom of this dialog box. Click the Select Frame icon to bring up the Target Frame dialog box as shown in Figure 13.14.

Figure 13.14.

Here's where you select which frame this link appears within.

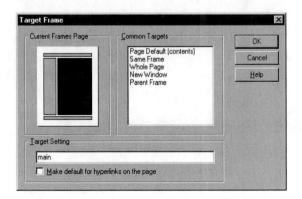

13

In the Current Frames Page box, you can choose within which frame you want this link to activate. By default, your browser will try to load the file you link into the current frame. So if you create this hyperlink from the header or footer, you aren't going to have much room to read the newly linked-to page. Instead, if visitors click on this link, you probably want it to appear in the main larger window in the middle right of the page.

Click on that window and FrontPage enters the name of that specific frame. You've now told this link to bring up the new page in a different frame. Click OK to close this dialog box; then click OK again to save and create your hyperlink.

Summary

Using frames is a great way to diversify the appearance of your Web site. They enable you to include multiple pages within the same screen. You'll find yourself using frames to build standard headers and footers across pages and as valuable navigational aids for visitors to your Web sites.

FrontPage 98 makes building Web sites with frames a breeze. Using the Frame Wizard, you can select from over 10 different frame templates and then build each page individually. You now know the entire step-by-step process required to create, edit, and then save your new framed site. Most importantly, you understand how to customize each frame's appearance and how to build links between the different frames in your site.

Q&A

Q I've created several links within my frames to other pages in my site. Sometimes I create a link to a different page on the WWW, but the link always appears within one of my frames. How can I avoid this problem and load the new page across the whole browser window, not in just one frame?

A When you create your hyperlink, you can select whichever target frame you'd like that new page to be loaded into. One of the target frame options within FrontPage 98 is a new window instead of any frame that is on your site. This lets your visitor "escape" the frames that might be trapping the linked page.

Q How can I delete a specific frame?

A Click your mouse in the frame you want to remove and choose Frame | Delete frame from the FrontPage Editor's menu. FrontPage verifies your request and then removes the frame.

13

Workshop

The Workshop contains quiz questions and an Activities section to help reinforce what you've learned in this hour. Try not to look at the quiz answers until you've tried to work them out yourself!

Quiz

1. How can you turn frame borders for the entire site on and off?

2. What is the difference between a frame and a frameset?

3. Can you create frames within frames?

Answers

1. Click the right mouse button within any frame and choose Image Properties. From there, click the Frame Page button to set frameset-wide changes. Click the Frames tab, and you can turn borders on and off for the entire set of frames.

2. A frameset is the main frame definition page that defines all the pieces and sizes of each individual frame. A frame is the specific area on the Web page that actually is a separate HTML file formatted to fit within a certain area.

3. Yes you can; in fact, there is no technical limit to the number of framesets you can build within frames. There is, however, a practical limit. Each frame carries some overhead by using screen space for the frame borders and taking longer to load within browsers because multiple HTML files must be downloaded. Try to never embed frames more than one or two levels deep, or your visitors might be dissatisfied with the time it takes to display the entire page.

Activities

1. Experiment with the handful of FrontPage frame templates. This hour introduced you to one of them in-depth, but there are nine more that are useful to your Web site.

2. Build a framed site that uses a navigational bar on the left side of the screen. Have a set of buttons or list of text on which you can click that brings up a variety of different pages into the main content window. For example, create a list of comic strips you like to read daily, then link that list into the comic strip's home page so that it appears on the right. Then you can easily check your favorite daily comics from one standard navigational bar.

3. Read Hour 8, "Linking Pages Together," for a more in-depth look at how to create hyperlinks to other pages and sites on the WWW.

4. Browse through Hour 19, "Managing Your Web Site," to learn other organizational tactics besides frames that can logically tie an entire set together.

13

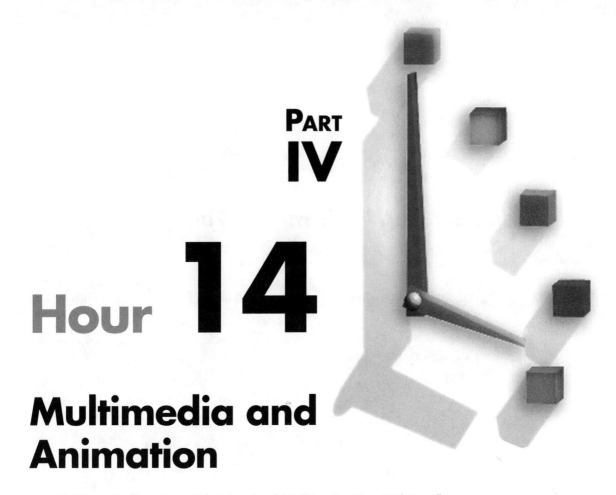

PART IV

Hour 14

Multimedia and Animation

In Hours 12, "Imagemap Education," and 13, "Framing Your Web Page," you learned all about using and building great graphics for your Web page. Graphics are critical to making an attractive Web page that interests visitors and keeps them coming back again and again.

Besides graphics, you also can include cool video and audio clips directly in your FrontPage Web. Audio clips play sound and music for visitors when they stop by, while video clips are displayed like graphics, except that they move. Besides audio and video clips, there is another way to add motion to your page—using animated graphics. Called animated GIFs, these images really are a concatenation of multiple Web graphics that automatically play. The effect is like flipping through a story book, in which standard Web graphics actually move.

FrontPage 98 includes true multimedia integration and support by enabling you to easily embed these exciting types of enhancements into your site. GIF animations can also be easily inserted and used as part of your Web page; in fact, several even come with FrontPage. This hour describes in detail the use of multimedia and animations in your FrontPage Web.

Specifically, this chapter shows you how to

☐ Understand the important audio and video file formats

☐ Use FrontPage 98 to include both types of multimedia on Web pages

☐ Learn about animated GIFs and where you can find some to use for yourself

Experiencing Multimedia Sites

Imagine making the movie *Star Wars*. George Lucas started with a plain old text manuscript. That manuscript might have been thorough, but it wasn't nearly as much fun as the actual movie. The great soundtrack and cool special effects make the movie fun and enjoyable. Without them, *Star Wars* might have been any old movie, and not the legend it is today.

With images, your Web page becomes a multimedia page because you combine graphics and text on one page. However, in today's terms, multimedia means including both audio and video clips in your home page.

Technically, your Web page is multimedia because you use text and images, but you won't qualify for a gold star unless you add audio or video clips to it. Fortunately, FrontPage makes including multimedia clips in a page relatively easy after you've gotten your hands on some audio or video clips you can use.

For a good idea of what a multimedia site is, stop by http://www.cnn.com. On this 24-hour news site, you can hear live reports, see real news footage, and view raw photographs. Figure 14.1 shows today's top stories.

Figure 14.1.

CNN is a true multimedia experience for all news junkies.

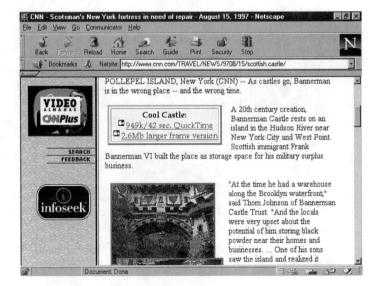

14

There are many different ways and reasons to use multimedia clips on a Web site. Another popular place you'll run across audio and video clips is in movie promotion sites. For example, in the `http://www.face-off.com` Web site, you can see previews of the Nicholas Cage and John Travolta blockbuster (see Figure 14.2).

Figure 14.2.

Many popular movies have supporting multimedia sites to attract viewers.

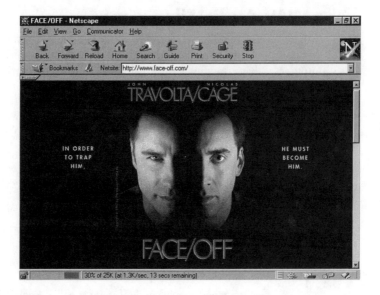

Understanding and Using Audio Clips

Now that you've seen some multimedia sites in action, it's time to learn how to update your own FrontPage Web site. The first type of multimedia you should learn how to add is audio clips. FrontPage makes it easy for you to include practically any type of audio clip or sound bite in your Web page. The most difficult part of using sounds is finding one that you like or one that matches your site.

Like adding images, putting an audio clip on your Web page embeds an actual file that downloads as the page is loaded. While images appear beside your text, the audio clip automatically starts playing in the background while you are browsing through a page.

JUST A MINUTE

To hear audio clips on your computer, you must have the correct hardware and software. If you are using a PC-compatible machine, you must have a sound card (preferably a SoundBlaster or compatible) and speakers hooked up. Most multimedia kits accompanying CD-ROM drives include all the necessary hardware to hear sound clips. Macintosh users, on the other hand, have less work to do. Mac's multimedia capabilities are built in.

14

This section describes the process for adding and using audio clips on your site. First, it describes popular audio file types you might run across; then it gives several suggestions for how you can find or make audio clips to use yourself. Finally, it shows you the relatively easy process of using an audio clip on your site.

The WAV Audio File Format

Throughout the WWW, you see a wide variety of audio clip file types and formats. These formats, representing the different methods used to electronically record the sounds into a computer, all have their own advantages and common uses.

Choosing from the different file types is like picking the right kind of film for your camera. You can use 35mm, disc, 110, or Polaroid instant film. Even though each film type works differently and requires a different type of camera, they all yield a similar result.

The most important type of audio format you should recognize is the WAV format. WAV files are the Microsoft Windows standard audio format. The .WAV extension is used for audio files created for use primarily under Microsoft Windows. WAV files tend to be of decent quality and are nearly ubiquitous around the WWW.

Both Netscape Navigator and Microsoft Internet Explorer include built-in support for playing WAV files that are embedded inside a Web page.

JUST A MINUTE

One other popular audio format is called RealAudio, which uses the .RA file extension. RealAudio is the pioneer of streaming audio files on the WWW. RealAudio sound files require special software to be loaded on the Web server; then they send audio files to the browser. Your browser is constantly receiving a stream of sounds and works much like a radio. You can learn more about this impressive way to use audio by visiting http://www.realaudio.com. You're more likely to use RealAudio for yourself rather than include these types of files on your Web page.

COFFEE BREAK

As you continue to explore the WWW, you'll run across several different types of sound files. Other popular formats include AU, developed for UNIX computers; AIFF, developed originally for Macintosh machines; and MIDI, developed for high-quality and large sound files.

In today's world, which type of audio file you use doesn't really matter; your browser can handle virtually all of them interchangeably. The WAV format has quickly become the default because so many people have and use Microsoft Windows, but feel free to download, listen to, or use any sound file you can get your hands on.

14

Finding Audio Clips to Use

Now that you are familiar with the WAV audio format, the next step is finding good sound files for your Web page. You have two options for getting audio clips: downloading them from the Internet or making some for yourself. You'll usually download and use clips that you find.

The Internet is a fantastic resource for all types of music and audio clips. You can download everything from Jim Carey ("Allllrighty then") to Martin Luther King Jr.'s "I Have a Dream" speech. The following is a short list of popular WWW sites where you can find, download, and listen to audio clips. These public archives enable anyone to download files.

☐ http://www.dailywav.com/—The Daily Wav Web Site. This site adds a new sound clip every day and has many popular and contemporary sounds that can be useful on a Web page.

☐ http://Web.msu.edu/vincent/index.html—Find famous people and speeches such as Martin Luther King Jr's "I Have a Dream" speech, among others, on this site.

TIME SAVER

When you click audio files at these sites, your browser automatically downloads them and plays them for you, without saving the file. Hold the Shift button down when you click audio (and video) files to save them permanently to your hard drive. After you save them, you can listen to them and add them to your Web with FrontPage.

CAUTION

Remember to keep copyright issues in mind when you download these audio and video clips. Just because you found them on the Internet doesn't mean that all copyrights have been obtained to make them available. If you are set on using these clips on your Web page, it is best to obtain permission from the original creator first. Companies often will let their likeness be used for a fan club of a particular television show or series.

COFFEE BREAK

Want to make your own audio clips from scratch? To do so, you must have a microphone hooked up to your computer's sound card. Most SoundBlasters and compatible systems let you easily plug in a $10 microphone directly to the back of your computer. In addition, you can directly plug in audio system components such as CD players, radios, and more by purchasing the correct cables at your local electronics store.

14

After you obtain a microphone, the next step is to digitize your voice and save it on your computer. Windows 95 comes with simple software you can use to record voices and sound effects directly into the WAV file format.

After you've saved the WAV files, adding them to your FrontPage Web is the easy step. See the next section for more details on including them in your site.

Adding Audio Clips to Your FrontPage Web

Actually, obtaining the correct clip is the hardest part of putting sound on your Web page. After you have an audio clip in hand, the FrontPage Editor lets you add it with just a few quick steps. Because sounds play in the background of a page after it loads, they don't actually appear on your Web page like an image (or video clip).

To add a background sound to your page, follow these steps:

1. Load your Web page into the FrontPage Editor, click the right mouse button, and choose Page Properties from the pop-up box. The Page Properties dialog box appears (see Figure 14.3).

Figure 14.3.

You can set sound clips with a single property from this dialog box.

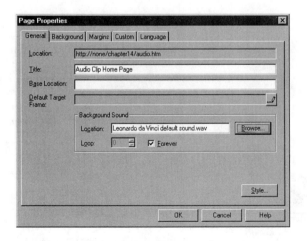

2. From the Page Properties box, you can use the Location box to set which audio file plays. You can type the name of a sound file or click the Browse button to scour your hard drive for a WAV file.

14

3. After you've selected a sound file to play in the background, FrontPage lets you decide how many times this clip should repeat. You can have the sound file constantly repeat, or play a set number of times (1–99).

4. When you are finished, click OK and the sound is embedded into your page. Don't forget to save the page.

JUST A MINUTE

> Another popular way to add sounds to a Web page is by building a hyperlink to the WAV files. When you create a hyperlink, you can point to virtually any file on the WWW, not just HTML files. By linking to WAV files, the sound isn't automatically embedded into the page and requires your visitor to take an extra step before they hear your sound file.

Understanding and Using Video Clips

Adding audio clips to your Web page is just the first step in making your FrontPage Web a true multimedia experience. The next step is embedding the video clips.

Video clips are combinations of moving pictures and sound, bundled together just like a movie. Video clips can range from snippets of actual films to home-created clips. Like audio clips, FrontPage lets you embed video clips into your page, but with one major difference. Audio clips play in the background while visitors explore your site, but video clips can actually be seen like standard Web graphics. Of course, the video clips contain motion and can include sound accompaniment as well.

Unfortunately, video clips have several drawbacks that make them difficult to use. The main problem is file size. Video clips are gigantic, usually at least 1–2MB in file size. Each video clip is a conglomeration of hundreds of images set to display one after another in rapid succession. A one-minute video clip can have as many as 1,000 different image frames. As a result, you'll usually find yourself using small and short video clips of just a few seconds in your FrontPage Web.

Downloading a 2MB file in ideal conditions and at the fastest speed your computer probably supports (28.8 baud) still takes 10–20 minutes. Millions of WWW users use 14.4 or slower baud modems. For these users, the large file size often means they won't take the time to download a video clip. But, often they are worth the added trouble and value. Imagine visiting a movie's home page. You'd be disappointed if there wasn't a video clip or two of that blockbuster, regardless of how long it takes to view.

14

JUST A MINUTE

> Viewing video clips on your computer requires the correct hardware and software. This means having enough RAM (8MB minimum) on a Windows-based computer to display the moving video images onscreen, plus a current Web browser.

Explaining Video File Types and Formats

Like the audio format, there is one main type of video file type you'll come across, AVI. The AVI format is the Windows Video format and is one of the standard video file types accepted worldwide.

This standard format is optimized to appear within Web browsers and on computers that run Microsoft Windows. You'll find that nearly all video clips come in the AVI format. Both Netscape and Microsoft fully support AVI files within their browsers so that the videos seamlessly appear within the constraints of a Web page.

Of course, there are other types of common video formats you might run across. The other most common format you'll use is called QuickTime. QuickTime (.QT extension) was developed primarily for Macintosh but can be used by all types of computers. Another popular video type is the MPEG standard, which was created for high-powered UNIX computers that have a lot of memory and horsepower.

Another format you'll start hearing more about in the future is called RealVideo. The RealVideo format is different from others discussed here, because your browser starts displaying the video clip as it streams down to your computer. This streaming format doesn't make you wait for extended lengths of time before you can enjoy the video clip for yourself. Developed by the same people who put together the RealAudio sound format, visit `http://www.realaudio.com` for more information.

Finding Video Clips to Use

Like audio clips, finding video clips to use on your Web page is the only challenging part of embedding multimedia into your FrontPage Web. Video clips are more difficult to find and create for yourself, so knowing where to look is important. You'll find several vast collections of video clips you can use on the Internet. Here's a partial list of some hot spots to find good MPEG and QT files on the Web:

- [ ] `http://www.video-links.com/`—Find a current collection of movies in several different categories here. These video clips range from episode shots of *Seinfeld* to popular commercials and trailers (quite a variety).

- [ ] `http://film.softcenter.se/flics/`—This is one of the most complete spots for digital video clips available, with over 1,300 clips. This is the one-stop clearinghouse for video sites on the WWW.

14

☐ `http://deathstar.rutgers.edu/people/bochkay/movies.html`—An ever-growing variety of movie clips. Here you find different video clips that contain Kathy Ireland, Barney the Dinosaur, and *Star Trek*.

TIME SAVER

Besides these listed multimedia collections, another popular way to find video clips is by purchasing stock video clips. Several companies sell CD-ROMs that contain royalty-free video clips you can use on your Web page. One of the best is FourPalms software (`http://www.fourpalms.com`). FourPalms distributes stock video clips, offering over 10 different CD-ROM titles full of video clips. It even sells a sampler CD for a few dollars so you can experience its quality for yourself.

JUST A MINUTE

Just a year or two ago, if you wanted to make your own video clips and put them on your home page, it would have been difficult and expensive. At that time, the equipment required to digitize and store video in electronic format was far too expensive and difficult to use.

Today, it's a different story. There are several affordable low-cost alternatives to creating your own video clips. Basic video cameras that connect directly to your computer come with hardware and software for under $200. In addition, you can make video clips from VCR tapes you already have. For about the same price range, you can purchase a digital converter enabling your VCR and computer to talk to each other.

Stop by your local computer store to learn more about your digitizing options. One stop that you won't want to miss is the Connectix QuickCam. For $100, Mac and Windows users can buy grayscale video cameras that take still images and full-motion video clips. These clips are digitized and saved automatically, ready for immediate use on your Web page. For around $199, you can also buy a color version of the best-selling QuickCam. Stop by `http://www.quickcam.com` for more info.

Another excellent low-cost camera is the WinCam. For about $200, you can order a color WinCam that looks a lot like an old Polaroid camera. It comes with a tripod and slide holder, as well as all the software you need. You can learn more about the WinCam at `http://www.wincam.com`. To get an idea of quality, several of the images at `http://www.shafran.com` were digitized with the WinCam.

To digitize a clip from a video tape, go to your local computer store and pick up a product called Snappy!. This product hooks into your VCR and computer and lets you add video clips from tape onto your hard drive for about $200.

14

Adding Video Clips to Your FrontPage Web

FrontPage 98 directly supports embedding a video clip into your Web page. In fact, FrontPage treats video clips essentially as it would a standard Web graphic, with just a few extra options to set.

To insert a video clip into your FrontPage Web site, follow these steps:

1. Start the FrontPage Editor and load the page you want to make multimedia. Then choose Insert | Active Elements | Video from the menu bar to bring up the Video dialog box (see Figure 14.4).

Figure 14.4.

With FrontPage 98, video clips are inserted just like standard Web graphics.

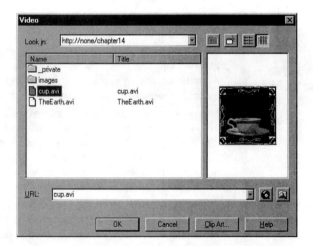

2. Choose the video clip you want to insert. You can select video files from the current Web, or browse the Internet or your hard drive for the perfect clip. After you've selected a clip, FrontPage adds a still image of it to your page (see Figure 14.5).

3. After you add the video clip to your page, you'll be able to watch it through your favorite browser. In addition, there are several video attributes you can set. Move your mouse over the embedded video clip, click your right mouse button, and choose Image Properties from the pop-up box that appears. FrontPage brings up the Video tab within the Image Properties dialog box (see Figure 14.6).

14

Figure 14.5.

Although it isn't moving, this is the embedded video clip.

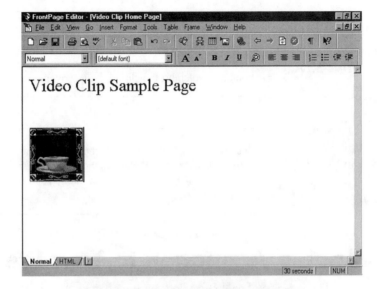

Figure 14.6.

FrontPage lets you set loop attributes and what triggers the video to start playing.

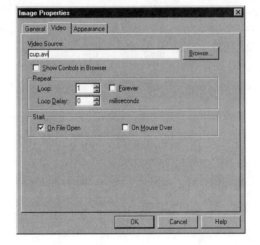

4. This is the standard dialog box that appears when you insert any image into your Web page. However, this tab becomes effective only when you are working with a video clip instead of an image. There are several properties to set, including the number of times the clip repeats and what event starts it initially.

   You can choose to have the clip repeat a finite number of times or let it play indefinitely. Don't forget to click one of the boxes in the Start part of this dialog box.

14

For longer video clips, you should always check the box labeled Show Controls in Browser. When this checkbox is selected, it adds Start and Stop buttons to the embedded video clip, enabling visitors to pause and continue watching the clip at their convenience.

JUST A MINUTE

Besides embedding a clip, you can also create a hyperlink to an AVI file. Choose Insert | Hyperlink from the FrontPage Editor's menu bar to create a new hyperlink from scratch. From here, you can link to an HTML file, or even a video clip.

Adding Animation to Your Web Page

The last type of cool effect you can use on your Web page is animation. Animated Web graphics have quickly become a staple among Web developers like you, because they are easy to create, simple to use, and fun to view when exploring a Web page.

Animated Web graphics are really an extension to the standard GIFs that you normally use on your Web page. A single animated GIF really is a combination of multiple GIFs mashed together into a single file. When your browser loads an animated GIF, it automatically starts scrolling through the entire file, loading the separate images making up that file as if they were multiple frames in a movie. The result is a lot like a flip book, in which you have animation-like effects because the browser takes care of displaying the animated GIF.

Using animated GIFs is easy because they are inserted onto your Web page like any standard Web Graphic. Choose Insert | Image from the FrontPage Editor's menu bar and you can add an animated GIF directly to your page.

The key to using animated GIFs is finding (or building) attractive and effective ones for your site.

COFFEE BREAK

When the GIF format was originally introduced in 1987, it contained many features that optimized it for sending graphics electronically through a modem. In 1989, the GIF standard was revisited and a little-used feature was added that lets you concatenate multiple GIF files into a single file, but has it display each separate file as if it were a frame in a movie. This feature produced an animation-like result, but was rarely used.

14

Sometime during 1995, it was rediscovered by the denizens of the Web, and GIF animation was reborn. Netscape and Microsoft soon started supporting it within their popular browsers. Today, several tools build animated GIFs for you without much hassle, but they really started out inauspiciously.

Finding Animated GIFs

The best way to quickly add and use an animated GIF on your Web page is to explore a collection of them online. There are several galleries of animated GIFs, but none as complete as the Animated GIF Artists Guild, which you can find at http://www.agag.com (see Figure 14.7). From here, you can learn more about the history of animated GIFs, view gallery upon gallery of GIFs you can use yourself, or find the techniques required to build them from scratch.

Figure 14.7.

The Animated GIF Artists Guild is the center of GIF information on the WWW.

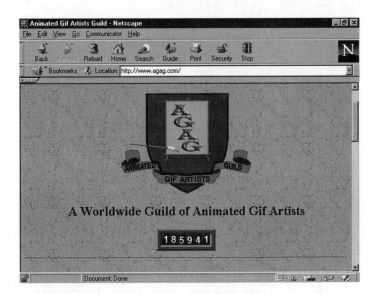

Mixing Multimedia and Animation

One new aspect that Web developers haven't had to deal with is incorporating true multimedia in a single FrontPage Web. In your Web pages, you can have text, images, sound clips, and video clips all being displayed (and heard) at the same time.

Working with multimedia is a new and difficult task to properly master. When you add a video clip to your FrontPage Web, you want to make sure it doesn't interfere with any background sounds that might be playing.

14

Here's a simple recipe that you should always follow when building a multimedia and animation-enabled Web page:

1. Plan what the final "experience" should be like. Decide whether the sound, images, animated GIFs, and video clips really go with one another. Consider the effect of the colors and styles of all the images, sounds, and video clips. Remember that you can change the color and appearance of any text as well.

2. Add all the text to your Web page. Format and colorize it properly. When using background colors and images, make sure that text is readable.

3. Add images next. Decide where to place the images and what size they should be. Make sure they are a reasonable file size to download, because multimedia-enabled pages quickly become large.

4. Decide whether you need GIF animations. GIF animations are easy to find on the WWW and come in all sorts of shapes and sizes. Because they work just like standard Web images, they are logical to place and embed.

5. Now add background sound. Sound is easier to work with than video because it's one-dimensional. Video clips often have their own soundtracks. Make sure the sound isn't too loud or obtrusive. Ensure that the sound clip you pick fits with the style of your FrontPage Web. For example, don't add the 1812 Overture to a Web page dedicated to Metallica.

6. Finally, mix in video clips. Often, you won't use background sounds on the same page with video clips because they could interfere with one another. Check the performance of your video/animation clip to make sure it downloads quickly.

Summary

Using multimedia and animation are two ways you can easily add excitement to your Web pages. Most visitors really enjoy when sounds play in the background, video clips automatically activate, or standard Web graphics transform into impressive animations.

This chapter introduced you to the basics of using sound, video, and animations on your Web page. You should feel comfortable with finding and using all three types of these interactive additions in any page within FrontPage. Fortunately, FrontPage supports multimedia in a coordinated and organized fashion, enabling you to add multimedia without much hassle.

14

Q&A

Q After looking at the HTML code behind my Web page, I noticed that my background sound was told to play –1 times. What does this mean?

A The –1 is really a trite way of telling the browser to repeat the sound clip forever and ever. By looking at the underlying HTML of a page, you can notice several neat tricks that FrontPage uses to get the browser to use the desired effect.

Q There must be a better way to manage all the different aspects of a Web page. By the time I color coordinate, add useful images, and change the text font, integrating multimedia clips is extremely difficult. How can FrontPage ease some of this confusion?

A By including many different Web themes, Microsoft anticipated the problem of managing and coordinating all the different aspects of a site. In Hour 21, "Applying Web Themes," you learn how to use themes to manage all the color and design coordination of a page, enabling you to concentrate on the proper places and pages to add background sounds, animations, and embedded video clips.

Workshop

The Workshop contains quiz questions and an Activities section to help reinforce what you've learned in this hour. Try not to look at the quiz answers until you've tried to work them out yourself!

Quiz

1. What's the difference between embedding and linking to sound clips from a Web page?

2. When using video clips, how can you add controls to the movie so visitors can choose to start and stop the movie at their convenience?

3. Why must you be careful about using both audio and video clips within the same Web page?

Answers

1. Embedding a sound on a Web page means that your sound plays automatically when the page is loaded. The sound actually becomes one of the default page properties. Conversely, you can also build a standard hyperlink to any type of sound file. In that situation, your browser would load and play the sound after the link was clicked. Linking to sound files is an excellent way to let users choose from a library of audio clips.

14

2. After inserting the movie into your page, bring up the Image Properties dialog box by clicking the right mouse button and selecting Image Properties. Then choose the box labeled Show Controls in Browser.

3. Because video snippets can contain sounds as well. These sounds could interfere or override the background sounds intended for that page.

Activities

1. As you continue to learn more about FrontPage, you'll quickly discover that themes are great tools because several of them use animated GIFs as part of their set style. Read Hour 21 to learn more about using and modifying a specific theme to fit your site.

2. Video clips can also be considered active elements within FrontPage 98. Check out Hour 15, "Activating Active Elements," to learn about different types of elements you can use to entertain visitors who stop by.

3. Besides finding them on the WWW, you can also easily build animated GIFs from scratch. Point your browser to http://www.group42.com to download and use a premier animated GIF construction tool to make these simple animations yourself.

14

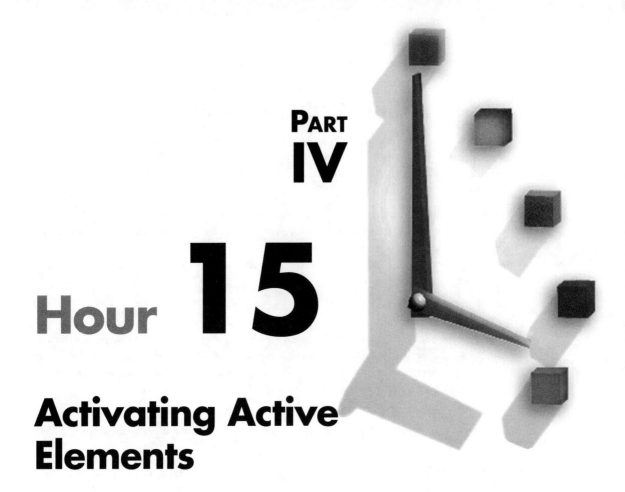

Hour 15

Activating Active Elements

There are several features within FrontPage 98 that make it the best tool available for building and managing Web sites. This hour introduces you to one of them, *active elements*. Active elements are embedded commands that add cool and useful special effects to your Web page. They come only with FrontPage and are a handful of tools that make your page interactive and exciting for users to visit. For example, you can create a special button for your page that changes color whenever a mouse moves over it.

This hour covers how to use and include active elements in your FrontPage Web. Specifically, you'll learn

- ☐ What active elements are
- ☐ How to include most of the default active elements in your FrontPage Web
- ☐ When, and when not, to use an active element
- ☐ Why you might want to customize a default active element

Understanding Active Elements

Active elements are a fantastic way to add interaction and special effects easily to your FrontPage Web. They go beyond standard HTML formatting features and let you add pre-packaged, small programs to your site. Microsoft enables you to use several different active elements within your site.

Normally when you create a Web page, you spend much of your time worrying about text formatting, image placement, and related issues. When a visitor loads that page, the browser then waits for a link to be clicked or some other action to occur. The browser is more or less sleeping until the user indicates its next command. This static page can be informative to visitors but often isn't very exciting.

Active elements combat this boredom because they are special Web pieces that add movement or interaction with your visitors even if they don't select a hypertext link or click the Back button in their browsers. For example, the Hover Button active element lets you add a sound effect that plays whenever a visitor's mouse moves over the button. So, you could include a button that looks like a small window and play a glass-shattering sound when the mouse moves over it, without waiting for a specific click or action from the user.

You'll find active elements entertaining and useful when building Web sites. They offer more advanced functionality that is difficult or impossible to accomplish with simple HTML codes.

NEW TERM Java is a popular language that programmers use to build interactive programs, called *applets*, that run directly from within a Web page. Java was created by Sun Microsystems and a consortium of developers. It is optimized to work specifically over the World Wide Web and works the same on all types of computers, including Macs, PCs, and UNIX machines.

JUST A MINUTE

Many of the active elements included with FrontPage are written in advanced Web programming languages. For example, the Hover Button active element was written in a computer language called Java.

Other active elements are written in a special format called Common Gateway Interface (CGI). CGI is a special format that lets Web pages communicate and share information with the server on which they reside. For example, the Hit Counter active element is a CGI script that updates a special counter on the server every time a visitor stops by a Web page that contains this special element.

Microsoft has included these active elements because they are commonly requested advanced features that normally would take significant knowledge and time to create yourself. Because they aren't written in HTML, they are much more advanced than most of the simple formatting and placement features you generally use in FrontPage.

15

Using Active Elements

Now that you understand how active elements work, the next step is to use them within your FrontPage Web. Active elements are easy to work with, and you can add them in the same way you incorporate a table or image into your site. You must create and embed them within the FrontPage Editor while you are editing or creating a new Web page.

This section describes several of the different active elements available through FrontPage and steps you through using them in your site. In general, active elements are relatively straightforward and are a fantastic way to add special effects without becoming an advanced programmer or HTML expert.

Hover Buttons

The first and easiest active element to create and use is a hover button. Hover buttons add some type of special interaction between your visitors and your Web page, when included within your Web. The Hover Button active element is so named because when included on a Web page, the button performs a special visual effect whenever the mouse moves over it. Hover buttons can appear as simple text buttons, link to other Web sites, trigger audio sounds when hovered over, and more.

To add a hover button to your FrontPage Web, choose Insert | Active Elements | Hover Button from the FrontPage Editor menu bar. The Hover Button dialog box appears as shown in Figure 15.1.

Figure 15.1.

There are many different effects to choose from when building a hover button.

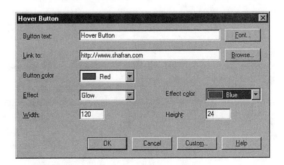

This dialog box lets you set how your hover button should appear. There are several different ways you can customize how the hover button appears within your page (see Table 15.1).

Table 15.1. Configuring your hover buttons.

Hover Option	Description
Button text	Controls what text appears on the hover button. You can click the Font button to change the text appearance.
Link to	Enables you to link this button to another page on the WWW. See Hour 8, "Linking Pages Together," for more information on URLs and hypertext links.
Button color	Selects the default starting color the button appears on the page. This color changes as the effect is applied to the button.
Effect	Decides which special effect the hover button will display when a mouse moves over it.
Effect color	The ending color after the hover button has finished showing the special effect. For example, if you select the Glow effect, the button starts out as one color and then glows the color specified in this setting.
Width	The width, measured in pixels, of the hover button.
Height	The height, measured in pixels, of the hover button.

Besides the standard hover button choices you can use, there are some advanced ways you can customize how this interactive button works with your visitors. Click the Custom button to bring up a set of four advanced features that can change the button's appearance and default actions (see Figure 15.2).

Figure 15.2.

Advanced customization lets you add sounds and images to your hover button.

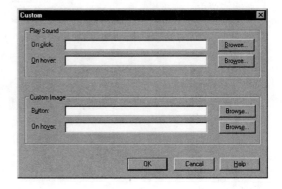

15

After you click OK, FrontPage automatically adds the hover button to your Web page. In addition, if you go to the FrontPage Explorer, you will see a new file in your Web, `fphover.class`. This file is a special program written in Java that creates the dynamic hover button on your Web page. Now when visitors stop by, their browser downloads the entire `.class` file and starts running the Java Hover Button program as an embedded part of the page. Figure 15.3 shows the hover button within FrontPage.

Figure 15.3.

The hover button changes depending on the colors and effect you selected.

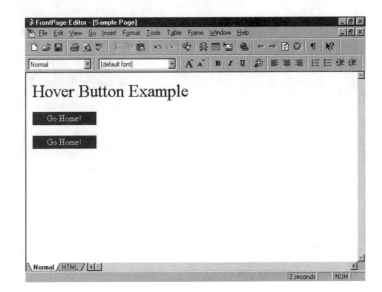

Any time you want to change the text, graphic, link, color, or effect of the hover button, right-click your mouse over the hover button within the FrontPage Editor and choose Java Applet Properties.

CAUTION

Not all browsers and visitors support Java applets running within a Web page. Even current versions of Netscape give you the option of not downloading the Java component to save download time and disk space. When you use the hover button or other Java applets, always include a notice on your Web page that this site uses Java.

Banner Ad Manager

Another great active element you'll want to use is the Banner Ad Manager. Although its name is confusing, you can use this active element in several spots on your Web site. This Java applet lets you display on your Web site a rotating set of images instead of a single graphic. When you add this active element to your FrontPage Web, visitors will continuously see a set of images you select rotating from one to another. It's a good way to add multiple images to the same spot on a Web page, because they constantly keep rotating.

Choose Insert | Active Element | Banner Ad Manager from the menu bar to bring up the dialog box in which you can set up this active element (see Figure 15.4).

Figure 15.4.

You have similar options with this active element as you do when you insert a hover button.

Similar to the hover button, there are several different settings and buttons you can choose when making a banner ad manager (see Table 15.2).

Table 15.2. Configuring your banner ad manager.

Banner Ad Option	Description
Width	The width, measured in pixels, of the applet that contains and displays the set of rotating images. FrontPage will resize each of the images to fit within these height and width settings.
Height	The height, measured in pixels, of the applet that contains and displays the set of rotating images.
Transition	Selects the special effect that loads one image after another. You can choose from six different transitions between images.
Link to	The URL where visitors should go if they click anywhere on this set of images.
Images to Display	The set of images FrontPage should load one after another. Click the Add button to insert another image into the rotating banner. You can include as many images as you'd like to rotate with this Java applet.

After you select all the images that should rotate in this applet, click OK. Again, FrontPage creates another `.class` file and the applet is automatically included in your page. When visitors stop by they will see the first image, and eventually all the images within this active element will scroll through.

Marquees

Another active element you can include in your FrontPage Web is a scrolling marquee bar. Marquees work just as you'd expect them to: words or phrases roll left or right across the screen.

You can insert a marquee banner on your page by choosing Insert | Active Element | Marquee from the FrontPage Editor menu bar. Figure 15.5 shows the Marquee Properties dialog box that appears.

Figure 15.5.

Marquees are very configurable Web elements, but work only within Microsoft Internet Explorer.

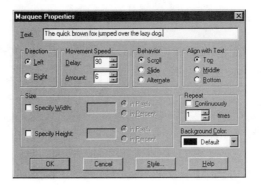

From the Marquee Properties dialog box, you can type in the Text box the information you want to scroll. You can set many other options pertaining to this scrolling marquee banner including direction, movement speed, behavior, color, repeating attributes, and text alignment. Set the marquee options you want to use, and then click OK. FrontPage shows the marquee within the Editor (see Figure 15.6).

To make changes to your marquee's text or behavior, click your right mouse button on it within the FrontPage Editor and choose Marquee Properties from the pop-up box that appears.

CAUTION

The Marquee active element is different from the previous two already discussed because it is not a Java applet. Marquees are HTML tags that were introduced by Microsoft in 1996. Unfortunately, it is a special Microsoft-only tag that is not recognized or supported by any other browser. Use Marquee elements only if you are absolutely sure that all visitors who stop by are using Microsoft Internet Explorer.

Figure 15.6.

This marquee keeps scrolling across the page for all visitors who stop by.

The marquee bar ———

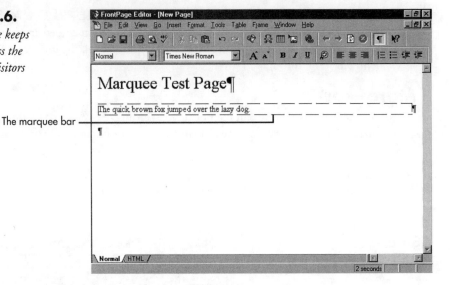

Site Searching and Hit Counters

There are two more types of active elements you can use and include within your site, Site Searching and a Hit Counter. Both add special elements to your page that give users more information about your site.

The Site Searching active element lets users issue a full text search across all the pages within your site. This is particularly useful if you have a large site that consists of many different HTML pages. If visitors can't find what they need, they can always search for the proper page.

The Hit Counter active element keeps a running tab of the number of visitors who stop by your site. An odometer-like counter appears on your page and is incremented every time someone new stops by.

These two active elements are useful but not always easy to include within a FrontPage Web. Both of them require your Web site to be running on a special server that has FrontPage extensions. Your Internet provider must explicitly support these advanced FrontPage features in order to work properly. For more information on uploading the FrontPage extensions and understanding whether your Internet provider supports them, check out Hour 17, "Publishing to the WWW."

To make your site searchable, choose Insert | Active Elements | Search from the Editor's menu bar. The Search Form Properties dialog box in Figure 15.7 appears and lets you set several default search site properties.

15

Figure 15.7.

Mainly, you can control which text appears within the search part of your Web page.

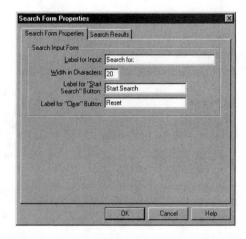

Customize the options you want to set, and click OK to add the search bar to your Web page. Figure 15.8 shows the Search active element within FrontPage.

Figure 15.8.

The Search bar is easy to use and powerful for visitors who don't want to browse your site.

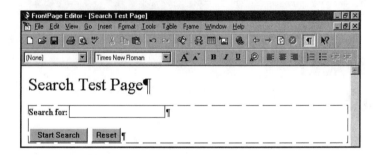

Almost as easy to create as the Search active element, hit counters are popular among many Web developers. Counters give you a good idea of how many people stop by your site, so you can tell whether you get a lot of visitors or nearly no traffic at all.

Add a hit counter to your page by choosing Insert | Active Element | Hit Counter from the Editor's menu bar. Figure 15.9 shows the Hit Counter Properties dialog box. From here you can choose between five different styles and fonts of numbers.

After you select a counter type, click OK and FrontPage adds an automatically incrementing GIF of a counter to your Web page. Figure 15.10 shows a counter on a sample Web page.

Figure 15.9.

Pick the counter type that best fits your page's style.

Figure 15.10.

For a nearly empty page, there sure have been a lot of visitors!

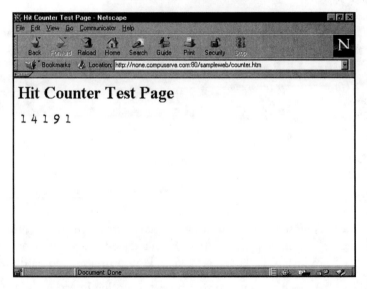

JUST A MINUTE

Not everyone will be able to use the FrontPage Hit Counter because their Web server might not support FrontPage extensions. If you still want to have a counter on your site, visit http://www.digits.com for information on adding a free counter to your Web page with simply a URL and nothing more.

15

Summary

Building a good Web site is a lot like building a house. You need a wide variety of tools and knowledge to create a sturdy, well-designed house. Active elements are new and useful tools that come in handy when you are creating a good and interactive Web site. Like any specialized tool, you'll want to be careful when you are using active elements so they make sense on the various pages within your site. For example, you don't need to add a counter to every page within your FrontPage Web, but you might want to always include scrolling marquees to send important information across each page.

This hour introduced you to the basics behind working with FrontPage 98 active elements. You should feel comfortable including these Web tools in your site and understand how each of them works. In addition, you learned that although some active elements are written in Java, some use CGI, and others require special FrontPage Web servers, they all have one thing in common: dynamic updates of Web pages that increase the interaction of your site.

Q&A

Q Where did the Banner Ad Manager active element get its name? Why isn't it called the "Rotating Image" active element instead?

A As you continue to explore the Web, you're likely to run across several sites that have advertisements on their set of pages. These advertisements are often a set of rotating images that link to a particular Web site. This Java applet was originally designed for that purpose but is much more useful to everyday Web developers than just including ads on a page. You can have rotating personal images, transforming logos, and much more, all by resizing and including this active element on your page.

Q How do I restart my hit counter at zero for a fresh beginning?

A After you insert a hit counter on your site, you can update its properties at any time. Simply right-click your mouse over the counter within the FrontPage Editor and choose Hit Counter Properties from the pop-up menu box. From here, you can restart your hit counter to any number including zero, and even set a fixed number of digits the counter should use on the screen.

Workshop

The Workshop contains quiz questions and an Activities section to help reinforce what you've learned in this hour. Try not to look at the quiz answers until you've tried to work them out yourself!

Quiz

1. How can you tell your hover button to slowly fill in red instead of glowing by default?

2. How can you include an incrementing odometer of visitors for your Web site?

3. Why might you not want to use a marquee on your Web pages?

Answers

1. When you insert the hover button, change the effect for this active element to be Color Fill instead of Glow, which is the default setting. Don't forget to change the Effect Color setting to Red so that the button fills in appropriately.

2. The first step is to make sure that your Web server is properly running the FrontPage 98 Web Server extensions. These extensions must be running in order for visitors to properly see the hit counter. Next, choose Insert | Active Elements | Hit Counter from the menu bar and pick the counter style you want to use. Don't forget to test the counter within your browser to make sure it works properly.

3. Because the marquee's tag is a very specialized tag that works only for Microsoft Internet Explorer browsers. Other popular browsers such as Netscape Navigator and Netscape Communicator will not display marqueed information.

Activities

1. Get a solid grasp on more advanced FrontPage elements by checking out Hour 16, "Embedding FrontPage Components." Components are similar to active elements but are less dynamic and interactive and are more focused on making Web management and creation easier.

2. Learn how to put all these concepts together into the complete site package by reading Hour 24, "Finale: Building a Home Page from Scratch."

3. For more advanced information on features such as counters, search http:// www.yahoo.com for counters and learn all about special CGI programs that can add counters for you without FrontPage extensions.

15

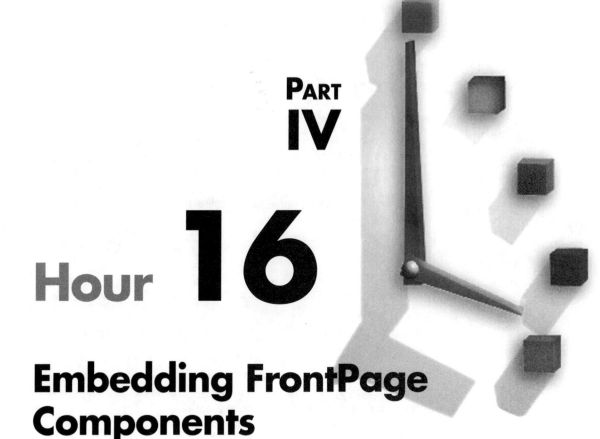

Hour 16

Embedding FrontPage Components

Active elements aren't the only cool way to add interactive special effects to your Web site. FrontPage also includes special embedded components that let you add advanced commands and information dynamically to your Web page. FrontPage components are small mini-programs that let you programmatically include information on pages within your site. For example, you could use the Scheduled Image component to display different images to visitors, depending on the day or time they stop by.

This hour introduces you to FrontPage components and shows you how to take advantage of their power and flexibility when you are creating more advanced, interactive Web sites.

Specifically, in this hour you'll learn how to

☐ Recognize the difference between components and active elements

☐ Include simple FrontPage components within your Web

☐ Have certain images and blocks of HTML appear during a specific schedule

Understanding Components

CAUTION

As you read through this chapter, you're likely to discover that components are fantastic tools for adding advanced features to your Web page. Unfortunately, FrontPage components work only when you publish your site to a Web server that supports the special FrontPage extensions.

FrontPage components require special interaction with Web servers that keep track and update components as they are inserted into one of their Web pages. If your Web provider does not support these special FrontPage-only extensions, components will not work properly for visitors who stop by.

For more information on understanding FrontPage extensions and how to find a Web provider that supports them, read Hour 17, "Publishing to the WWW."

FrontPage components are special variables that can be inserted anywhere within the various pages of your FrontPage Web. These special variables enable you to include dynamic pieces of information that can change every time a visitor stops by. When you add a component to a page, FrontPage stores the component type and description.

Every time a visitor stops by that page, FrontPage re-evaluates that component and adds information to the page as it is sent back to the browser. For example, one of the main components lets you embed another HTML file into any page within your Web. When a visitor loads the original page, FrontPage retrieves the full set of HTML and sends it back to the requesting browser. As it comes across the embedded component, it realizes it is supposed to find and include a separate page of HTML and pretend it is part of the original page. The user never notices a difference. The component variable is automatically translated into the embedded page of HTML.

FrontPage always includes the current version of the embedded HTML page. Therefore, if the embedded page changes and a new visitor stops by, FrontPage will include the new HTML page instead of the original. This entire dynamic process enables different visitors to see different information even when they all stop by the same Web site.

Hit counters operate in the same way. Every time a new visitor stops by, the FrontPage server increments the counter by one and sends a new number back to the browser. No visitor sees the same number because it is dynamically updated and tracked automatically by the FrontPage server.

Using the FrontPage Components

Now that you understand how components work, the next step is to understand when you should use them. The tricky part behind using components is understanding how they work, because FrontPage makes it easy to include them on your Web pages.

You insert all FrontPage components into your Web page in the same way. First, start up the FrontPage Editor and load the page you want to edit. Then, choose Insert | FrontPage Component from the menu bar to bring up the Insert FrontPage Component dialog box (see Figure 16.1). FrontPage then lets you select the component you want to add to the current Web page.

16

Figure 16.1.

A list of all the components you can include on your page.

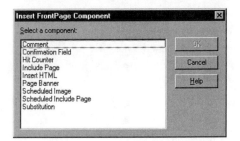

This section steps you through adding most of these components to your Web page. Each FrontPage component operates slightly differently and requires different options to work properly. You'll learn how to insert and configure each component to fit your particular need.

Inserting a Comment

The first and easiest component to work with is a comment. FrontPage comments are key words and phrases that appear only in FrontPage and the HTML file, but aren't displayed in a Web browser. You use comments to make notes to yourself about important changes in the Web page, or to add additional information about who created the page or when it was last edited.

Comments are particularly useful when you must include information that might come in handy when the page is edited in the future, but doesn't need to appear for all visitors who stop by. When you have more than one person editing a page or update certain pages only every few months, comments let you include instructions about how you built a particular page, why you included certain information, and what changes must be made in the future.

To add a comment to your Web page, choose Comment from the Insert FrontPage Component dialog box. The Comment dialog box appears (see Figure 16.2).

Figure 16.2.

This information appears in the Web page but not within the Web browser.

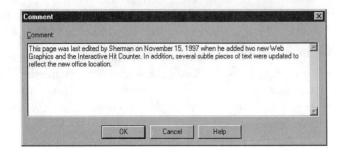

From here, type the information you want to appear as a comment within your Web page. When you are finished, click OK and FrontPage adds the information you typed in a special color to your page. Figure 16.3 shows the newly inserted comment.

Figure 16.3.

All FrontPage comments are clearly identified so you know what will and will not appear within a browser.

Comment identifier —

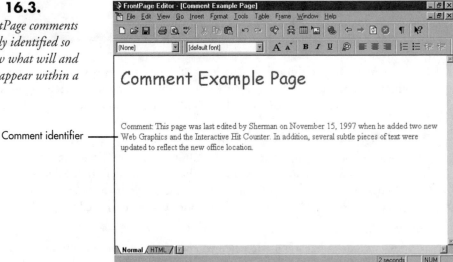

Remember, the commented information won't appear directly in the browser when visitors stop by, but they can read it by looking at the HTML source code behind the page. Therefore,

16

don't put confidential or compromising information into comments, because any visitor can read them if they want to.

You can edit your comment at any time by double-clicking on the comment within the FrontPage Editor.

Include Page Example

The Include Page component is probably the most useful component within FrontPage. It enables you to automatically include HTML pages within other pages in your FrontPage Web. For example, you can create a standard footer page that must appear at the bottom of every page within your site. On each page you can create a FrontPage component that automatically attaches a certain HTML file every time a visitor stops by.

In the future, when you must change the footer for every page, you must update only the standard footer page of HTML. FrontPage dynamically includes the footer every time a visitor requests the page, so your changes are immediately reflected throughout the entire site. You don't need to visit each page and make the same change over and over again—this is a great time saver.

Follow these steps to use the Include Page component:

1. The first step in using this component is to build the Web page you want to include inside other pages.

2. Next, load the page that will contain the included page, and bring up the Insert FrontPage Component dialog box. Select Include Page from there, and the Include Page Component Properties dialog box appears (see Figure 16.4).

Figure 16.4.

You can dynamically include literally any Web page using this component.

3. Choose the file you want to include by typing its filename or URL, or by clicking the Browse button and picking a page from your current Web. Figure 16.5 shows FrontPage browsing for a file to include.

Figure 16.5.

Pick the specific file you want FrontPage to include in your current page.

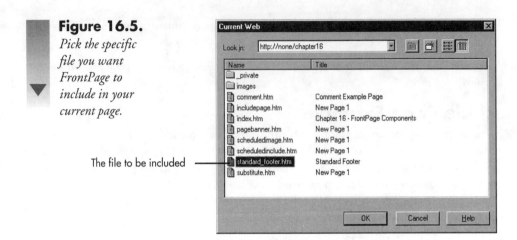

The file to be included ——————— standard_footer.htm

4. Click OK, and FrontPage includes that page automatically by attaching the entire file. You can't edit the inserted page or make any changes to it from the containing file. To update the included file, you must load it separately within the FrontPage Editor. Then, any changes you make are automatically reflected within all the other pages that contain that HTML file. Figure 16.6 shows the new HTML page with an included file.

Figure 16.6.

FrontPage adds this included file as a section of non-editable HTML code.

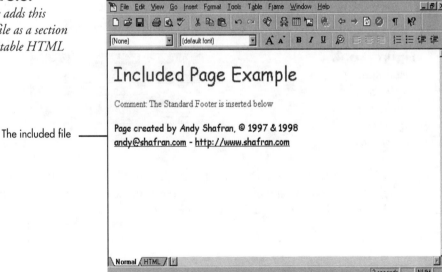

The included file ———————

FrontPage uses the Include Page component extensively within its default templates and wizards. Read Hour 3, "Quickstart: Using the FrontPage Templates," for more information.

Insert HTML

The next FrontPage component lets you embed specific bits of HTML code into your page. It is your responsibility to make sure the HTML is accurate and will not adversely affect how the page appears. The Insert HTML component is used only by HTML experts who want to dynamically include specific pieces of code rather than edit their pages with FrontPage. You'll rarely use it unless you must add a special piece of HTML code that FrontPage doesn't support.

To use the Insert HTML component, choose Insert HTML from the Insert FrontPage Component dialog box. FrontPage brings up the HTML Markup dialog box (see Figure 16.7), in which you can type your HTML directly. When you are finished, click OK and FrontPage inserts the snippet of HTML right into the current page.

Figure 16.7.

You can add any type of HTML code imaginable from here.

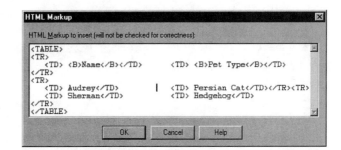

Page Banner

One of the most enjoyable components to work with lets you include graphical banners to the top of your FrontPage Web pages. By choosing the Page Banner component from the Insert FrontPage Component dialog box, you include a dynamically generated graphic that changes depending on the title of a specific page. In general, you will use this component only when you work with FrontPage themes, because the banner image always matches the specific theme you've selected for your Web site.

To learn more about using page banners and setting the text that appears within them, see the section labeled "Adding Themed Banners" in Hour 21, "Applying Web Themes." That hour discusses page banners in significant detail and shows you how to use them all over your site.

Scheduled Images and HTML Files

The most powerful FrontPage components you can use let you include specific images or HTML files on a certain date or time schedule. FrontPage lets you specify a specific image or file to dynamically include on a page, and then set a starting and ending time at which the included component should appear. During the specified time, visitors will see the image and file indicated. However, if they stop by your page before or after the scheduled time, the FrontPage server does not dynamically include that image or file into the Web page.

This technique is very useful when you are including time-sensitive information on a page. For example, if you are building a Web page for a travel agency, you might want to include information about a special promotion for tickets booked during the month of August. You can use FrontPage to include a special HTML file full of promotional information that appears only until midnight on August 31. Because the server dynamically adds the included file or image, you don't have to worry about editing your page at the exact minute the promotion ends—FrontPage does it automatically.

Scheduling an image or file to be included within a specific page is a straightforward process. You can either choose Scheduled Image or Scheduled Include Page from the Insert FrontPage Components dialog box. FrontPage brings up the Scheduled Image Properties dialog box (see Figure 16.8).

Figure 16.8.

Scheduling included images and files is the most advanced FrontPage component you'll use.

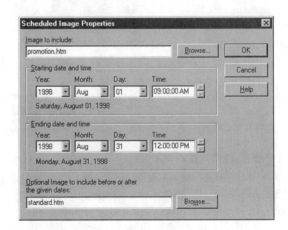

From here, you can select the image or file you want to include on a scheduled basis, configure the scheduling parameters, and even tell FrontPage to display a separate file when visitors stop by outside the scheduled time.

After you configure the schedule in which you want the image or file to appear, click OK. FrontPage adds the included file to the current page and lets you continue editing. During the scheduled time, FrontPage treats the embedded file as it would treat standard included files within FrontPage Webs.

16

You can change the schedule or included file at any time by double-clicking the embedded component to bring back the Scheduled Image Properties dialog box.

Summary

You use FrontPage components to add information to your Web that can dynamically change with each visit. FrontPage components are special notifiers that make the server insert additional files or information into a Web page to ensure that each visitor will always see current information, regardless of when they stop by.

You'll use FrontPage components in several places to create dynamic HTML pages. By including other HTML files, comments, and images, you have complete control over how your pages appear and can manage your site easier.

Q&A

Q There were several other components to insert that you didn't cover in this lesson. Which ones do I need to worry about?

A Microsoft is constantly changing and updating its products, so there might be additional components available for you to use when you try to insert one for yourself. Feel free to experiment and explore how to use these other components to see how they fit your specific needs. All components share one common theme: They are special variables that FrontPage fills in each time the page is called so it doesn't store the same information within a single page. Don't forget that FrontPage components require the special FrontPage server to be used when hosting your Web site. Otherwise, they won't work properly for your visitors.

Some standard components not discussed in this hour include the hit counter and confirmation field. Both of these components are covered in detail in other chapters within this book. The Hit Counter component is covered in Hour 15, "Activating Active Elements," and the Confirmation Field component is discussed in Hour 23, "Forms."

Q How do the scheduled image times work? Do they depend on the time of the server that contains the page or the local time of the visitor who stops by?

A Scheduled images and files depend on the date and time of the server that contains the original HTML file. Because the WWW is truly global, and people from all around the world might stop by, this is a great point to keep in mind when you are scheduling times to include files. Removing a file at 5:00 p.m. EST means that people in San Francisco can't see your entire Web page for 3–4 hours according to their local time, and this problem only magnifies when you deal with individuals who are on the other side of the International Date Line. As a general rule, when you include timed material on a Web page, always indicate the date, time, and time zone when the material no longer will be available.

Workshop

The Workshop contains quiz questions and an Activities section to help reinforce what you've learned in this hour. Try not to look at the quiz answers until you've tried to work them out yourself!

Quiz

1. How do comments operate?

2. How can you add a special image to appear only between the hours of 9:00 a.m., September 1, 1998 and 12:00 p.m., October 1, 1998 (EST)?

Answers

1. Comments are phrases that can be read within the FrontPage Editor, but aren't seen when that page is loaded in a browser. The commented text does appear if you look at the source HTML code of a particular page.

2. a) Open the FrontPage Editor to the proper page.

   b) Choose Insert | FrontPage Component from the menu bar.

   c) Select the Scheduled Image component and click OK.

   d) Type the image that is to be scheduled, and then edit the date and time that the server should use to decide whether to include the image on this specific page.

Activities

1. FrontPage components are very similar to active elements. Check out Hour 15, "Activating Active Elements," to learn the differences between components and elements and when you'll use each technique with your Web.

2. Make sure you understand how to build and insert Web graphics into your Web before you try to schedule the appearance of them. Read Hour 9, "Understanding and Using Web Graphics," for more information.

3. FrontPage comes with several other types of related features that are beyond the scope of this book. Try experimenting with the Insert Table of Contents and Insert Navigation Bar menu items from the Editor for some advanced and interesting component-like features.

PART V

Advanced FrontPage Techniques

Hour

PART V

Hour 17

Publishing to the WWW

Most of this book so far has focused on creating exciting Web pages within your site. You know how to edit text, add images, build tables and frames, and even use FrontPage components. All the modifications and changes you make to your FrontPage Web are saved and registered on your personal computer. Because you run FrontPage 98 on your computer through Windows 95, each HTML file and image is saved somewhere on your hard drive. Having these files on your computer is useful only up to a point. You must send them to another computer that is connected to the Internet, so that millions of people across the world can see the pages you've spent so much time designing.

This entire process is called *publishing* and is the critical link required to making your Web pages available on the World Wide Web. This hour introduces publishing and shows you how FrontPage facilitates much of the hard work for you.

Specifically, in this hour you'll learn how to

☐ Understand the entire Web publishing process

☐ Find a spot on the Internet to store and publish your FrontPage Web

☐ Configure FrontPage to upload your entire web to a computer on the Internet

Understanding How to Publish to the Web

As you create and edit individual pages with FrontPage, they are automatically saved on your personal computer's hard drive. This is convenient for you because all the files you must work with are simply in some subdirectory. When you view your site with the FrontPage Explorer, you see a listing of all the HTML pages, images, and related files within a single subdirectory.

Unfortunately, when these files are on your personal computer, you are the only one who can access them. You must make them available to all the users on the WWW by uploading, or publishing, them to the Internet. When you publish your files, you are sending them electronically to a computer, called a *Web server*, that is connected full-time to the Internet. Web servers usually have names—that's where www.shafran.com and www.samspublishing.com come from.

Therefore, when you publish your FrontPage Web, you are copying all the files on your computer onto a specific Internet computer. This Web server has a full-time job of hosting your pages and sending them back to browsers every time a visitor stops by.

The publishing process is quite easy to understand. On your Web server are the same files that are saved within your FrontPage Web. You even have the same subdirectories as well. In essence, you are creating a synchronized copy of your FrontPage Web on two computers. You can edit and test all the changes on your PC without affecting the site everyone sees when they use their favorite browsers. When you're satisfied with your changes, you can republish your pages, and all your changes become available on the Web server.

Figure 17.1 graphically depicts the Web publishing process.

17

Figure 17.1.

A chart of how Web publishing works.

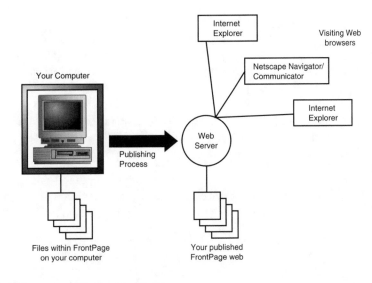

What You Must Have to Publish

Before you can publish your FrontPage Web to the Internet, you must have an account on a Web server that will host and save your individual files. Hundreds of different companies will rent you space on their servers for monthly fees. These companies are called *Web presence providers.*

For a nominal fee (ranging from about $10 to $30 a month), a Web presence provider will give you a certain amount of disk space on its server with which you can publish your FrontPage Web. It assigns you a special URL on its site that will contain your entire FrontPage Web. You can then upload and publish your web as often as you'd like, keeping it up to date.

In fact, you probably already have a Web presence provider, even if you don't know about it. Most companies that provide Internet access also double as Web presence providers. Your Internet access provider probably comes with rented space on its server at no additional cost. For a detailed list of affordable Web presence providers, visit http://budgetweb.com.

FrontPage Web Presence Providers

As you might imagine, not all Web presence providers are created equal, particularly when you build sites with FrontPage 98. FrontPage 98 has several powerful and flexible features that will make your pages look great and interact with your users. However, these special features will work only with Web presence providers that have announced they support FrontPage Web sites.

In order to properly use and display several of your FrontPage-specific features, Web presence providers must install special software called *FrontPage extensions* on their Web servers. These FrontPage extensions enable you to create dynamic Web pages that use advanced features such as components, active elements, and interactive forms. Microsoft charges Web presence providers a fee to use these FrontPage extensions on their servers, which is why not all providers support them. In addition, they are optimized to work only with Web sites created specifically with FrontPage. Therefore, no other HTML editor out there can take advantage of these special features.

To publish your web and make it available to the entire world, you don't need to use a Web server that has FrontPage extensions, but not all the advanced features in your site will work. If you enjoy using FrontPage and all the features it has to offer, your best bet is to stick with some of the many Web presence providers that support FrontPage extensions.

Microsoft provides a list of FrontPage-supporting Web presence providers online at `http://www.microsoft.com/frontpage/hosting.htm` (see Figure 17.2).

Figure 17.2.

Many companies around the world support affordable FrontPage extensions.

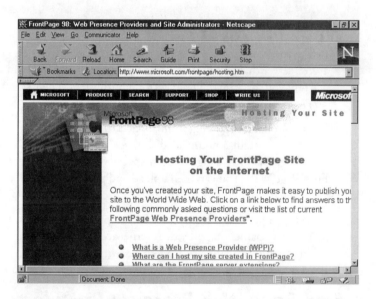

Don't be afraid to explore several of the different sites listed; their prices and services vary widely. As a good rule of thumb, you shouldn't need to pay more than $25 a month for a decent-quality Web presence provider that supports FrontPage extensions. Be aware of hidden charges with Web providers. Some of them charge large extra fees for additional disk space, and others tack on costs when you have a very popular Web site with a lot of traffic.

17

Uploading Your Web Pages with FrontPage 98

Now that you understand how Web publishing works and you're sure you have space on an Internet, it's time to learn how to send your pages to the Internet. FrontPage actually simplifies the process for you. The first time you upload your pages, you must enter important information about where you're sending it and enter your username and password. On subsequent uploads, FrontPage remembers all this important publishing information and automatically uploads all the needed files to the Internet with a single click of the button. In fact, FrontPage uploads only those files that have changed since the last time you published your site!

 FrontPage sends files to the Internet with a built-in tool called the Web Publishing Wizard. This tool is invoked automatically every time you click the Publish button from within the FrontPage Explorer.

JUST A MINUTE

The integrated Web Publishing Wizard is another reason why FrontPage 98 is the best Web creation tool out there. FrontPage is the complete package—site creation tools, site management tools, and even site publishing tools. Few other editors come with all the pieces required to take a concept from scratch to a published Web.

Uploading for the First Time

This section helps you configure FrontPage to upload and publish your web for the first time. Before you can upload your files, remember that you must have an account on a Web server (preferably one that supports FrontPage extensions).

 Within the FrontPage Explorer, click the Publish button. The Publish dialog box appears as shown in Figure 17.3.

Figure 17.3.

Choose the location where your web is to be published.

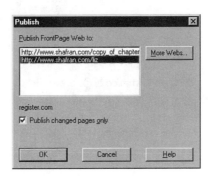

17

The Publish dialog box asks you where on the Internet you want to upload and publish your current FrontPage Web. Your listing might be blank if this is the first time you've published a site using FrontPage. Click the button labeled More Webs to bring up the Publish FrontPage Web dialog box (see Figure 17.4).

Figure 17.4.

First you must tell FrontPage the URL of your site.

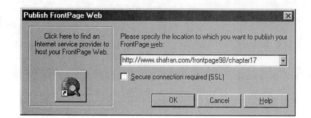

This dialog box lets you specify which server on the Internet you are using to upload your current FrontPage Web. Type the URL that your Web presence provider gave you, and then click OK.

If the server to which you are uploading supports FrontPage extensions, your Web site automatically starts to upload. However, if your Web presence provider doesn't support FrontPage extensions, the Microsoft Web Publishing Wizard dialog box appears, asking you to type an FTP server name (see Figure 17.5).

Figure 17.5.

Sites that don't support FrontPage extensions need additional information before you can upload.

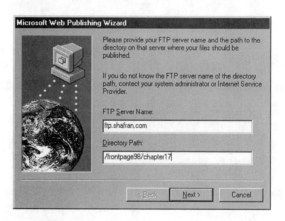

FTP is short for *File Transfer Protocol*, which is the default way two computers on the Internet send files back and forth to each other. Servers that don't have the FrontPage extensions on them must use FTP as the method for uploading your web from your computer to the Internet.

17

Your FTP site is provided by your Web presence provider. Type the computer name where you will be sending files and any appropriate subdirectories, and then click the Next button.

The last question the Web Publishing Wizard asks you is for your FTP username and password. Again, this is information your Web presence provider will give you when you sign up with it. If you have any questions about your FTP server name, username, or password, call your Web presence provider's technical support line, and they should be able to help you immediately. Figure 17.6 shows FrontPage asking for my username and password.

Figure 17.6.

FrontPage hides your password so no one else can see it on your monitor.

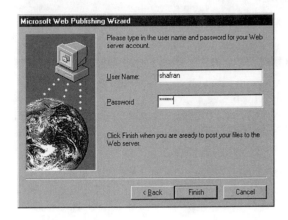

When you have typed your username and password, click on the button labeled Finish. FrontPage immediately connects with your Internet server and sends it your entire site. Figure 17.7 shows your upload in action.

Figure 17.7.

Publishing your web happens immediately.

File being uploaded

FrontPage status bar

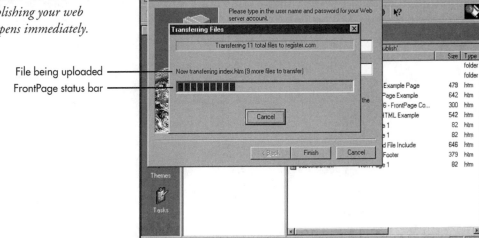

Now you can browse your newly published Web site with Netscape Navigator/Communicator or Microsoft Internet Explorer, along with the millions of other users who have access to the WWW.

CAUTION

> If you try to upload pages that use FrontPage-only features to a site that doesn't support the FrontPage extensions, a warning box will appear during the upload process. This warning box reminds you that not all features you use in your site are supported.

Subsequent Publishing Attempts

After you've set up your site, publishing changes and updates to your FrontPage Web is an absolute breeze. Every time you make a change to a web file or set of files and want to publish to the Internet, all you must do is click the Publish button within the FrontPage Explorer. FrontPage remembers all the server and user information and immediately starts to send your files to the Internet.

FrontPage is smart enough to upload only pages that have changed or been modified in any way, keeping your publishing time to the bare minimum.

Summary

FrontPage is a complete self-contained Web-publishing tool. Besides being a fantastic editor and site management tool, FrontPage 98 also comes with all the software required to upload your web to computers on the Internet.

Publishing with FrontPage 98 is easy; you simply tell it which server on the Internet will host your web and then let it start sending the files. You should now feel comfortable sending your web to the Internet so it can be seen by you and the millions of people who constantly browse the World Wide Web.

17

Q&A

Q **There are so many different Web presence providers out there that all cost about the same. What qualities should I look for to select one over the others?**

A Besides the price, your number one concern is technical support. Uploading web pages is usually easy, but you want accessible technical support in case you run into problems and need help troubleshooting. In addition, before you pick a provider, try visiting its site several times during different periods of the day. Make sure the site is consistently up. In addition, you might want to ask the provider what type of connection it has to the Internet. The larger the connection, the faster downloading files is for you and all the visitors who stop by. A T3 connection is the best type to have.

Q **How does FrontPage know which files have changed that it should upload?**

A FrontPage keeps a log of every transaction it has with your Web presence provider. Each time you click the Publish button, FrontPage checks each file in your web against that log to see whether you made any recent changes to it. If so, it sends the file to the Internet. Otherwise, it skips that file and continues checking the rest of the current FrontPage Web.

Q **After I upload my web, how can I get visitors to stop by?**

A Generating publicity and attracting visitors to your Web page requires a lot of planning and attention. Your first step should be registering your site in the main Internet search directories. Visit `http://add.yahoo.com/fast/add?` to learn how to add your page to the Yahoo! catalog.

Workshop

The Workshop contains quiz questions and an Activities section to help reinforce what you've learned in this hour. Try not to look at the quiz answers until you've tried to work them out yourself!

Quiz

1. What's the difference between publishing and uploading?
2. What are FrontPage server extensions and why are they important?

Answers

1. Not much. Uploading is the physical act of sending a file from your computer to a computer on the Internet. Publishing is what Web developers call the entire process of making a site available online and consists of uploading many files.

2. FrontPage server extensions are special pieces of software that extend the behavior of Web servers on the Internet. They enable you to use advanced pages of HTML that include several FrontPage-only features, such as using components. Without them, you won't be able to create a site that fully uses all the FrontPage features discussed in this book.

Activities

1. Make sure that you have an Internet account where you can upload and store your FrontPage Web. Preferably you'll have an account that supports the FrontPage extensions. Try uploading your web to this account, and then visit your URL with your favorite browser to verify that your files uploaded properly.

2. Publishing your Web site is strictly related to Web management techniques. Read Hour 19, "Managing Your Web Site," to learn more about organizing and structuring your site so that visitors can enjoy it more.

3. Now that you can publish a page, skip to Hour 24, "Finale: Building a Home Page from Scratch," which steps you through the entire process of building a set of pages and publishing them to the Internet.

17

Hour **18**

Enabling Style Sheets

Cascading Style Sheets are one of the new and improved features built into FrontPage 98. Recently approved by the World Wide Web Consortium (`http://w3c.org`), style sheets give you significantly more control over the appearance and layout of your Web pages than standard FrontPage editing techniques do.

Using style sheets, you can change the default way text, graphics, lines, and tables appear within a Web browser, even if you use standard HTML tags and FrontPage 98 features. In fact, you probably use style sheets today because they are an integral part of how FrontPage themes work. This hour introduces you to style sheets and shows you the rudimentary steps involved in creating them with FrontPage 98. Specifically, in this hour you'll learn

- ☐ The history behind style sheets
- ☐ How style sheets affect the way browsers present information
- ☐ When you should use style sheets on your site
- ☐ How FrontPage makes building your own custom style sheets easy

Understanding Style Sheets

Cascading Style Sheets (CSS), usually referred to as *style sheets* within FrontPage 98, give you extreme flexibility in the appearance and layout of information within your Web pages. Style sheets enable you to set font and display attributes that are applied to all information across an entire page, or even across an entire Web.

Normally, when you use the FrontPage Editor to add text to a page, you select a standard style for how that information appears on the page. This style controls the font used, text size, and even the color. You can choose from several different text styles, including normal, headlined, or bulleted text. Browsers automatically know how to display and format text in each of those styles.

Style sheets let you change how all normal text appears—its color, font, and size—by setting certain attributes in one central location. Then, when you change your style sheet, all the text associated with that style changes, so you don't need to update its appearance by hand individually.

Similarly, style sheets work on practically all elements you can include on a Web page—lists, tables, and graphics. You can assign special display attributes and characteristics to these different Web elements. Style sheets then let you share those attributes with the rest of your page.

Style Sheet History

Style sheets were created and standardized to improve how information within a Web page can be published. Although HTML is a flexible language, you have limited layout and font control over the information on a page—something desktop publishers and advanced Web developers don't like. Therefore, the Cascading Style Sheets standard was adopted by the international organization that improves and enhances HTML and other Web standards: the World Wide Web Consortium, or W3C (http://w3c.org).

By pre-setting advanced font and layout options, you can drastically change the way text appears on a page. For example, look at Figure 18.1, the W3C home page for Cascading Style Sheets (http://w3c.org/Style/).

Although this page looks like a big Web graphic, it isn't. Each word or phrase is a simple piece of text within this HTML file that uses a different style than the other words or phrases. Some styles make the text appear large and bold, while others use smaller fonts with brighter colors. All the different styles have layout controls that set how far from the left and right margins the text should appear. In fact, some text even overlaps.

18

Figure 18.1.

Each phrase is simple text with a different style sheet applied to it.

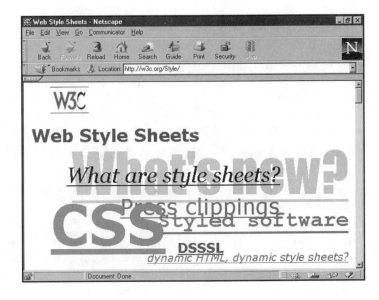

With patience and perseverance, you can customize your FrontPage Web using vivid styles for your text, tables, and lists.

COFFEE BREAK

In general, style sheets are normally used to control how different pieces of text appear within a Web browser. Before style sheets existed, you could use only the default HTML settings for working with text. You could set font, color, and text size, but you could never modify margins, change layout, or apply to your entire page a style you like.

Style sheets help cross the bridge between Web publishing and desktop publishing. Desktop publishers use tools such as Adobe PageMaker to control exactly how a page or screen should be printed. PageMaker was used with this book to lay out each page's margins, incorporate screen shots, and add special elements such as this Coffee Break. With PageMaker, you can drag and drop information across the screen, deciding exactly where it should appear when you press the Print button.

As Web publishing became more advanced and more and more companies wanted to create great-looking sites, they realized they were hampered by the limited layout and formatting capabilities of HTML.

Unfortunately, style sheets are complicated to create and use, particularly when compared to the simplicity of HTML. Because style sheets are new to the Web, only a handful of Web creation tools even support them—FrontPage 98 is among the best. And, visitors must use a current browser—Internet Explorer 3.0 or Netscape Communicator/Navigator 4.0—to see the new and improved pages that use Cascading Style Sheets.

Looking at Style Sheets

Style sheets can be saved as separate files, using the `.css` extension, or embedded as part of any standard HTML file. FrontPage 98 comes with a whole slew of cascading style sheets, enabling you to improve the way pages in your Web appear. But FrontPage hides its use of style sheets and calls them *themes* instead. FrontPage lets you set a theme for an entire site to coordinate how all text, lists, tables, and headlines appear within the Web. For more information on FrontPage themes, see Hour 21, "Applying Web Themes."

By using style sheets, FrontPage can ensure that headlines and text appearance are controlled from a central CSS file. Figure 18.2 shows a sample CSS file from one of the Microsoft FrontPage themes. Notice how it is more difficult to understand and read than a standard HTML file.

Figure 18.2.

Style sheets are much more difficult to interpret because they use more advanced and confusing codes to specify how information should appear.

```
graph0.css - Notepad
File  Edit  Search  Help
<!DOCTYPE HTML PUBLIC "-//IETF//DTD HTML//EN">
<html>

<head>
<meta http-equiv="Content-Type"
content="text/html; charset=iso-8859-1">
<meta name="GENERATOR" content="Microsoft FrontPage 3.0">
<title>theme template</title>
<style>
<!--

.mstheme
{
        separator-image: url(arcsepd.gif);
        list-image-1: url(arcbul1d.gif);
        list-image-2: url(arcbul2d.gif);
        list-image-3: url(arcbul3d.gif);

        nav-banner-image: url(arcbannd.gif);

        navbutton-horiz-normal: url(arcnavhd.gif);
        navbutton-horiz-pushed: url(arcnavhs.gif);

        navbutton-vert-normal: url(arcnavhd.gif);
        navbutton-vert-pushed: url(arcnavhs.gif);

        navbutton-home-normal: url(archomed.gif);
```

FrontPage and Style Sheets

As previously stated, style sheets are complicated to use and create because they are so flexible. FrontPage lets you assign a certain style to virtually every different piece of information you can include in your Web, and create page-wide defaults.

18

To Do

Page-wide style sheets are the easiest to build and configure because they control all the text and information for that HTML file. To set a page-wide style sheet, follow these steps:

1. Start the FrontPage Editor and load any HTML page from your current Web. Click the right mouse button anywhere on the page, and select Page Properties from the pop-up box that appears. Figure 18.3 shows a standard Page Properties dialog box.

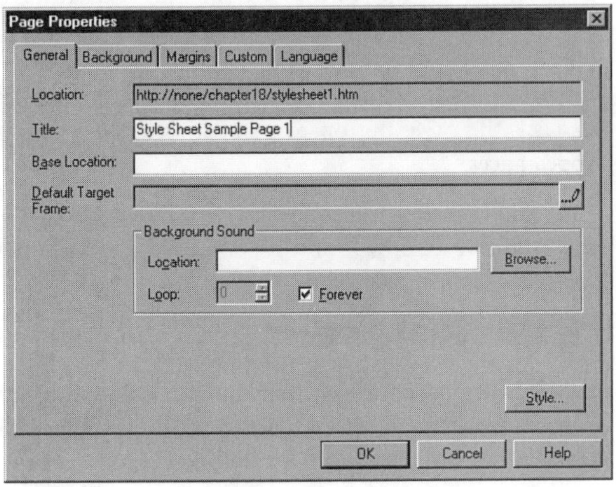

Figure 18.3.

Look for the Style button, which lets you coordinate style sheets within most property boxes in FrontPage.

2. Click the Style button to bring up the Style dialog box (see Figure 18.4). There are six different tabs that enable you to set style attributes.

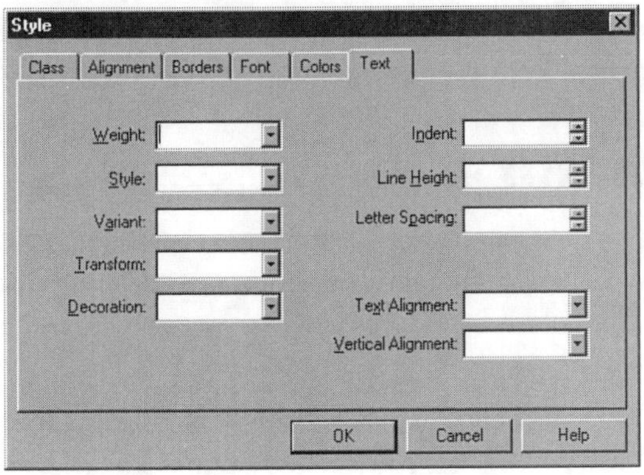

Figure 18.4.

Among these six tabs, there are over 30 different attributes you can set when working with Web style sheets.

18

3. Click the different tabs within this Style box to change the default appearance of information on your page. For example, if you click the Text tab, you can affect the way text appears across the entire page.

4. Click OK when you've finished setting your styles. FrontPage returns you to the Page Properties dialog box, where you must click OK again to save your new page-wide style sheet settings.

Besides setting page-wide styles, you can also create a style sheet for a specific piece or paragraph of text. The process is very similar to setting page-wide styles. Using your mouse, select the text you want to modify and click the right mouse button. Select Font Properties from the pop-up box that appears. You can set standard font attributes from this dialog box, or click the Style button to make a style sheet and control advanced layout and font appearances.

After you've inserted a set of styles into your Web page, you can click the HTML tab within the Editor to see how FrontPage saves the attributes you've selected.

Further Reference

Entire books have been written about using and optimizing style sheets within your Web pages. You can build advanced sets of attributes that can be shared with and referenced across many pages within your site by linking HTML pages with independent style sheets.

For more information on learning how to build and use style sheets, check out *Web Designer's Guide to Style Sheets*, written by Steven Mulder and published by Hayden. Or, for a comprehensive reference that describes advanced ways you can use style sheets within FrontPage 98, check out *FrontPage 98 Unleashed*, by Sams Publishing. This book is the complete reference to everything about FrontPage you'd want to know and includes a detailed section on using style sheets within your Web.

Summary

Style sheets are advanced tools that can dramatically change the way text appears within a Web browser. By controlling fonts, margins, and colors, style sheets can turn a standard page into a colorful and well-designed site.

FrontPage 98 includes reasonable support for building and including style sheets within your Web sites. In fact, you'll use style sheets extensively because they are an important aspect of FrontPage themes. You should feel comfortable understanding what style sheets are and how they are generally set within FrontPage 98.

18

Q&A

Q **What's the difference between style sheets and FrontPage themes? You mentioned them both and said they were related, but I still don't understand how.**

A Style sheets are collections of font and layout attributes that can be applied to pieces of a Web page as a single group. Style sheets can be embedded into a single Web page or saved as a separate .css file and then linked to by many different Web pages within your site. You can create a style sheet to change how text appears in your whole page, instead of editing its font, color, and size individually.

Themes are collections of style sheets and graphics that coordinate all the pages within an entire site to match each other. Using a theme means that every page within your FrontPage Web uses the same background graphic and applies text style sheets to all the information you type into your page.

Realistically, you'll use themes more often than individual style sheets because they are much less complicated, easier to set, and create an attractive, well-designed site.

Q **What happens when I create a page-wide style sheet and then build another one just for one paragraph of text? Which style sheet does the browser use to display that piece of text?**

A Page-wide style sheets are always superseded by sheets created and used for specific paragraphs and pieces of text. Think of the order of precedence as a pyramid, with the page-wide settings at the top, paragraph settings next, and word settings at the bottom. Your browser will always use the top style sheet from that pyramid.

Q **When editing a table, I customized some of the other settings in my Style property box to change the way table borders appear. FrontPage showed the changes in the table properly, but Netscape simply showed the same old boring table. Does Netscape support all parts of style sheets?**

A The style sheet technology and standard are much further ahead of Netscape and Microsoft at implementing and supporting all the features you can customize. Netscape Communicator/Navigator 4 supports many style sheet options, but not nearly all of them—the same with Internet Explorer 3 and 4. As new versions of Web browsers are released, you'll find significantly more support for displaying information that uses style sheets. A good rule of thumb: Most style sheet attributes that affect text appearance are supported.

18

Workshop

The Workshop contains quiz questions and an Activities section to help reinforce what you've learned in this hour. Try not to look at the quiz answers until you've tried to work them out yourself!

Quiz

1. Who created the Cascading Style Sheets standard?
2. How much support does FrontPage 98 have for styles sheets?
3. How do I set styles when I'm editing a Web page with the FrontPage Editor?

Answers

1. The style sheet standard was created and managed by the World Wide Web Consortium. The W3C is a group of individuals and companies that set worldwide standards such as the HTML standard. By setting these global standards, there is a better chance they will be accepted and implemented in popular browsers and HTML editing tools. You can keep up on the Web Consortium's progress by regularly visiting http://w3c.org.

2. FrontPage 98 has rudimentary support for basic and advanced style sheets. Unfortunately, FrontPage doesn't easily let you separate styles into separate CSS files (yet) or graphically create and manage your styles. However, FrontPage is the best of the tools out there and has significantly more support for style sheets than competing products. Expect better support for the CSS standard in subsequent releases of FrontPage as they become more popular for Web developers to use.

3. You always set FrontPage styles from within a property box. Most property boxes include a button labeled Style with which you can create and edit style sheets to fit your own specific need.

Activities

1. Style sheets are closely related to FrontPage themes. Learn more about this coordination technique in Hour 21. You'll learn how themes work, how to use them, and what types of modifications you can make to them.

2. WebReference.Com is the clearinghouse for all hip new technology for creating Web pages. It offers design tips and advanced technical resources. Visit http://www.webreference.com/dev/style/index.html for a complete tutorial and overview on using Cascading Style Sheets within your set of Web pages.

18

Hour 19

Managing Your Web Site

Most of this book focuses on building and editing individual pages from scratch. The FrontPage Editor is a fantastic and flexible tool that really simplifies the Web creation process.

This hour changes focus by showing you several FrontPagewide options that enable you to easily manage and organize your entire Web. Instead of editing and configuring a single page within the Editor, you'll use the main FrontPage Explorer in this hour to learn about Webwide spell checking, hyperlink tracking, and more. You'll learn that there's a lot more involved in building a Web site than simply creating each individual page.

Specifically, in this hour you'll learn how to

☐ Keep track of larger Web sites with the FrontPage Explorer

☐ Perform systemwide spell checking through each page in your site

☐ Verify hyperlinks within your site and to other pages across the world

☐ Set Webwide properties that affect the entire site

Spell Checking and Thesaurus

If you're like most people, you'll occasionally make spelling mistakes and typos when you create each of your Web pages. Typos are just a natural part of working with word processors, Web editors, and other programs that require you to type. And even armed with a fine-tooth comb and a good dictionary, you're not likely to catch all your mistakes with a simple re-reading of all the pages within your Web.

Fortunately, FrontPage includes a high-quality spell checker that takes a significant amount of pain out of the editing process. FrontPage can spell check individual pages or your entire site, depending on whether you initiate a check within the Editor or Explorer.

Another important tool that comes in handy for most people is the built-in thesaurus that lets you look up related words and synonyms.

Spell Checking Within the FrontPage Editor

As you create and edit each of your individual pages within the FrontPage Editor, you should add a new step to your file-saving routine. Each time you are finished editing a page, start the FrontPage spell checker to perform a final run-through of your document to correct any glaring typos, misspellings, or common mistakes.

 Start the spell checker by choosing Tools | Spelling from the FrontPage menu. FrontPage starts up the built-in spell checker and begins reading through your current file. When it finds a word it doesn't recognize, it brings up the Spelling dialog box (see Figure 19.1).

Figure 19.1.

Spell checking is a quick way to improve the quality of your page.

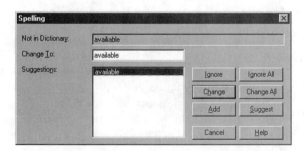

FrontPage shows you the word it doesn't recognize and then suggests several alternative spellings. You can select an alternative spelling of the highlighted word, add the new spelling to the FrontPage dictionary, or verify that the word in question is really spelled properly and have FrontPage ignore it.

When you're finished spell checking your document, don't forget to save the newly edited version.

19

JUST A MINUTE

A good spell checker doesn't replace a careful re-reading of the text on every one of your pages. Spell checkers check only mechanical mistakes; they don't locate missing words, incomplete sentences, bad grammar, or a host of other mistakes. Always make sure you re-read your Web page one final time before saving and publishing it to the WWW.

Cross-File Spell Checking with the FrontPage Explorer

Besides running the spell checker across one file at a time, you also can perform a cross-file spell check throughout selected (or all) files within your FrontPage Web. By issuing the Spell Check command in the FrontPage Explorer, you'll search through each of the HTML pages in your Web looking for unrecognized and misspelled words.

To run the cross-file spell check, follow these steps:

To Do

1. Within the FrontPage Explorer, Choose Tools | Spelling from the menu. FrontPage brings up a different Spelling dialog box that asks you which files you want to search through (see Figure 19.2).

Figure 19.2.

You can select certain files to spell check, or look through the entire Web.

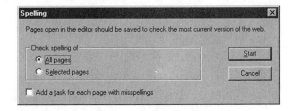

2. Choose whether you want FrontPage to check all the files within your Web or only files marked within the Explorer view.

3. Click the Start button to begin. FrontPage brings up a status bar that shows you all the pages it has looked at and counts all the unrecognizable words it has found. Figure 19.3 shows the cross-file spell checker in action.

4. After FrontPage has gone through all the pages in your site, you have two options for correcting your mistakes. FrontPage can lead you through each file, one at a time, and bring you to each misspelled word, or you can create a new task for each page containing misspelled words. This new task reminds you to correct the misspelled page before publishing it to the Web.

   To correct your mistakes immediately, click the button labeled Edit Page. FrontPage starts the Editor and loads the first HTML page within your Web that contains an unrecognizable word.

19

Figure 19.3.

FrontPage lets you check your entire site easily.

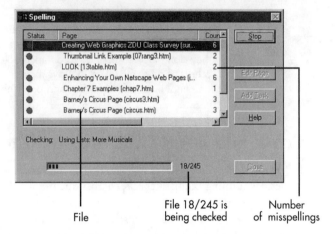

File

File 18/245 is being checked

Number of misspellings

5. Conveniently, FrontPage brings you directly to the first word you must check and brings up the same Spelling dialog box that lets you correct, ignore, or add this word to your dictionary.

6. When you are finished editing all the misspelled words on this Web page, FrontPage brings up the Continue with Next Document? dialog box and lets you start correcting mistakes on the subsequent page within your Web (see Figure 19.4).

Figure 19.4.

Do you want to correct misspelled words on the page within your Web?

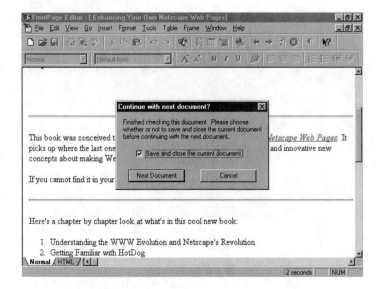

7. Repeat steps 5 and 6 until all the misspelled words in your Web have been corrected.

TIME SAVER

If you want to create a spell-checking task for future processing, you can click the Add Task button in step 4 instead of editing each specific page at that moment. FrontPage generates a special task labeled Fix Misspelled Words within the Tasks view in the FrontPage Explorer. Figure 19.5 shows the information this task contains.

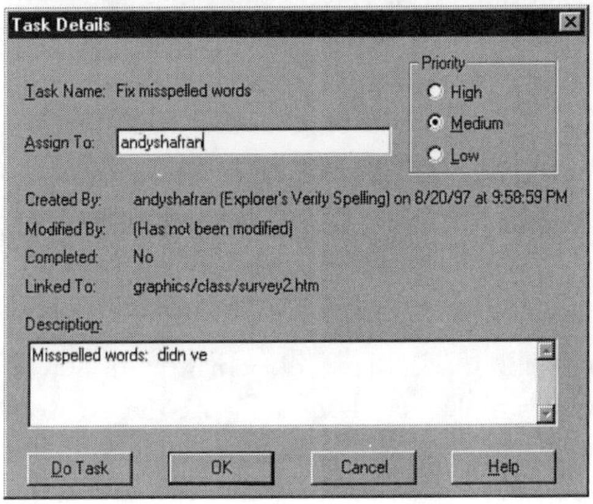

Figure 19.5.

Spell-checking tasks store the HTML page, all the misspelled words, and the assigned person for this task.

Task Details	
Task Name: Fix misspelled words	Priority: ○ High ● Medium ○ Low
Assign To: andyshafran	
Created By: andyshafran (Explorer's Verify Spelling) on 8/20/97 at 9:58:59 PM	
Modified By: (Has not been modified)	
Completed: No	
Linked To: graphics/class/survey2.htm	
Description:	
Misspelled words: didn ve	

[Do Task] [OK] [Cancel] [Help]

Using the Thesaurus

Besides the built-in spell checker, another popular FrontPage tool is the thesaurus. The thesaurus lets you highlight certain words and look for related words or synonyms to upgrade your page's vocabulary.

To use the FrontPage thesaurus, start the Editor, and then use your mouse to highlight the word you want to look up. Then choose Tools | Thesaurus from the menu. FrontPage looks up the highlighted word and displays several related words or synonyms to replace the original word with. Figure 19.6 shows the FrontPage thesaurus looking up *conceive*.

Select the synonym you want to use, and click the Replace button. Your old word is automatically transformed into the new synonym.

19

Figure 19.6.

FrontPage offers several suggested synonyms for conceive.

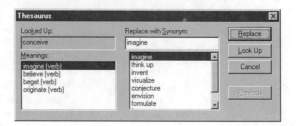

Tracking Web Hyperlinks

As your site increases in size and complexity, you'll find it harder and harder to keep track of all the different pages, graphics, and hyperlinks crisscrossing the entire Web. Managing medium- to large-sized Webs had been historically difficult before FrontPage, because keeping the entire set of pages organized, up to date, and linked properly with one another was challenging.

To combat this problem, FrontPage has included several different views you can use to track and manage your Web site. You can graphically see how all the pages in your site link to one another to identify the logical path visitors can take when exploring your Web site.

To use this special hyperlink management system, open any FrontPage Web, and then click the Hyperlinks view. Look at Figure 19.7. It shows a simple Web site that has three different HTML pages and a few separate multimedia files.

Figure 19.7.

By graphically viewing your site, you can see how visitors can step through your pages.

Links to subpages

The main home page

In Figure 19.7, all links start from the main home page, index.htm. From there, two additional pages are hyperlinked, each containing links or embedded files of their own. At any point in your creation process, you can visually see how all the files in this Web are linked to one another. This technique is useful because you get an idea of how visitors can explore this Web site. When they start at the main page, they can only go to one or two other subpages. Mapping this route through your site is important because you always want visitors to be able to logically find their way from page to page within your site.

Although the Hyperlinks view is useful for small Webs, it really comes in handy when your Web site consists of many different pages, all related to one another. Because each page can contain hyperlinks to several other pages inside and outside the current Web, you have no way to track all the links between pages. It is very easy to overwhelm yourself with too many hyperlinks, just because it is so easy to create them.

One common mistake Web developers make is overlinking their pages internally to one another. For example, if you have a site with 10 different pages, you probably don't need to build hyperlinks between all 10 of them on each page. Instead, you should create a hierarchical plan so that your visitors can logically flow from one page to another, instead of randomly jumping around between unrelated pages.

Therefore, it is always a good idea to track how all the hyperlinks in a medium-to-large Web site are organized using the Hyperlinks view in FrontPage. Look at Figure 19.8, which shows a sample customer support Web (built from the FrontPage template) and shows how all the pages are logically linked to each other.

Figure 19.8.

There is a clear path through the pages within this site.

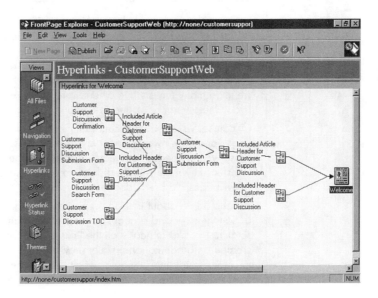

Now look at Figure 19.9 for a much more confusing example. This figure shows a large and complex Web site that clearly overlinks between pages. There are dozens of links on each page. Some of the links lead recursively back to the original home page whereas others lead to far-off, obscure files.

Figure 19.9.

What a confusing mess of a site!

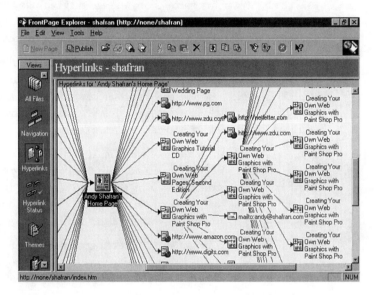

COFFEE BREAK

Interestingly, the hyperlink view shown in Figure 19.9 is the author's original Web site. Over the past year, I had slowly been adding new sections to my home page (http://www.shafran.com) until suddenly the whole structure of the site was a mess. Just looking at Figure 19.9 shows you how confusing it was to navigate my site. Some pages were accessible too many times while others were hidden away in hard-to-find areas. It took me several hours just to decipher all the links in this view.

Of course, visitors didn't seem to mind; they always went to the new pages and didn't worry about my apparent disorganization. The problems arose when I needed to remove one set of pages. There were so many incestuous hyperlinks that I didn't know where to start because by deleting a few pages, I'd break dozens of hyperlinks.

What did I do about it? After importing my old Web into FrontPage, I began the slow and arduous process of reorganizing my Web from scratch. I got rid of nearly all the links on my home page and slowly re-created an organizational system. Every time I built a new hyperlink within the FrontPage Editor, I would switch back to the Hyperlinks view to see how the pages were organized and related to one another.

19

Eventually, I was able to restructure the whole site and come up with a new navigational plan. Visitors now can go to one of five different pages from the original site. From there, I limited myself to five more hyperlinks on most subsequent pages. It was a painful process that took long hours to accomplish. Now, I have a well-organized Web site that is easy to manage, easy to navigate through, and demonstrates the techniques described in this book.

Now that you've seen several different Webs graphically organized and represented, it is easy to see why you want to be careful when building hyperlinks between pages.

Without constantly checking the Hyperlinks view in the FrontPage Explorer, you can easily lose track of how confusing your site becomes for visitors to navigate. Developing this navigational plan then makes it easier for you to add new sections to your Web. You can simply look at your Web map and then figure out where a new section belongs graphically.

Then, you can create new pages within your Web and build a limited set of hyperlinks to those pages. FrontPage makes it easy for you to build each of these new pages because of the dynamic relationship between the Editor and Explorer. Every time you must edit or fix up a page, you can simply double-click it within the Hyperlinks view, and the Editor loads that file immediately.

Setting Sitewide Properties

The final section in this hour shows you how to change some standard administrative settings for your current FrontPage Web. Properties such as the name and location of the Web can easily be modified any time in the future, regardless of the name you give it when you first start FrontPage.

19

Within the Explorer, choose Tools | Web Settings from the menu bar. The FrontPage Web Settings dialog box appears with the Configuration tab selected (see Figure 19.10).

The two options you might want to set are Web Name and Web Title. The Web Title is the word or phrase that describes this particular FrontPage Web. Usually, it is a couple of descriptive words so you can identify this Web from others on your computer. Similarly, the Web Name is the filename of the directory containing all the files for this Web. This filename becomes part of the URL for viewing these Web pages.

You can change the Web Title or Web Name at any time to reflect the current Web contents. Always keep these two fields up to date so that you can easily identify the subject and contents of all the Webs on your machine.

Figure 19.10.

You can rename and retitle your FrontPage Web at any time.

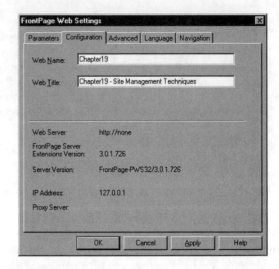

Summary

FrontPage is a fantastic tool for managing and building all types of Web sites from small to large. As your simple Web page expands and becomes a Web site, there are several powerful FrontPage tools you'll want to take advantage of. Starting with the cross-file searcher and spell checker to the Hyperlinks view within the Explorer, there are several techniques you'll need to use to manage your site.

This hour introduced you to some of the special FrontPage features that come in handy when managing multi-page sites. You shouldn't have a single misspelled word in your entire site after finishing this. Similarly, you should be confident that your visitors will have an easy time navigating through all the pages within your site; otherwise, you have several important changes and modifications to make in your site.

Q&A

Q **When I originally ran the cross-file spell checker through my whole site, FrontPage told me there were hundreds of misspelled words across all 30 of my pages. But after going through the page-by-page correction process, I only fixed 100 or so different mistakes. Now FrontPage tells me there are no misspelled words. What happened to all the others?**

A You probably expanded the dictionary of words FrontPage recognizes. Each time FrontPage finds a word it doesn't recognize, it provides several suggested alternatives. If none of the alternatives is correct, you can type your own correction or choose to ignore the unrecognized word; it might be an acronym of some type or

19

someone's name, for example. In addition, you can also click the Change All or Ignore All buttons. When you click these two buttons, FrontPage remembers the action you picked for this word and then reapplies it every time it finds the same word within any page. Often, many of the misspelled words FrontPage finds are really names, acronyms, or other words spelled correctly. When you click the Ignore All button, FrontPage will never prompt you for the same word again, thus dramatically reducing the number of words that it doesn't recognize.

Q Coming up with a navigation plan through my Web site is harder than I thought. What types of suggestions can you give me for organizing all the pages within my Web?

A There are many different ways you can link and organize multiple pages within a single Web. Here are some of the best methods:

The Waterfall method: Water can flow in only one direction, and so can your visitors. On each page, you include only one or two links to subsequent pages within your Web. You never include hyperlinks outside your Web until the visitor reaches an ending point of your site.

The Elevator method: Your page is categorized into several different sets of pages, all relating to one another. On the main page, the visitor can choose a specific category (or floor, to continue the metaphor). Then, within each category, there is a set of links to related pages and then another link back to the original home page.

The Web method: Anarchy rules when creating hyperlinks between all pages in this site. Any page can be linked to any other page. This method is great for visitors who want to jump back and forth between all the pages on your site, but nearly impossible to maintain if you have more than 10 pages in your Web.

19

Workshop

The Workshop contains quiz questions and an Activities section to help reinforce what you've learned in this hour. Try not to look at the quiz answers until you've tried to work them out yourself!

Quiz

1. How can you search for synonyms of a specific word when editing within FrontPage?

2. Why would you use the Hyperlinks view within the FrontPage Explorer?

3. When doing a spell check, if FrontPage comes across a word it doesn't recognize but is spelled correctly, what should you do?

Answers

1. Select the word you want to look up, and then choose Tools | Thesaurus from the FrontPage Editor's menu. There is a variety of related words and synonyms to choose from.

2. You'd use the Hyperlinks view within Explorer to see how all the pages within your Web are related to one another. All links and embedded files show up in this graphical setting, which expands and contracts every time you click the + on a specific Web page.

3. You can click the Add button to include the word permanently in the FrontPage dictionary, click Ignore to ignore its current spelling for this one instance, or click Ignore All to always bypass checking this word throughout the entire page or FrontPage Web.

Activities

1. Managing your Web site is just the first step in creating a well-designed site. Read Hour 22, "Site Design Tips," to learn other techniques for capturing visitor interest and attention when they stop by.

2. Create a new FrontPage Web. Choose to import it from a site instead of building it from scratch. When importing it, point FrontPage to one of your favorite sites—try http://www.shafran.com if you are really daring. After the site is imported, experiment with the Hyperlinks view to see how it is organized and structured. Learn which sites are easy to navigate and which ones aren't; you can probably tell just by exploring the site and not importing it into FrontPage.

Hour 20

Under the Hood with HTML

Throughout this entire book, you've learned all sorts of techniques to use when building Web pages. Each of these techniques has been accomplished using commands found within Microsoft FrontPage. When you want to make text appear bold, you click the bold icon within FrontPage, and when you want to add an image, you chose Insert Image from the menu.

Every time you issue some command within the Editor, FrontPage is actually building and editing a separate file. This file, written in Hypertext Markup Language (HTML), contains all the codes necessary for browsers to display a page properly. Therefore, when you mark text as bold in FrontPage, you are actually adding a special HTML code to the HTML on which you are working.

This hour uncovers some of those details FrontPage usually hides from you. You learn more about HTML, when you'll need to understand it, and how to make simple changes yourself without using the FrontPage Editor. Specifically, this hour teaches you how to

☐ Understand how HTML works when building Web pages

☐ Recognize common HTML tags when you come across them

☐ Make changes by hand to the HTML in your FrontPage Web

☐ Insert special FrontPage components designed for inserting straight HTML

Understand HTML's Role in Building Web Sites

HTML is the programming language behind the WWW. Relatively easy to understand, HTML is made of numerous codes, called *tags*, that are embedded into a standard text file. Each of these tags has a specific purpose and is used to mark up information as it should appear within a browser.

For example, the following piece of code is written in HTML:

```
<TITLE>Welcome to Andy's Home Page</TITLE>
<H1>Visitors are welcome to stop by.</H1>
There is a lot of information on <B>computer books</B> I have written,
my professional interests, and my <B>family</B>.
```

Take a moment to carefully read through the previous snippet of code. There are three different HTML tags used there. Notice how the first line is surrounded by the <TITLE> and </TITLE> tags. This pair of tags is used to tell your Web browser what piece of text belongs in the title bar. Next is a large headline surrounded by the <H1> and </H1> tags; this text appears much larger and bolder than standard text. This is the HTML tag used whenever you choose a Heading 1 style within the FrontPage Editor.

Finally, there is a small paragraph of text. In this section, the same tag is used twice to make certain phrases appear in boldface. The <B> and </B> tags are commonly used. Look at Figure 20.1 to see how this very simple Web page looks within Netscape.

Generally, HTML is easy to understand if you take a few moments to carefully read through all the specific tags found on a particular page. Fortunately, you won't need to concern yourself with that level of detail very often because the browser takes care of all the difficult interpretation work for you.

You can look at the underlying HTML for any page you visit directly from your Web browser. To see the HTML, choose View | Page Source from your browser's menu. Immediately, a box appears that shows you all the behind-the-scenes codes that make up that particular Web page. Figure 20.2 shows a sample Web page with its HTML code.

20

Figure 20.1.
After learning the three different HTML tags, you can predict how all the tags appear.

Title text ——

Size 1 headline ——

Bold text ——

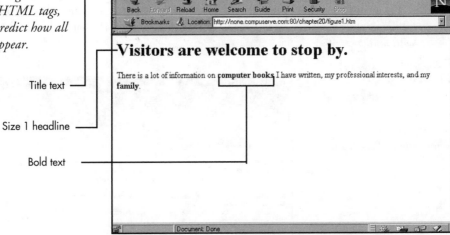

Figure 20.2.
With enough patience, you can probably decipher the HTML from this page.

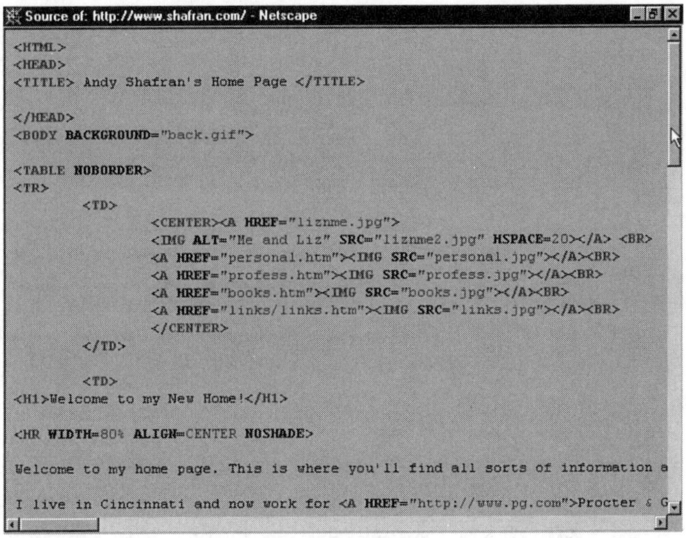

20

HTML and FrontPage

Because FrontPage is an HTML editor there is a similarity, naturally, between all the commands available to you within the editor and the markup tags that make up HTML. Start the FrontPage Editor and load any Web page into it. At the bottom of the screen, you should notice several different tabs. Normally, you create your page while using the Normal tab, which emulates how the page will look within a browser. But this time, click the HTML tab (see Figure 20.3) and you will immediately see the raw HTML that makes up the page you are looking at.

Figure 20.3.

You probably haven't explored this tab too much because it requires you to know HTML.

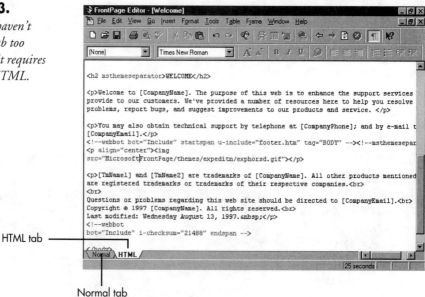

HTML tab

Normal tab

Editing HTML by Hand

When you are in the HTML tab within the FrontPage Editor, you can manually type or change any text or tag. FrontPage lets you edit the HTML just as if you were in a simple text editor such as Notepad or Wordpad.

Unless you are very proficient in HTML, making big changes to the raw HTML within FrontPage isn't a good idea. Because the HTML language relies on precise use of tag pairs, it is very easy to accidentally delete a closing tag, use a new tag improperly, or make unwanted changes to your page. The biggest drawback to editing an HTML file directly is that you cannot immediately see the effects of your changes as you can when normally using the FrontPage Editor.

FrontPage 98 is a very robust program and supports virtually every HTML code and tag. Because of this, you'll find yourself rarely editing HTML directly, unless you prefer to

20

memorize and write the tags yourself. Typing HTML codes yourself doesn't save much time, leaves a lot of room for error, and requires a large amount of knowledge behind each element you can use within a Web page.

For example, creating a table within the FrontPage Editor is pretty easy. You can specify the table size you want to build, and then use your mouse to resize any cell. Making a table by typing HTML requires intimate knowledge of nearly 10 different tags, not to mention the special order in which each tag must be used, or else the table won't show up. On top of that, you must size each cell in the table according to its pixel dimensions, meaning that you must guess how tall and wide you want the table to be, instead of simply using your mouse to drag and drop the borders.

As a result, more and more people are shying away from learning and developing Web pages by hand. Instead, they are opting for easy-to-use tools such as FrontPage 98 or other programs in this general class of tools called *HTML editors*.

TIME SAVER

HTML editors come in two different breeds, textual and WYSIWYG (What You See Is What You Get). Microsoft FrontPage 98 is a WYSIWYG editor. This means that every time you add a Web element to your page, FrontPage displays it exactly how it will appear within a browser.

Textual editors are just advanced versions of Notepad. They show you the complete text of the file you are editing and add simple buttons that will generate certain pieces of HTML for you, but still show all the tags on-screen.

For more information on the WYSIWYG capabilities of FrontPage and the advantages of using this type of HTML editor, check out Hour 2, "Installing and Using FrontPage."

When to Edit HTML by Hand

20

Although editing Web pages by hand can be difficult, sometimes it is the easiest and only way to fix a particular problem or tweak the way some information appears within a page. This section describes several situations in which you might consider using the Editor's HTML tab to make some changes to your Web page by hand.

Using Notepad

One common situation in which you might hand edit a Web page is when you have just a single small change to make. In that case, you might even consider using your computer's Notepad or Wordpad instead of starting FrontPage 98 at all.

Because FrontPage takes so long to start and consumes quite a bit of a computer's resources, many people find it much easier and quicker to start Notepad, load the page into editing, and then make the simple change. The next time you start FrontPage, the changes you make are automatically displayed within the Editor. Of course, by making changes to a page outside FrontPage, your new page still must be uploaded or sent to the Internet so visitors can see your changes.

To start Notepad on your computer, click the Windows 95 Start button and choose Programs | Accessories | Notepad. Figure 20.4 shows Notepad updating a file.

Figure 20.4.

Notepad isn't the best editor, but it works for quick and small changes.

```
index.htm - Notepad
File  Edit  Search  Help
<HTML>
<HEAD>
<TITLE> Andy Shafran's Home Page </TITLE>

</HEAD>
<BODY BACKGROUND="back.gif">

<TABLE NOBORDER>
<TR>
        <TD>
                <CENTER><A HREF="liznme.jpg">
                <IMG ALT="Me and Liz" SRC="liznme2.jpg" HSPACE=20></A> <BR>
                <A HREF="personal.htm"><IMG SRC="personal.jpg"></A><BR>
                <A HREF="profess.htm"><IMG SRC="profess.jpg"></A><BR>
                <A HREF="books.htm"><IMG SRC="books.jpg"></A><BR>
                <A HREF="links/links.htm"><IMG SRC="links.jpg"></A><BR>
                </CENTER>
        </TD>

        <TD>
<H1>Welcome to my New Home!</H1>

<HR WIDTH=80% ALIGN=CENTER NOSHADE>

Welcome to my home page. This is where you'll find all sorts of information at

I live in Cincinnati and now work for <A HREF="http://www.pg.com">Procter & Ga
<P>
```

Borrowing a Technique

Another common time you'll want to edit HTML for yourself is when you run across a cool technique on the WWW that you want to use for yourself. For example, if you visit http:// www.shafran.com, you might decide you really like the two-column format but don't have the time or knowledge to build it for yourself. Therefore, you could copy the HTML making up that page and paste it directly into FrontPage by using the HTML tab within the Editor.

Then, you just need to change the content of the pasted page so that it discusses information relevant to you, and your page is complete.

To "borrow" HTML tricks and code from another page, follow these steps:

1. Use your browser to point to the site you want to use.
2. Choose View | Page Source from the browser's menu to see the underlying page of HTML that the browser is interpreting for you.

To Do

20

3. Using your mouse, select the section of HTML you want to copy for your own use.

4. Copy the HTML to your computer's clipboard by pressing Control+C on your keyboard or choosing Edit | Copy from the menu bar.

5. Switch back to FrontPage and click the HTML tab.

6. Move your cursor to where you want the copied HTML pasted, and select Edit | Paste (Ctrl+V) from the FrontPage menu.

Formatting the HTML Code

If you look at the HTML tab within the Editor, you'll quickly notice how complicated and difficult a page appears simply because of the way each line is formatted. Although FrontPage does a great job of creating the page of HTML for you, it isn't very good at making the raw HTML readable. Important sets of tags are hard to identify because they might flow across multiple lines, and long tags might scroll off the right of the screen.

Many people like to format their pages to make the HTML readable in case they must update it by hand, or to make it clear for visitors who might look at the HTML behind a specific page. Therefore, they add tabs, carriage returns, and spaces to make the page of HTML much more accessible and readable.

Click the HTML tab within the Editor to see an example of a confusing-looking page. Figure 20.5 shows a sample home page that was created with the Editor. Notice how it is difficult to interpret and read.

Figure 20.5.

This unreadable page could really use some reformatting.

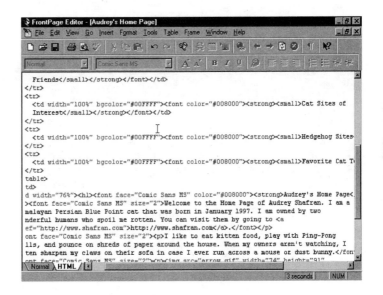

20

Carefully reformat the appearance of the HTML tags in this page. You can add carriage returns, tabs, and spaces without affecting how the page appears within FrontPage or a browser because browsers ignore all extra spaces found within HTML files. For example, if you press Return to separate two paragraphs of HTML, Netscape wouldn't care, because it separates paragraphs on the screen only if it finds the special <P> tag.

By separating the logical markup of a page with tags from the physical formatting of its spacing, you can easily make each page of HTML more readable and understandable. Figure 20.6 shows the newly reformatted page you originally saw in Figure 20.5.

Figure 20.6.

This page is much easier to read and understand.

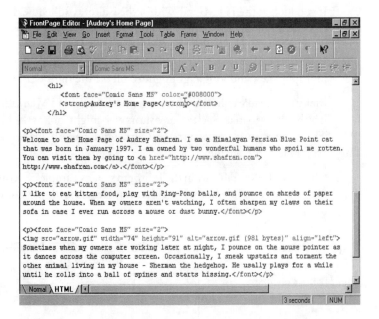

When reformatting your HTML page, you must ensure that you change only the formatting and don't accidentally erase an opening or closing tag. For example, when you use tables on your page, if you accidentally erase or move a single <TD> tag, the entire table might not appear within FrontPage or the browser might become confused. When you edit HTML pages, you should constantly switch back to the Normal view to make sure the page still works properly.

Advanced Page Tweaking

Even though FrontPage 98 is a truly comprehensive Web editing program, sometimes it can't be used to add advanced or difficult aspects to a Web page easily. Like all HTML editors, FrontPage has its flexibility limitations when you are building a page.

You might want to add a specific HTML feature or characteristic to one page that is difficult to do with FrontPage or can't be done at all. Here's an example of when you would need to add a line or two of HTML to achieve your desired effect.

Figure 20.7 shows a simple home page that is formatted properly. Normally, to add a simple background color to your table, you could select the cell you want to edit, click the right mouse button, and choose Cell Properties. But this table is different because it is actually an embedded table within a table.

Figure 20.7.

Editing embedded tables sometimes requires you to manually add HTML tags.

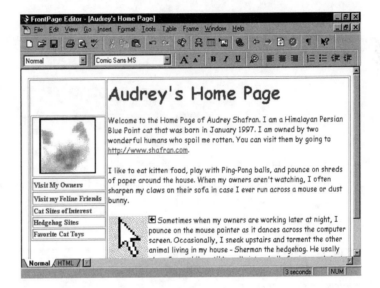

The screen is split into two cells of the table. The left side contains navigational information, and the right side contains the data. However, each navigational link on the left is part of a second, embedded table that is completely contained within that cell. Changing the cells with the cat image and the navigation links is easy enough, but changing the default characteristics of the cell that contains that second table is more difficult.

Whenever you try to update the cell properties, FrontPage never lets you select the entire cell covering the left side of the screen. Therefore, to change the background color of that cell, you must click the HTML tab, and then add the following snippet of HTML in the correct spot:

```
bgcolor=blue
```

This piece of HTML simply tells FrontPage and the browser that the entire cell should have a blue background color. Figure 20.8 shows where this particular line was added.

20

Figure 20.8.

Always format your HTML to make it readable before trying to tweak how your page appears.

The added HTML ——

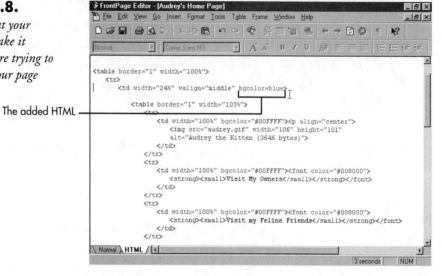

After the HTML is added, Figure 20.9 shows how the new page appears within FrontPage; the two tables on the left each have different background colors. Even though FrontPage couldn't make the change graphically, it recognizes the newly added HTML and reformats the page properly.

Figure 20.9.

Normally, you can't achieve this type of effect unless you manually edit the HTML.

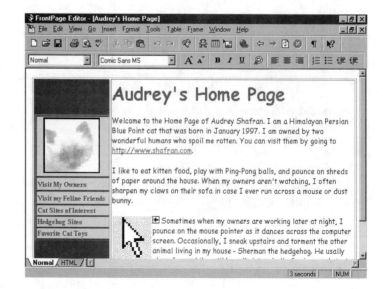

20

In general, you will be able to accomplish most editing functions directly with the FrontPage Editor. But sometimes you will run across tasks that require you to manually type HTML. For these tasks, you must be careful when editing your Web page to make sure you include legal HTML and make appropriate changes.

Summary

When you are building Web pages, it is important to have a basic understanding of HTML. Although FrontPage hides most of the difficult details from you, occasionally you might need to immerse yourself in the more advanced details of working directly with HTML.

This hour introduced you to the basics of HTML as a language and gave you several situations in which you might—or might not—want to edit the underlying codes of your page for yourself. You should feel comfortable flipping between the Normal and HTML tabs within the FrontPage Editor and recognize some basic tags.

Q&A

Q Is there really no way to use the Table features in FrontPage to make changes to a cell when there is an embedded table inside it? That seems awfully short-sighted of Microsoft.

A The particular problem highlighted in this hour occurs only when the only thing inside a cell is another table. If there were any other text or images, you'd easily be able to change the cell properties. FrontPage isn't a perfect program, and sometimes you'll run across idiosyncrasies such as this one. Fortunately, those idiosyncrasies are few and far between, and 90 percent of most Web developers won't need to worry about them.

Actually, this situation is only a problem because of the order in which the table was built. You could easily set the background color of the original table before creating the second, embedded table. But that requires significant planning, and thinking of every detail ahead of time is difficult.

Q When exploring the rest of FrontPage, I came across a component that lets you insert HTML directly into your page. When would I want to use this component instead of just typing the HTML directly into the Editor?

A The Insert HTML component is covered in more detail in Hour 16, "Embedding FrontPage Components." This feature lets you add a special set of HTML code that the server adds dynamically, as a browser requests that page. This technique works only when you use a special FrontPage Web server and offers no significant advantages over typing the HTML tags directly into the page.

20

Workshop

The Workshop contains quiz questions and an Activities section to help reinforce what you've learned in this hour. Try not to look at the quiz answers until you've tried to work them out yourself!

Quiz

1. Name three reasons why you might hesitate to edit raw HTML in one of your Web pages.

2. When browsing through the Web, if you find a really neat table or other HTML trick, how could you look up and copy that HTML directly into your own set of pages?

3. Do extra spaces, carriage returns, and tabs affect the way a page appears within a Web browser?

Answers

1. You must make only a simple, very small change and don't want to have to load up all of FrontPage.

    Reformatting the underlying HTML to make it more readable.

    Making changes that aren't readily available through the standard FrontPage Editor.

2. To take a section of HTML code from another site, follow these steps:

    a) From your browser, view the HTML source code.

    b) Select the section of HTML you want to copy for yourself and copy it to the Clipboard (Control+C).

    c) Within the HTML tab of FrontPage, paste (Control+V) the copied text. You now have the information available for your own use.

3. No. Browsers only recognize single spaces to separate words and sentences. Beyond that, they require special spacing tags instead. Therefore, reformatting HTML doesn't create any problems.

20

Activities

1. Editing HTML code directly requires a more acute knowledge of HTML and building Web pages from hand. You probably will need another book to give you more advanced details of using HTML for yourself. Try *Teach Yourself HTML in 24 Hours* by Dick Oliver (published by Sams), or *Creating Your Own Web Pages, Second Edition* by Andy Shafran (published by Que) for introductory guides to learning HTML for yourself.

2. Read Hour 16, "Embedding FrontPage Components," for a more in-depth discussion of some automated tools that are useful when editing your page. One of them even lets you insert blocks of HTML.

3. Read Hour 24, "Finale: Building a Home Page from Scratch," where you'll go through the entire process of making your site. This hour gives you a good idea of the type of interactive page you can create with FrontPage without worrying about difficult and advanced HTML details.

20

PART VI

Interacting with Your Visitors

Hour

Hour 21

Applying Web Themes

As you continue to build and expand your own Web sites, you'll start to learn how to make a good-looking site great. It takes a lot more than building simple pages to create a site that is attractive and impressive to visitors who stop by. One way FrontPage makes it easy for you to build great-looking Web sites is through the concept of *themes*, or a cohesive set of graphics, buttons, and icons that are designed to go together.

Using different themes, you can completely change the appearance and experience of your site. By assigning a theme to a FrontPage Web, you instantly change the way all bullets, colors, and text appear in a site so that they coordinate with one another.

FrontPage has several themes to choose from, each of which can be customized to fit your specific Web requirements. This hour introduces you to FrontPage themes and shows you how to use them to your advantage when building a Web.

Specifically, in this chapter you'll learn how to

- ☐ Understand how themes work
- ☐ Add a FrontPage theme to your site
- ☐ Customize a theme to fit your particular site
- ☐ Take advantage of advanced theme capabilities

Understanding FrontPage Themes

Themes are a new innovation in FrontPage 98 and drastically improve the cohesiveness and coordination of an entire Web site. Themes take Web design one step further than previously possible because they automate the coordination between background graphics, colors, bullets, headlines, and horizontal lines.

When you use a theme, FrontPage replaces standard items such as bullets and horizontal lines with graphical icons associated with the particular theme you select. Therefore, instead of the standard round bullets, you might have miniature leaves if you choose the Nature theme, or a compass for the Global Marketing theme. Themes change the effect of the entire Web page. They customize text font, color, height, and characteristics so that your information fits with the way graphics appear.

You'll find yourself using themes often because they add so much character to a standard page. Otherwise, you'd have to customize text font and graphics yourself, a slow and painful process for pages that are large and edited often.

Themes actually change the way you build Web pages. For example, if you want to add a horizontal line to a standard Web page, you would choose Insert | Horizontal Line. Then, you could edit the line properties to set its thickness, color, and more. When you choose the exact same menu command for a themed page, FrontPage inserts a long thin graphic that resembles a horizontal line but is much more enjoyable to look at and use on your page.

FrontPage does the same thing with bulleted lists, headline text, and background graphics. It actually replaces those elements for you automatically with one that matches a particular theme, saving you significant time.

FrontPage 98 comes with several different default themes from which you can select. With the FrontPage CD-ROM, you'll find nearly 60 different themes, each with its own set of graphics, icons, fonts, and colors. Each theme has its own personality. The same page will look dramatically different when assigned to a different theme.

For a better understanding of how themes work, look at the following example. Figure 21.1 is a standard, boring Web page for a fictional travel company. It's not very exciting; it has only a headline, a table, some text, and bullets.

Now take a look at Figure 21.2. This is the exact same page as before, only set to use a theme named Arcs. You assign a theme to a particular page or the entire Web by issuing a single command, which significantly changes a page's appearance in a matter of moments.

21

Figure 21.1.

If you ran across this page on the Web, you'd be bored stiff.

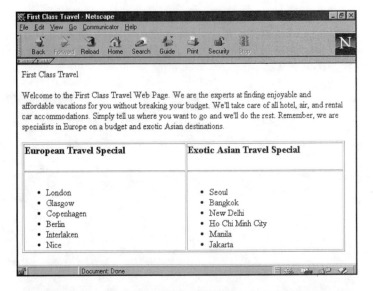

Figure 21.2.

What a difference the theme made to this page!

Pretty amazing, isn't it? Notice how the theme knew exactly how to replace the bulleted list, the horizontal line, and even change the font of the text and banner at the very top. Themes are very thorough and include virtually every aspect of a Web page. Sometimes, they even use animated GIFs for bullets and lines.

21

Look at Figures 21.3 through 21.8 to see the same Web page in six different themes. Notice how each theme matches its name by using coordinating graphics and font styles. Some themes make sense for this travel agency, while others are more appropriate for a different type of Web page.

Figure 21.3.

The In Motion theme.

Figure 21.4.

The Construction Zone theme.

21

Figure 21.5.

The Expedition theme.

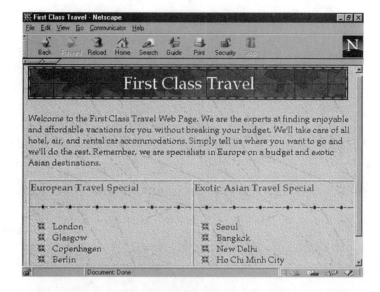

Figure 21.6.

The Global Marketing theme.

21

Figure 21.7.

The Nature theme.

Figure 21.8.

The Sumi Painting theme.

JUST A MINUTE

Although interesting to look at in this book, themed pages are much more impressive when you can enjoy their full color and graphics. You can see each of these themed pages and more by visiting this book's home page at http://www.shafran.com/frontpage98.

21

Using Themes for Your Web

Now that you understand a little bit more about how themes work and how they can look, the next step is to use them for yourself. Adding a theme to a FrontPage Web is easy. You can use either the FrontPage Explorer or Editor to assign themes to your Web pages, but they work slightly differently from one another. Setting a theme in the Explorer makes every page within the whole Web use the same theme. Conversely, you can set a theme to a single page if you use the Theme command within the FrontPage Editor.

Using the FrontPage Explorer

To set a Web-wide theme, first open the FrontPage Web you want to change. Then click the Themes icon within the Explorer Views bar running down the left side of the screen (or choose View | Themes from the menu). Figure 21.9 shows the theme options you can set.

Figure 21.9.

FrontPage lets you preview each theme before you apply it to your Web.

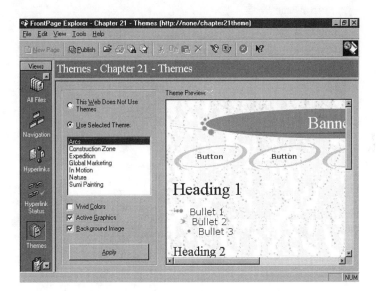

You can select any theme in the list box. FrontPage automatically sets the Use Selected Theme radio button whenever you choose a theme to use Web wide. FrontPage shows you a preview of the aspects a theme changes in the Theme Preview box.

There are several variations you can choose in a FrontPage theme. Right below the theme list box is a set of three checkboxes that enable you to pick and use only certain parts of a theme if you want. FrontPage lets you turn on and off the use of bright and vivid colors, animated GIFs, and background images. Usually you'll want to use all three theme aspects unless you really have an adverse opinion of the way the theme appears by default. Microsoft spent a lot of time customizing and configuring the various components of each theme, and the themes tend to look much more exciting when all three checkboxes are marked on.

21

After you've selected a theme, click the button labeled Apply, and FrontPage goes through your entire site and adds the themed components to each page.

TIME SAVER

If you want to remove your theme attributes, click the radio button marked This Web Does Not Use Themes, and then press the Apply button. All themed characteristics will be automatically removed, and your Web is returned to plain vanilla.

Using the FrontPage Editor

You also can use the FrontPage Editor to set a particular theme to use within your Web. In addition, the Editor lets you set a theme for a specific page instead of just for the whole FrontPage Web.

Start the Editor and load the page whose theme you want to set. Then choose Format | Theme from the menu to bring up the Choose Theme dialog box (see Figure 21.10).

Figure 21.10.

Setting a theme within the Editor lets you use multiple themes within one Web.

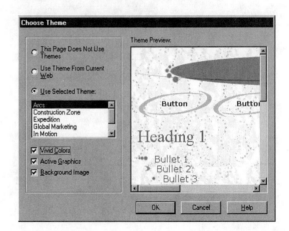

You have similar options available here as when you select a theme with the FrontPage Explorer. The only difference is the set of radio buttons in the top-left side of the box. From here, you can set this single page to not use a theme, set a Web-wide theme, or just a page-wide theme. Setting Web-wide themes means that FrontPage will update every page in the entire Web when you click OK.

21

Adding Themed Elements

After you've selected your theme, FrontPage converts the entire theme to the font, color, and text attributes associated with it. All bullets are converted into icons, all horizontal lines become long, skinny images, and headings and linked text are reformatted.

Every time you add new information to your themed page, FrontPage automatically formats the text and icons appropriately. Therefore, if you click Insert | Horizontal Line from the menu, the matching line icon appears instead of the standard HTML horizontal line. What's impressive is that when you edit the horizontal line properties by clicking the right mouse button and choosing Line Properties from the pop-up box, FrontPage grays out all options that are inappropriate to the themed line (see Figure 21.11).

Figure 21.11.

Because it isn't a standard HTML line, only the alignment options can be set.

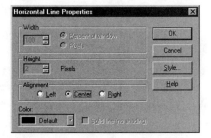

Even more impressive is that FrontPage doesn't treat the inserted line graphic as a standard Web graphic. Normally, you can resize and change any graphic inserted into your page by double-clicking it or by dragging its edges to make it larger or smaller. But a theme-inserted horizontal line is a static picture that comes as-is and can't be resized. Bullet and button icons work in the same manner.

Adding Themed Banners

One of the best parts of using a theme enables you to add a large, screen-width banner to your Web page that serves as a highly graphical headline. A headline banner actually is an automated FrontPage component (see Hour 16, "Embedding FrontPage Components"), but it is really geared toward being used in conjunction with Web themes. A headline banner automatically transforms a page headline into a graphically matching banner that matches the selected theme. All the headlines shown in Figures 21.3 through 21.8 were actually automated banners.

21

To add an automated banner to your page or pages, follow these steps:

1. Load your page into the FrontPage Editor and choose Insert | FrontPage Component from the menu (see Figure 21.12).

Figure 21.12.

A page banner is just one of the many components you can use.

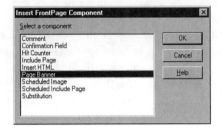

2. Select Page Banner from the Insert FrontPage Component dialog box and click OK. The Page Banner Properties dialog box appears (see Figure 21.13).

3. Select Image for the type of page banner you want to create. Only the Image type uses the current Web theme to customize the way the graphical banner appears. Click OK, and a graphic looking similar to that shown in Figure 21.14 appears.

4. For now, the text that appears on the banner is blank; you must set the text within the FrontPage Explorer. Switch to the Explorer and click the Navigation view (see Figure 21.15).

Figure 21.13.

Banners can be boring text or become graphic-like and use the current page's theme.

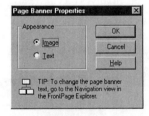

5. You use the Navigation view to build links between multiple pages within a FrontPage Web. The text that appears on the FrontPage page banner is the same text that appears on each page icon within the Navigation view. You can rename any page by clicking the right mouse button over the page and choosing Rename from the pop-up box that appears. After you rename your page, switch back to the FrontPage Editor. The text on the page banner changes automatically.

21

Figure 21.14.

This is a new banner on a blank page using the Sumi Painting theme.

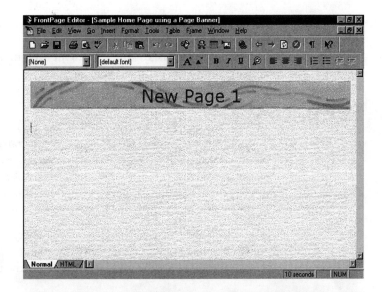

Figure 21.15.

You've used the Navigation view very sparingly so far in this book.

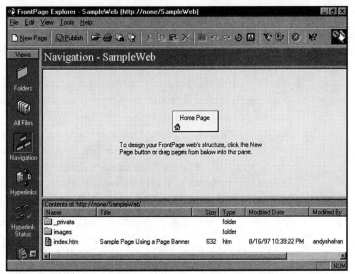

TIME SAVER

Before you can rename a page, it must be an icon within the Navigation view. You can drag any HTML file from the Contents listing onto the Navigation view before you rename it.

21

After you insert a page banner, FrontPage automatically creates the appropriate Web graphic for you. When visitors stop by this page, they download a graphic that shows the headline on top of the matching theme image. This is much more exciting than a text-only headline and adds character and professionalism to your site.

Summary

This hour introduced you to FrontPage themes and demonstrated how you can use them to create a completely coordinated Web site. Using themes is like using an interior decorator on each page of your site and ensuring that all the pages pleasantly match one another. Themes enable you to build a complete site that has every page displaying a consistent look, which benefits your visitor and makes you appear like a better Web developer.

You should feel comfortable setting and using themes within any page or Web in FrontPage. In addition, you now should understand how the Page Banner component works and why you'd want to use it instead of a standard Size 1 heading at the top of your pages.

Q&A

Q Besides aesthetics, are there any additional benefits to using themes on my Web site?

A Using a set of themes can improve the appearance and sometimes even the download time of your Web site. If you try to emulate the way themes work by adding lots of graphics and images to your pages, you'll quickly find that downloading each page can take a while. FrontPage themes, on the other hand, take advantage of browser caching and enable you to download many graphics only once, but see them on multiple pages. For example, a visitor must download a button or horizontal line only once, and then the visitor's browser displays it for each subsequent page within that themed site, without downloading it anew each time.

Another benefit of a themed site is that it helps visitors understand and navigate through all of your pages. Page consistency is important because it helps visitors know what text color is important, what the different buttons look like, and more. By establishing a common look to your entire site, a visitor instantly knows whether he is still on one of your pages each time he clicks a link.

21

Q **What else is the Navigation view used for? It seems to be important, but it looks confusing and difficult to understand.**

A The Navigation view primarily is used to dynamically generate link relationships between multiple pages in a FrontPage Web. By dragging multiple pages into the Navigation view, you are creating a hierarchical listing of how each page can refer to another. You can set certain pages to be parent documents while others appear below them as children. FrontPage keeps track of these relationships for you just as a family tree keeps track of who is related to whom. Then in the Editor, you can add dynamic navigation bars that generate links to all child documents, parent pages, sibling pages, and more. Navigation bars are advanced topics and out of the scope of this book.

Workshop

The Workshop contains quiz questions and an Activities section to help reinforce what you've learned in this hour. Try not to look at the quiz answers until you've tried to work them out yourself!

Quiz

1. What's the difference between setting a theme within the FrontPage Explorer and setting one within the Editor?

2. How are page banners created?

Answers

1. When you set a theme within the FrontPage Explorer you create a consistent look across every page within your Web. The Editor enables you to go one step further and set (or remove) a theme for a single page without affecting the entire Web, if you want.

2. Page banners are FrontPage components that must first be inserted into a Web page and then edited within the FrontPage Explorer Navigation view.

   To create a page banner, choose Insert | FrontPage Component from the Editor's menu bar and then select Page Banner from the Insert FrontPage Component dialog box that appears. Select an image or text page banner from the Page Banner Properties dialog box, and your banner is added to the current page. Don't forget to edit the text that appears within your banner by using the Navigation view in the FrontPage Explorer.

21

Activities

1. Everyone has his or her own personal taste when it comes to using themes. Create your site and evaluate several, if not all, the themes in FrontPage. Make a list of the ones you prefer and assign one of them to your Web. Don't be afraid to change your page's theme periodically to spice up your site for visitors who stop by repeatedly.

2. Check out Hour 22, "Site Design Tips," for another discussion on good design within a Web site. Using themes is only the first step in creating a coordinated, well-designed site that piques visitors' interest when they stop by.

3. Themes are used thoroughly within FrontPage templates and wizards. Read Hour 3, "Quickstart: Using the FrontPage Templates," for a more thorough discussion of how templates operate.

21

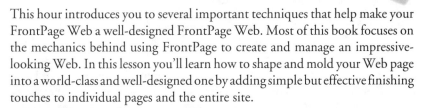

Hour 22

Site Design Tips

This hour introduces you to several important techniques that help make your FrontPage Web a well-designed FrontPage Web. Most of this book focuses on the mechanics behind using FrontPage to create and manage an impressive-looking Web. In this lesson you'll learn how to shape and mold your Web page into a world-class and well-designed one by adding simple but effective finishing touches to individual pages and the entire site.

You'll learn how to control visitors' lines of sight and improve the way they experience your page. These simple design tricks add up to create a more impressive and more enjoyable FrontPage Web for you and each of the millions of potential visitors who might stop by.

Specifically, in this hour you learn how to

☐ Make sure your Web page has a consistent look to it

☐ Keep your Web page current and exciting to attract repeat visitors

☐ Structure your HTML file so it can be read and maintained in the future

☐ Add comments to your HTML file

☐ Validate your Web page with an automated HTML checker

Home Page Design Tips

As you've learned throughout this book, you can use FrontPage 98 to create a Web page in just a matter of minutes. If you use templates, wizards, and FrontPage's intuitive Web-building interface, you can create individual pages and sites simply by typing your information. However, although creating a basic Web page isn't very difficult, you should keep several things in mind when you are designing how individual Web pages, and the entire site, appear. In this section you'll learn a few popular but simple design tips that will help keep your Web pages looking great.

Measure Your Page's Consistency

All telephones work in the same way. You pick up the receiver and dial the person you want to reach. When you're finished, you hang up the receiver to end your conversation. Sure, some phones require you to dial a special number (such as 9) to work, and others hide their buttons in hard-to-find spots, but all of them generally work the same. This consistency lets you know how to use a phone from anywhere in the world.

Visitors to your Web site will appreciate that same type of consistency on your pages, so all your Web pages should have a consistent style about them. After a while, visitors will know where to find information on your Web pages without consciously thinking about it.

The following are some examples of consistency:

☐ Use the same size and font for headlines on every Web page. If you use a Size 1 heading and color it blue on one page, then you should use that same style for all the pages in your site. Soon visitors will recognize that large blue text represents a headline. Using different sized headlines on different pages will look odd and make your Web look inconsistent. One tactic you can use to keep your page consistent is to work with FrontPage themes. See Hour 21, "Applying Web Themes," for more details.

☐ Add graphics and images in similar ways throughout your home page. If some of your graphics are hyperlinks to other Web sites and some are simply placed on your page, visitors might not recognize which graphics are hyperlinks and which are not.

☐ Include consistent information in the page's footer. At the bottom of every Web page, include important data about when it was created and whom to contact for further information. Add this same default footer to every page in your site. You can learn more about standardized footers in Hour 16, "Embedding FrontPage Components."

Brevity Is a Virtue

Some people like to compare the World Wide Web to a book that you can read and jump around in from page to page. Although this metaphor works for some pages, most visitors compare the Web to glossy magazines you can buy in a store. Instead of reading each article with significant detail, visitors simply flip through each page quickly until they notice something that is interesting or catches their eyes. For the most part, readers flip pages about as fast as their hands can click their mouse buttons. Because of this short reader attention span, magazines (and Web pages) must present information in a short and usable nature.

With this in mind, it's a good idea to keep your Web page concise and to the point. People browse through Web pages quickly. If something looks long and boring to read, most keep going until they see something that is broken down and easy to read.

Think of your own browsing techniques. It's easy to run out of patience when you are browsing the WWW. If there is too much information or something doesn't jump out and grab you, you're more likely to jump to another page before slowly reading and digesting several paragraphs of text. Figure 22.1 shows how a home page looks when it has too much text on it.

Figure 22.1.
Nobody will bother reading this; it's boring and long-winded.

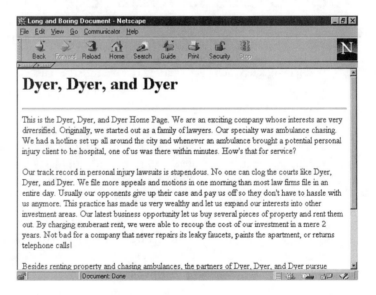

If you have a lot of information to put on your Web page, consider splitting the information onto several different pages, or at least using tables, lists, or frames to organize the page better. This keeps your visitors from becoming information overloaded.

To keep readers interested and your home page brief, try using this simple rule of thumb: the *three-by-three* rule. Basically, the three-by-three rule tells you to never place more than three paragraphs (each with three sentences) together on a single page under normal circumstances. After three paragraphs, readers become bored and move on. Instead, use lists and tables to bring out important information and catch visitors' eyes.

Of course, this rule can't always be followed—you might have a long paragraph of text or simply need to have a lot of data within a single page.

TIME SAVER

> Also keep in mind that every person who visits your Web page must download everything that's on it (including all the text and pictures) before reading it. The smaller your page, the less time people have to wait, twiddling their thumbs, for your Web page to download. Remember that text downloads much faster than images. An entire page of text can download faster than a single image.

Don't Overdo Your Web Page with Glitz

Along the same lines, don't let your Web page get out of hand with too much glamour and glitz. Everyone knows that you can add lots of pictures, sound clips, forms, and clickable maps to your FrontPage Web, not to mention all the embedded components and active elements that let you keep each page fresh. Don't overuse these neat and impressive aspects built into FrontPage; otherwise, your site could look like a bad parody of Times Square in New York (a lot of hype but nothing substantial).

When your FrontPage Web uses many different features at once, it becomes difficult to read and hard to even look at. Keep in mind that this rule is even doubly important when you are mixing and matching more than images and graphics. Forms, scripts, components, audio files, and video clips are all fantastic but are tremendously difficult to add to Web pages without overdoing it.

Don't be afraid to ask for an honest opinion about your page from a friend or relative. If they don't seem to appreciate all the features you've included, try splitting each page into multiple pages. Each page could take advantage of one or two FrontPage features but still maintain consistency and relevance for visitors stopping by.

Keep Your Web Page Alive

Every Thursday night, a new episode of your favorite television show comes on. Every week when you turn on the TV, you know that you aren't going to see the same episode you watched last time because that would be boring. Except in the summer, new episodes are weekly occurrences. Can you imagine if there was only one episode, and the TV station

22

22

played it over and over again? You'd watch it the first time and maybe see the rerun once, but after that, you'd switch channels. The reason you keep coming back week after week is because you know you'll see something new.

You should practice this same philosophy on your Web page. If you create a basic FrontPage Web and never update it or make changes, why would anyone come back? After one or two stops, they've seen everything there is to see on your site and will start visiting other WWW spots instead.

The key to getting visitors to come back again and again is to constantly update your pages to keep information fresh and new. One great example of a constantly updating site is the Weather Channel's home page (http://www.weather.com), shown in Figure 22.2. Even though the Weather Channel doesn't use FrontPage, you can still appreciate how important it is to keep current information available. Every time you visit, you see current weather maps and information.

Figure 22.2.

Can you imagine if this page was never updated?

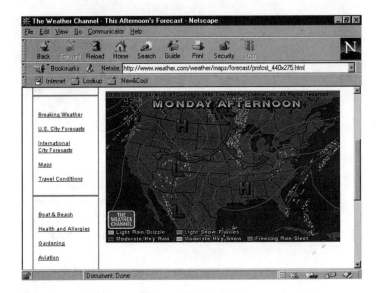

After you've built a basic Web page, keeping it fresh, new, and exciting is difficult but well worth the trouble. For example, lawyers might keep a list of links related to landmark precedents and decisions in which their clients might be interested. Accountants might note recent tax changes and offer regular tips on how to prepare for the tax deadline. Even if you think your particular Web site doesn't need to be updated often, think again.

Figure 22.3 shows one zany example of a fantastic Web site, the Cologne Answer Guy (`http://www.cologneguy.com/`). It is a good Web site because the author clearly spends a lot of time keeping the latest and greatest information online. Not only can you learn everything there is to know about cologne, but there are current sales figures, exciting promotions, and special tie-ins with other smell-oriented sites.

Figure 22.3.

The Cologne Guy keeps you coming back for another whiff.

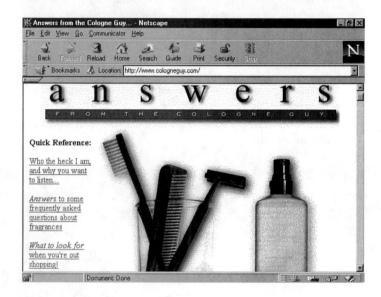

Image Visioning

One common design characteristic comes into play whenever you use images and pictures on Web pages. Normally, you don't need to think about it, but *image visioning* can be a powerful yet subtle way to update your page. Image visioning is the concept of placing a Web graphic on a page in such a manner that it draws a visitor's line of attention toward the center of the screen, not to the edge.

Figure 22.4 shows an example of image visioning in action; it shows a sample Web page describing a European vacation. Notice the picture at the top of the screen (a person—me—standing in front of Napoleon's tomb). See the cannon behind me pointing to the right? It's important that this image be placed on the Web page properly. Logically, when someone sees this Web page, he or she will notice the picture at the top.

Because the cannon points to the right, most people's eyes automatically look in the direction the picture is pointing. In this case, they are immediately drawn toward the title of the Web page on the right side of the picture. Simply put, when someone looks at an image, they logically look in the direction toward which a picture is pointing.

22

Figure 22.4.

Design your Web pages with your images in mind.

Now look at Figure 22.5, which is just about the exact same Web page. But notice how the image has switched sides, and the page just doesn't have the same effect. When you look at this page, your line of vision moves toward the right off the screen, and visitors aren't drawn into reading the rest of this page.

Figure 22.5.

This layout doesn't exploit the visitor's logical line of vision.

Image visioning is an old concept among newspaper editors and layout artists. This is another example of how a new type of media can use the same time-honored tactics that newspapers and book editors have used for years to help the reader locate and enjoy information.

Today, most newspapers employ these techniques to help guide visitors' eyes through long stories, toward related photos, and into important advertisements. Readers are subtly guided without their knowledge.

There are many other similar techniques you can use to build Web pages. One includes using smaller, sub-headlines (called kickers in the newspaper biz) above the large size-1 headlines on your page. Another technique wraps the body of a page around an image (this can be carefully done using FrontPage tables).

Navigation Bars

One of the best design features in FrontPage 98 is the capability to dynamically create and use graphical navigation bars throughout your Web. Navigation bars let you create hyperlinks to different pages in your site, depending on how you structurally organize them. Navigation bars enable you to create hierarchical listings of how your Web pages are related. Then, you can insert special navigation bars that build links to other files (in your Web) that are at the same level or sublevel as your current file.

Navigation bars can be confusing to understand, so here's a visual example of exactly how they work. First, create a new FrontPage Web from the Customer Web template. This template is useful because it includes dynamically generated navigation bars. After you create your sample Web, click the Navigation view from the FrontPage Explorer. This view shows you the hierarchical relationship between all the pages within this Web. Figure 22.6 shows the default setting; there are only two navigational levels in this Web.

You can change and modify the page hierarchy so that some pages become higher or lower than others in this view. Simply select a page and drag it to a new level in the window. You now are changing how FrontPage dynamically generates links between pages within this Web. FrontPage lets you insert special components that build links between different levels of documents. Figure 22.7 shows the same Web, only hierarchically organized better.

22

Figure 22.6.

This sample template assigns each page to only two hierarchical levels for FrontPage navigation bars.

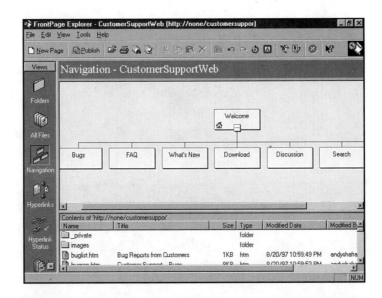

Figure 22.7.

Now there are only three links from the main page in this Web.

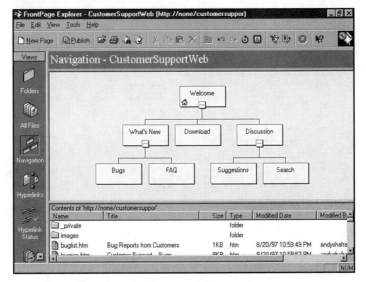

After you've rearranged how your pages should be linked to one another hierarchically, start the FrontPage Editor and open any page in this site. Then choose Insert | Navigation Bar from the FrontPage 98 menu. The Navigation Bar Properties dialog box appears (see Figure 22.8).

Figure 22.8.

This dialog box lets you control how the pages in this Web link to one another.

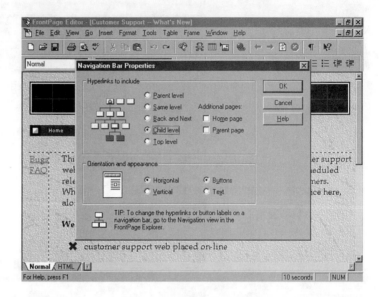

From here, you can add a dynamically generated navigation bar that builds hyperlinks to other pages within your Web. Notice that there are several different options from which you can select. You can choose to build hyperlinks to other pages at the same level as this current page, only to child documents, only back to the top page, and many more. FrontPage even graphically shows in the Preview section where the navigation bar will link you.

This dynamic navigation bar changes when you add new pages to your Web or restructure the hierarchical relationship between your pages from within the FrontPage Explorer. When you click OK, FrontPage builds the navigation bar for you automatically (see Figure 22.9). It even uses special graphics and buttons if you've selected a theme for this site.

Of course, you can update how the dynamic navigation bar appears at any time by clicking your right mouse button over it within FrontPage and selecting the Edit FrontPage Component Properties choice from the pop-up dialog box that appears.

TIME SAVER

Navigation bars are just one of many advanced FrontPage features that aren't fully covered within this short introductory book. In fact, they deserve a whole chapter or two just for themselves because they can be very advanced and complicated, particularly for large Web sites. Check out *FrontPage 98 Unleashed* by Sams.net Publishing for a more in-depth discussion on creating, using, and editing dynamic navigation bars for your FrontPage Web.

22

Figure 22.9.

Compare the What's New page with its level within the Navigation view pane and you'll see it links only to child pages.

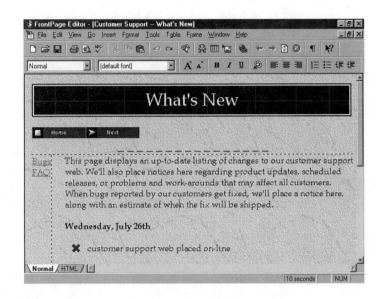

Test Your Web Page

Before you submitted a term paper in college, you always gave it one final run-through and look-see. You'd break out the spell checker and give the paper to friends to read before submitting it to your professor. Even though you spent a lot of time creating the perfect term paper, you almost invariably found small errors and silly mistakes that could cost you credit.

Can your Web page make the grade? Before you put your Web page on the WWW and start announcing it to millions of people to visit, you want to run a final check on your home page as well. You should check it with a fine-tooth comb for common and easily preventable errors. This section shows you how to check your home page for common mistakes before your visitors locate them for you.

Preview Your Page

Likely, you've got one of two popular browsers loaded onto your computer, Netscape Navigator/Communicator or Microsoft Internet Explorer. Most people in the world use one of these two browsers. As you develop your pages, you probably will use a browser to see how your site will appear. Even though FrontPage is a WYSIWYG editor, some tags look slightly different in an actual Web browser. In fact, after finishing the initial page editing, you should review every page in your site.

When you view each page, look it over thoroughly and read each word. Here's a list of simple but important things to check when you look at your home page, and how to fix the problems:

☐ *Look for grammatical errors and typos:* Missing small typos and grammatical errors within a page—such as incorrect punctuation, spelling, and of course, the dreaded homonym—is very easy. Use the FrontPage spell-checker and thesaurus generously; that's why they're included. Misspelled words signify that you didn't take the necessary time to check out your page.

☐ *Make sure your paragraphs are split up properly:* A common mistake is to forget the carriage return between paragraphs. If you don't press Enter, some paragraphs run right into Web graphics or other elements on your page.

☐ *Make sure images appear where they should:* When you start adding images to your Web pages, it is easy to set appearance properties incorrectly. Make sure your image is properly placed and sized on your Web page and that all the placement properties work correctly.

☐ *Make sure all of your links work correctly:* If you are going to include hypertext links in your FrontPage Web, make sure they work correctly; otherwise, visitors see a screen that looks like Figure 22.10. Mistyping URLs is a common mistake that can easily be avoided. FrontPage even comes with a URL checking tool, the Hyperlink Status View within the Explorer.

Figure 22.10.
Web surfers hate to see this screen, which means a link has been broken.

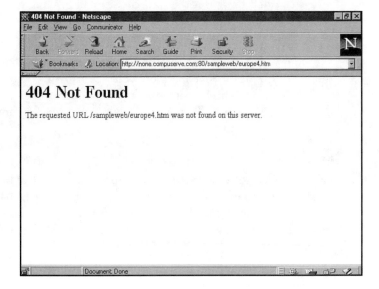

22

22

Use Another Browser

Although this book is geared toward optimizing your home page for all types of browsers, it's a good idea to check out your page using both the Microsoft and Netscape Web browser. Your Web page might look fantastic in Netscape, but impossible for Microsoft users to read. You want it to be read by anyone on the WWW, without looking improper or out of place.

Download the latest version of Internet Explorer at http://www.microsoft.com, or download the latest version of Netscape at http://www.netscape.com.

TIME SAVER

Older browsers typically don't support all the new HTML and Netscape extensions. They might display items such as tables in a jumbled fashion. For example, older versions of Internet Explorer (before 3.0) don't support frames—this can be a real problem for some of your users.

Summary

Designing for the WWW takes more care and planning than simply typing paragraph after paragraph of information into a single page. It requires forethought, planning, and a keen eye.

This chapter introduced you to several different design techniques that novices and professionals can use to significantly improve the way FrontPage Web sites appear and work for all types of visitors. You should feel comfortable remolding some pages in your site to take advantage of these techniques, without spending a lot of time re-creating each page from scratch.

Q&A

Q You showed me how to create navigation bars, but how do I get rid of them on a page? Even when I deleted them from within the FrontPage Editor, there seem to be some remnants of the navigation bar remaining.

A You can't delete navigation bars simply by taking them off the screen. You can remove navigation bars one page at a time by clicking the right mouse button and selecting Page Properties from the pop-up dialog box that appears. Then click the Custom tab to see the specific FrontPage variables assigned to this page. Select the variable named Microsoft Border, and then click the Remove button. All traces of the navigation bar are now removed from the page.

Q I'm now paranoid about using all the FrontPage features you talked about throughout this entire book. It seems really easy to create a page that is too busy or confusing to my visitors, and I need my page to be accessible to everyone. Are there any other hints you have to keep the page designed well?

A First, remember that good taste and design are completely subjective. You won't be able to create a page that everyone thinks is fabulous; everyone has their own preferences. The best way to create a well-designed site is to spend a lot of time exploring the Web for yourself. Make notes about sites you do and don't like. Identify sites that seem to have visitors always coming back. What advanced features do they use? How is the site structured? Over 2/3 of the time, a well-structured site dramatically improves the site's quality without using a single cool or advanced feature.

Workshop

The Workshop contains quiz questions and an Activities section to help reinforce what you've learned in this hour. Try not to look at the quiz answers until you've tried to work them out yourself!

Quiz

1. Why should you always try following the three-by-three rule when creating pages within your site?

2. What does image visioning mean?

Answers

1. To keep your pages concise, organized, and to the point. By constraining yourself to a few short paragraphs of text, you must make every word count. By taking care of the words and phrases you use, you are likely to increase the usefulness of your site for visitors who stop by.

2. Image visioning is the concept of lining up the action in your Web graphics so that your visitor's line of sight naturally flows into the rest of your page.

Activities

1. Sit down with your local newspaper and look at each page without reading any stories. Identify which stories are given prominent positions and how they are displayed. Look for different headline sizes, integration with charts and photos, and other layout techniques. Try to apply some of those standard concepts to your FrontPage Web.

22

2. Read Hour 19, "Managing Your Web Site," for more advanced information on keeping all your pages organized, spell checked, and easy to work with.

3. Navigation bars are really advanced FrontPage components that you can use on your page. Read Hour 16, "Embedding FrontPage Components," for more information on how these automatic processes work and other types you can use within your Web.

22

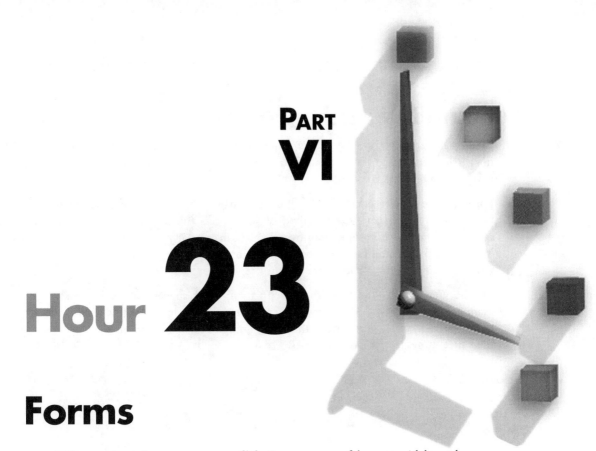

Hour 23

Forms

Filling out forms is a necessary part of life. Forms are one of the most widely used ways people communicate information and their personal facts and opinions. Credit card applications, income taxes, surveys, and questionnaires are all important parts of tracking information. Some forms are easy to fill out, whereas others are difficult, asking questions (such as, "Under which category do your income taxes fall?") requiring thoughtful responses.

Regardless of how forms are used, all forms have one thing in common: They are a standardized way to gather several pieces of information in a short amount of space. Forms ask the same questions from many different people, and then that information can be consolidated and compared.

FrontPage 98 lets you create your own electronic forms that ask people to type information on your Web site. There are several different reasons why you might use a form; to solicit feedback from visitors, for example.

This chapter introduces you to building and configuring FrontPage forms for your own Web sites. Specifically, you'll learn how to

- ☐ Use forms to get visitor feedback
- ☐ Add different types of form fields to your FrontPage Web
- ☐ Configure several form-specific options for your site

Building Interactive Forms

Normally, visitors who stop by your Web page only get to read the text you type and see the images you include. The Web typically is a one-sided conversation. Visitors simply browse and click on different hyperlinks.

Forms change the Web paradigm slightly by enabling visitors to answer certain questions and type in data when they visit certain types of Web pages. You can ask visitors to leave their comments and answers to questions from a site or take a poll allowing users to choose one item or another. You'll find that forms are an integral part of communicating with your visitors and letting them participate at your site.

On the Web and in FrontPage, there are many different shapes and types of forms. For example, look at Figure 23.1, a straw poll from the Official Doonesbury Web site (http://www.doonesbury.com). Periodically, this entertaining Web site asks visitors pertinent questions that always have a Doonesbury-ish flavor.

Figure 23.1.

Is Elvis a fad or fading? You decide at this interactive poll.

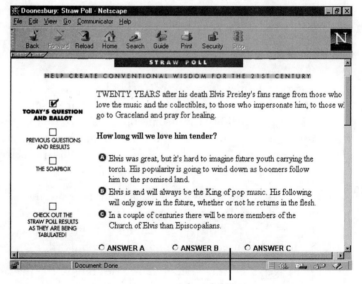

A form field letting you vote

After reading the quiz, you can cast your own vote in a special Web element called a *form field*. This field lets you select an option and then submit your choice electronically. After you select an answer, scroll down to the bottom of the screen and click the button labeled Submit. After you submit your electronic form, your vote is tallied, and a current list of voting results is displayed (see Figure 23.2).

23

Figure 23.2.

Not many people have faith in Elvis anymore.

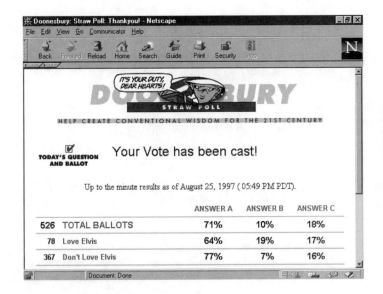

Web forms can look completely different than the Doonesbury straw poll, and let you type in all sorts of different data. Look at another example in Figure 23.3. This electronic form is an interactive guestbook that visitors can sign as they stop by.

Figure 23.3.

This guestbook lets you type your name, e-mail address, and location.

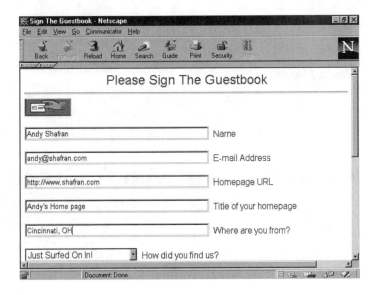

Processing Forms with FrontPage

Now that you've seen a few different types of forms, this section explains exactly how they work. As you edit and create new Web pages, FrontPage 98 lets you add special items to your page called *form elements*. These elements enable you to build different types of interactive questionnaires for your visitors.

In addition to the different fields on the page, each form has a special button labeled Submit. The Submit button lets visitors indicate when they're finished typing their information, and sends that data back to the Web server hosting the page.

From there, the Web server takes the data you enter on a form and performs some type of action on it. Web servers can create consolidated files from each form, send e-mail containing the results, or publish the data to an entirely new results page that everyone can see.

FrontPage makes building and including forms and form elements on your Web pages easy. You can graphically insert various form elements into your page, and then easily decide what to do when each visitor clicks the Submit button. The key to using forms properly is to understand their relationship with your Web server. Forms are another feature that work primarily with Web servers that support FrontPage extensions. FrontPage even expands the traditional use of forms by letting you build online discussion areas by using standard form functionality.

JUST A MINUTE

> Actually, you don't always have to use a special server that supports the FrontPage extensions in order to get forms to work properly. However, you must have special permission from your Web provider to use this interactive feature. Check with the company that hosts your Web site to see if it allows you to use forms on your Web page. Otherwise, nothing will happen when visitors click the Submit button.

Building Forms with FrontPage

Creating a form with FrontPage is easy because all the different types of elements can be graphically included on your page. When you add form elements to your page, you'll use the special Form toolbar found within the FrontPage Editor. Choose View|Forms Toolbar from the menu to see the different types of form elements you can use (see Figure 23.4).

Figure 23.4.

Like most actions in FrontPage, there are icons to shortcut your work when creating forms.

The form toolbar ─┐

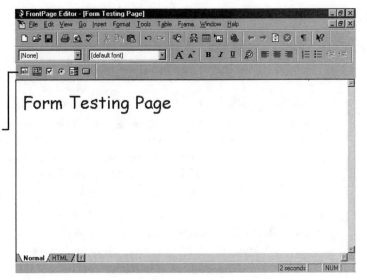

Adding a Text Box

The first and easiest form element you'll work with is the one-line text box. To add a one-line text box to your form page, you can use the Form toolbar or choose Insert | Form Field | One Line Text Box from the menu. FrontPage adds several elements to your Web page (see Figure 23.5).

Figure 23.5.

This is the most basic form you can create.

The form boundary lines ──
One-line text box ──
Submit button ──
Reset button ──

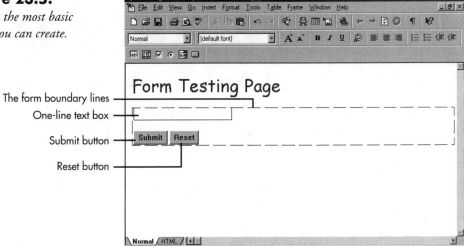

Even though you added just a single field, FrontPage added four different items to the current page:

One-line text box	An empty field in which visitors can type a single line of information. You must type some text next to this field to label it properly for your visitors.
Submit button	Sends the form off to the Web server to be processed.
Reset button	Erases the contents of all elements within this form when clicked.
Form boundaries	This dotted line surrounds all the elements associated with this specific Submit button. You can have multiple forms on the same page, but each has its own Submit button, and these boundary lines help you distinguish them.

Save this page, and you have created your first form. One-line text boxes are the most common form element because they are so simple, but they appear as simple blank boxes on a Web page. You must add a text label next to the box, describing what your visitors should do within that box.

Finally, there are several different properties you can set to control exactly how this field appears within a browser. You can set these characteristics by clicking your right mouse button on the empty field and choosing Form Field Properties from the pop-up box that appears. This opens the Text Box Properties dialog box, shown in Figure 23.6.

Figure 23.6.

Each form element has special properties you can set.

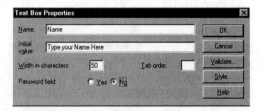

Most of these properties are too advanced for this book, but there are two you'll probably want to use, Initial Value and Width in Characters. The Initial Value property lets you specify a word or phrase that appears by default in this particular field. And, as you can guess, the Width in Characters field specifies how many characters this blank field can contain.

Scrolling Text Fields

Scrolling text fields are nearly identical to one-line text fields except that they can span multiple lines. You can insert this field element by choosing Insert | Form Field | Scrolling Text Box from the menu.

23

TIME SAVER

> Make sure that your cursor is inside existing form boundaries before you insert this field; otherwise, FrontPage will assume you are creating a new form within the same Web page and add another set of form boundaries and submit or reset buttons.

You can set similar properties to the scrolling form field (width and default text), as well as control how many lines tall the field should appear within a Web page.

Checkboxes

So far, you've seen two similar types of fields that let visitors type a lot of information to be submitted. This next form field type, a checkbox, lets your visitors select items from a list instead of typing the information themselves.

You probably are familiar with how checkboxes work. Mark a checkbox and its value is recorded as on, unmark one and its value is a negative, or off. On Web pages, checkboxes are useful for letting visitors select one or multiple related items from a list.

You must add each checkbox item individually. Add an empty checkbox to your page by choosing Insert | Form Field | Check Box from the menu. A small, unchecked box with no label appears within your current form. Immediately type a word or phrase that identifies this specific checkbox. Repeat this process until all the checkbox selections have been included on your page, as in Figure 23.7.

Figure 23.7.

Include as many checkboxes as you want within a specific page.

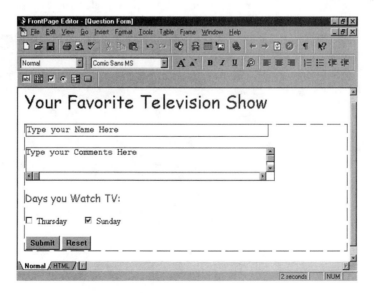

By default, all checkboxes on a Web page appear unmarked, waiting for visitors to click them. You can change this default setting by bringing up the Check Box Properties dialog box, shown in Figure 23.8.

Figure 23.8.

Check Box Properties lets you set the initial checkbox appearance when loaded in a Web browser.

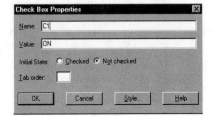

Radio Buttons

Radio buttons are similar to checkboxes, except that you can select only one item at a time from a list of radio buttons. To understand exactly how radio buttons work, think of how your car radio operates. At any given time, you can listen to only one station. Similarly, at any moment, visitors can mark only one radio button from a list.

To add a set of radio buttons to your Web page, follow these steps:

1. Choose Insert | Form Fields | Radio Button from the FrontPage menu. FrontPage generates a small round button and places it on your Web page. This is a radio button. You must type a label yourself, indicating what value is associated with this radio button. Figure 23.9 shows a single radio button added.

Figure 23.9.

Adding a radio button is essentially the same process as adding a checkbox.

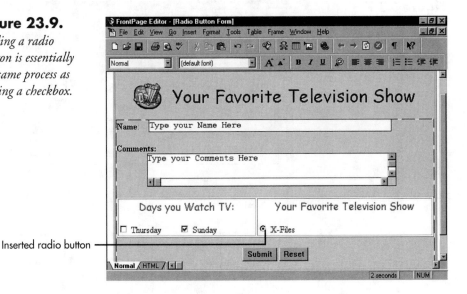

Inserted radio button

23

2. Repeat step 1 until you've added as many radio buttons as you'd like. Don't forget to add a text label next to each button. Remember, this label isn't saved when a visitor submits the form, it is just used to let them know which button they've selected.

3. Using your mouse, double-click the first radio button you added. This brings up the Radio Button Properties box, shown in Figure 23.10.

Figure 23.10.

Here's where you set properties for each individual button.

4. Change the Group Name box to be something relevant to the question you are asking. For this example, the group name will be TVShow. It is important that all radio buttons have the same group name. That's how FrontPage and the browser know that each radio button option is related to one another.

5. Change the value of this radio button to be similar to the text label you assigned it. It is this value that is saved when visitors click the Submit button for the form. Click OK when you are finished.

6. Repeat steps 4 and 5 for each radio button you've inserted on your page. Make sure that you give each button the same group name but a different value name.

After you've added and configured all the radio buttons to your Web page, you're just about finished. There is only one more type of form element you can use, a drop-down menu.

Drop-Down Menus

The final type of form element you'll commonly use in your site is the drop-down menu. Drop-down menus let your visitors select one item from a list of information you provide. They are intuitive and easy to use. To insert one on your page, follow these steps:

1. Choose Insert | Form Field | Drop-Down Menu from the FrontPage Editor's menu. Figure 23.11 shows how the empty drop-down menu appears on a Web page.

2. After you've added the drop-down menu to your form, the next step is to add choices for your visitors to select from. Double-click the empty drop-down menu to bring up the Drop-Down Menu Properties dialog box in Figure 23.12.

Figure 23.11.
Drop-down menus let users graphically select from a list of items.

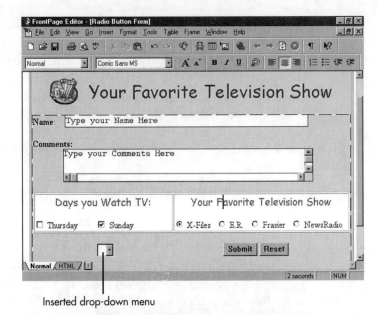

Inserted drop-down menu

Figure 23.12.
Adding a drop-down menu is the same process as adding a checkbox.

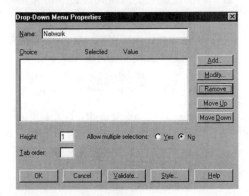

3. From here, you must add selectable items to the drop-down menu list. To add a new element to this list, click the Add button to bring up the Add Choice dialog box, shown in Figure 23.13.

Figure 23.13.
Every item in the drop-down list must be added individually.

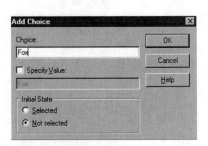

23

4. Type a phrase that your visitors can select from this drop-down menu and click OK.

5. Repeat step 4 until you've added all the necessary elements to your drop-down menu. Don't forget to name your drop-down list so that FrontPage can associate a pertinent name with the data your visitors select in this field.

6. After you've added all the elements to your drop-down list, click OK and FrontPage builds your drop-down menu box for you. Figure 23.14 shows how this final form with the drop-down menu looks.

23

Figure 23.14.

The completed form with nearly every type of field.

Drop-down menu

TIME SAVER

By default, drop-down menu lists are only one element tall, making you click the down arrow to see the entire list. With FrontPage, you can resize the drop-down box by dragging its bottom boundary down and expanding its size onscreen. The drop-down list then becomes a scrollbox in which you can see all the items available to choose from.

Submitting and Processing Your Form

After you've created all the elements on the form, you're nearly finished. All you have left to do is tell FrontPage what you want to do with your form data every time a visitor clicks the Submit button. After you've programmed the Submit button, this form page is finished and you can integrate it as part of your standard FrontPage Web. That's all there is to it.

By default, when visitors click your form Submit button, FrontPage sends them a standard message letting them know that their submission was complete, and then saves the visitors' answers in a private file on your Web server. Figure 23.15 shows the standard confirmation screen FrontPage shows when you click the Submit button within Netscape.

Figure 23.15.

FrontPage regurgitates everything that you selected so that you know what you've submitted.

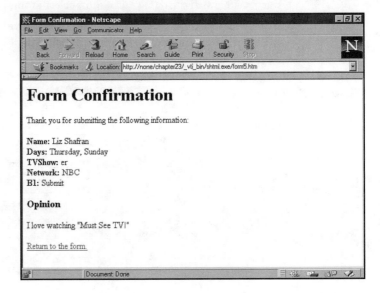

Then FrontPage takes the results of your form and writes them to a private file within your FrontPage Web called `form_results.txt`. You can find this file in the `_private` directory of your FrontPage Web. At any point, you can go through this result listing and see a tally of all your results.

You can change this default action to do several things instead of creating this `form_results.txt` file. Within the FrontPage Editor, move your mouse anywhere within the form boundaries and click the right mouse button. Select Form Properties from the pop-up box that appears. FrontPage brings up the Form Properties dialog box (see Figure 23.16).

There are several options available here, but only two that are critically important: the Send To box and the Options button. As you can tell, the default behavior when a form is submitted is to send the results to a specific file. You can easily change the results file that is created to a different name or directory. Or you can have the form results mailed to you at a particular e-mail address—very handy for receiving comments as soon as they are submitted.

The other choice in this dialog box that you'll want to worry about immediately is the Options button. This button configures exactly how the results are formatted as they're submitted (to a file or via e-mail). Figure 23.17 shows the Options for Saving Results of Form dialog box that appears when you click the Options button.

23

Figure 23.16.

You can change the default form action from here.

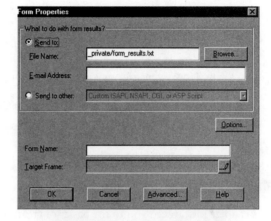

Figure 23.17.

Results can be saved to text files, HTML files, or even HTML bulleted lists.

You can explore the different options available to you when choosing the format and information to save as the Submit button is clicked. Click OK to save your form action options. After you set the submit action to your particular liking, your form is now finished!

TIME SAVER

A lot of people like to add interactive forms to their Web pages to act as guestbooks for people stopping by. They ask several questions from visitors and then post everyone's results publicly. Creating a guestbook-like application with FrontPage is easy; you've already done the difficult part by building the form.

You must configure two options within the Form Properties dialog box. First, save the submitted results to a file outside the _private directory. Try saving it to a file called `guestbook.html` (no subdirectory). Then click the Options button and choose HTML Bulleted List under File Format. Click OK to save your modifications.

Now, whenever anyone clicks the Submit button, your FrontPage Web server will save your changes to the `guestbook.html` file in a simple list format. Then elsewhere in your FrontPage Web, you can build a hyperlink to the `guestbook.html` file.

Summary

This chapter introduced you to the basics of creating interactive forms for your FrontPage Web. Forms are fantastic ways for you to gather data from your visitors on a variety of topics. Many people like to include comment forms from visitors that are e-mailed as soon as they're completed. Other developers build simple guestbooks or voting mechanisms to their sites.

You should feel comfortable with the different types of form elements discussed in this hour and understand how to assign a special action for FrontPage to complete when your visitors click the Submit button.

Q&A

Q Is there any way to rename the Submit button? I'd like it to say something like Sign Guestbook.

A Yes. You can replace the text label on the Submit button with just about anything you'd like. To change the text on the Submit button, double-click it to bring up the Push Button Properties dialog box. In the box named Value/Label, replace the word Submit with anything you want.

Q Why are the different form elements named? Can't FrontPage use the text labels I type next to each button and field?

A FrontPage has no way to identify that the text next to a radio button or checkbox is associated with a particular button, which is why you must name your form elements. When visitors click the Submit button, you are assigning a standard name to each form field and can look at the results and understand what they mean.

Q What were some of the advanced options available in the Form Properties dialog box that you didn't cover in this hour?

A In general, the Form Properties dialog box is geared toward controlling what happens after the Submit button has been clicked. There are several advanced options that let you configure your form to work with all sorts of different Web servers. In addition, you can add hidden fields, such as a date/time stamp to the submitted information that visitors don't even know gets included with every submission.

Workshop

The Workshop contains quiz questions and an Activities section to help reinforce what you've learned in this hour. Try not to look at the quiz answers until you've tried to work them out yourself!

Quiz

1. What's the overall process for creating an interactive form on any Web page?
2. What's special about radio buttons that requires them to use the same group name?
3. Why are all form elements contained within the dotted form boundary line?

Answers

1. a) Decide what type of form you want to create.

   b) Start adding appropriate form elements—text boxes, checkboxes, radio buttons, and drop-down menus. Configure each form element properly to fit your specific needs.

   c) Configure exactly what should happen when visitors click the Submit button. Decide whether you want the results saved to a file or e-mailed directly to your account.

2. You must group all radio button items together under the same name so that only one element can be selected at a time. Otherwise, FrontPage and your browser won't know that the radio button elements on your form are related to one another.

3. The form boundary lines, which appear only within the FrontPage Editor, group all elements on a specific form together with a single Submit button because you can have multiple forms on a single page.

23

Activities

1. Create the same form generated at the end of this chapter. Make sure that you add the same elements and try to format it similarly. This will give you experience in making all the different form elements and including them within tables as well.

2. Create a guestbook for your Web page that lets visitors publicly submit and see the results from all other visitors to your site.

3. Read Hour 24, "Finale: Building a Home Page from Scratch," to learn how to put all these important and useful concepts together to build a good-looking interactive Web site.

Hour **24**

Finale: Building a Home Page from Scratch

Welcome to the last hour in this book. This hour focuses on putting together all the lessons you've learned so far and helping you build your own great-looking Web site with FrontPage.

As you've learned in the last 23 hours, Microsoft FrontPage is a high-quality, flexible tool that makes Web building a relatively simple task. Whether you are formatting your text or creating advanced interactive forms, FrontPage usually is the right tool for the job. This hour puts all those features together to provide a step-by-step guide to building a cool FrontPage Web for yourself.

Specifically, in this hour you'll learn how to

☐ Build a step-by-step plan to create a complete Web site from scratch

☐ Use FrontPage themes, templates, and wizards in a practical manner

☐ Check for any last-minute important details for your site

Building Your Site—Step-by-Step

This hour takes you through the actual process of building a personal Web site, something you're likely to do with FrontPage. Each step is described in full detail so that you can see how quick and easy building a site is when you are familiar with how FrontPage works. After you complete this chapter, you should be able to apply the same concepts when you build a small business or corporate Web site to represent you on the WWW.

JUST A MINUTE

This chapter assumes that you have properly installed FrontPage on your computer and that it works without any difficulties. In addition, you must have a current Web browser installed and an Internet connection to which to publish your site.

Step 1: Starting FrontPage

The first step in creating your new personal Web is to start FrontPage from your computer. By default, FrontPage adds an icon to the Start menu in Windows 95. Click the Start button, and then choose Programs and Microsoft FrontPage (see Figure 24.1).

Figure 24.1.

Before you can create your site, first start FrontPage.

Step 2: Building the Default Site

After you click the FrontPage icon, the Getting Started dialog box appears, as shown in Figure 24.2. From here, you can choose to open an existing web or make a new one. For this example, select the radio button labeled Create a New FrontPage Web.

When you click OK, the New FrontPage Web dialog box appears. This dialog box, shown in Figure 24.3, asks you several important questions about the new Web you are creating.

Figure 24.2.

Do you want to open an existing Web or make a new one from scratch?

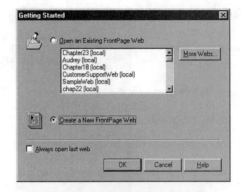

Figure 24.3.

What type of FrontPage Web do you want to build?

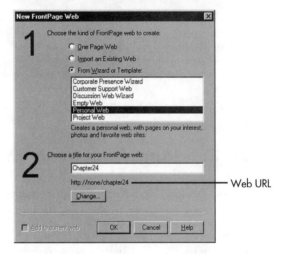

Web URL

FrontPage lets you select the type of new Web you want to create and then lets you assign it a name. For this example, you'll make a Web from a wizard or template, and then select the Personal Web option.

In addition, you can assign a specific name to this Web to keep it separate from the others you create with FrontPage. Type a title for your Web in the bottom of this dialog box. Notice how FrontPage builds the correct URL to this new site right below the title you type. When you are finished, click OK and FrontPage automatically creates a default site for you. Figure 24.4 shows your newly created Web site within the FrontPage Explorer.

Figure 24.4.

FrontPage takes care of building the initial Web pages for you.

The Web name ———

Your Web files ———

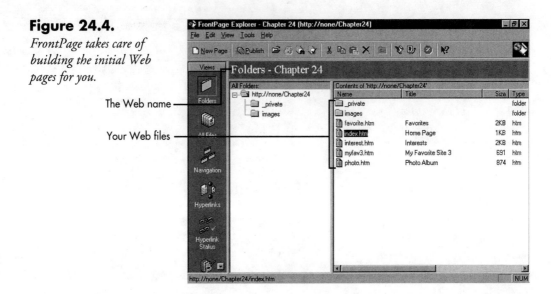

Take careful note of the URL that FrontPage lists for this site. You'll need it to use Netscape to browse your site.

Step 3: Setting Your Web Theme

After you create your initial set of Web pages, the next step is to assign an appropriate theme for your personal site. Remember that themes are coordinated sets of fonts, colors, and graphics that help make all the pages within a site fit with one another.

In the FrontPage Explorer, click on the Themes view (one of the icons scrolling down the left side of the screen). Click the button labeled Use Selected Theme, and then pick a theme from the list. FrontPage shows you a preview of each theme as you select it.

JUST A MINUTE

You might have more or less themes available for you to choose from depending on how you've installed FrontPage. The downloaded version of FrontPage comes with only a handful of different themes, whereas you get over four dozen different themes from which to choose when you install from a CD-ROM.

Figure 24.5 shows the Sumi Painting theme selected for this Web site.

24

Figure 24.5.

This theme adds class to your personal FrontPage Web site.

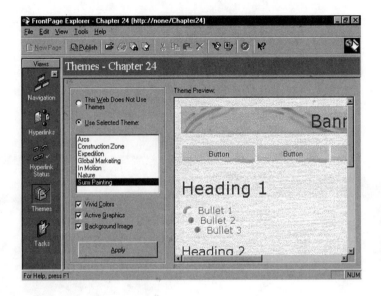

Step 4: Editing Your Home Page

In the FrontPage Explorer, switch back to the Folders view. A list of all the files in your Web appears on the right side of the screen. FrontPage has created five pages for this Web.

Using your mouse, double-click the file named index.htm; this is the default home page for your Web. FrontPage automatically starts up the Editor with index.htm ready to be edited (see Figure 24.6).

Figure 24.6.

You can add any text and images to this main home page.

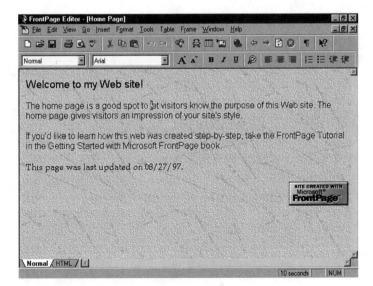

Now add a headline and a few paragraphs of text about yourself, replacing the default text FrontPage placed there for you.

Step 5: Add a Button Bar

After you've added text to your initial home page, build a button bar that links together all the pages in your Web. Within the FrontPage Editor, choose Insert | Navigation Bar from the menu. The Navigation Bar Properties dialog box appears (see Figure 24.7).

Figure 24.7.

Navigation bars dynamically build hyperlinks between all the pages in your Web.

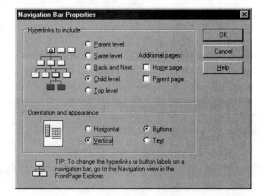

Select the type of navigation bar you want to include. The standard navigation bar builds hyperlinks to all child pages for each file in your Web. Click OK, and FrontPage inserts a set of graphical buttons that match the theme associated with your site. Figure 24.8 shows this nearly completed Web page.

Figure 24.8.

With matching buttons, headlines, and text, this initial page is almost complete!

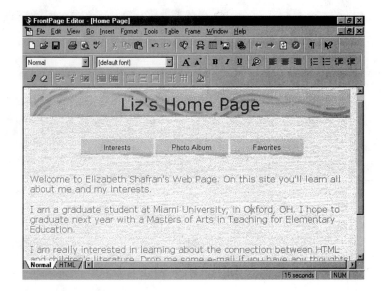

24

You can set which buttons appear in your navigation bar by looking in the Navigation view from the FrontPage Explorer. This view lets you graphically organize how the different pages in your Web are organized. The navigation bar changes depending on how the files in this view are hierarchically structured. For more information on navigation bars, see Hour 22, "Site Design Tips." Figure 24.9 shows the Navigation view for this personal FrontPage Web.

Figure 24.9.

The navigation for this small Web is relatively simple; all the other pages link off the main home page.

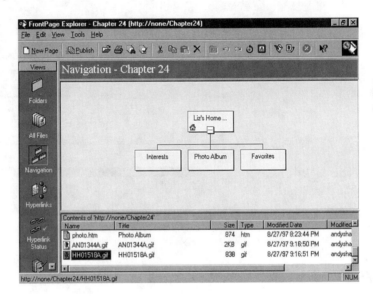

TIME SAVER

You can change the text that appears within each button on your pages by editing the label for your pages within the Navigation view in Figure 24.9. Click one time on a page with your mouse, and FrontPage lets you edit and change each page's label.

Step 6: Add Graphics

After you build your navigation bar, it is time to include some Web graphics in your site. Within the FrontPage Editor, choose Insert Clipart from the menu. The Microsoft Clip Gallery 3.0 dialog box appears (see Figure 24.10). Click the tab labeled Clip Art, and scroll to the bottom of the clip art categories. FrontPage added six new clip art categories geared specifically toward your Web pages.

After you've selected an image, FrontPage adds it to your page automatically. Now save your page and load it with your favorite browser. Figure 24.11 shows the nearly completed page in Netscape, complete with clip art, navigation bar, and information.

Figure 24.10.
There are hundreds of different clip art images you can easily use within your Web page.

Figure 24.11.
This page is just about finished!

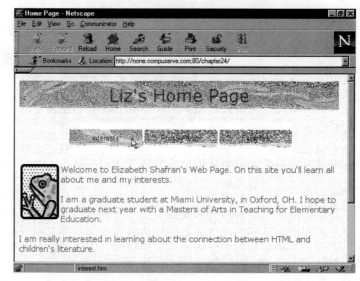

Notice how the button bars change their appearance when your mouse moves over them; this is a built-in Java program that helps you interact with your visitors.

Step 7: Finishing the Other Pages

After you've created the initial Web page, go back and edit the other pages that this FrontPage template built for you. They all look similar to your main home page but need your own specific information on them. There are three additional HTML pages you must edit:

Interests	Add a simple headline and a bulleted list of your favorite activities.
Photo Album	Include scanned photographs of you or important items.
Favorites	Link this page to other personal favorite sites across the WWW.

When you've finished editing these other three pages, you're ready to make your FrontPage Web accessible to the rest of the World!

JUST A MINUTE

> If three pages aren't enough for your own personal site, click the New Page icon within the FrontPage Explorer and add additional pages to your Web. Some people like to have special pages dedicated to their favorite bands, their family, or even about their job or business. You can include as many different pages as you'd like in your personal FrontPage Web.

24

Publishing Your Web

After you've created your initial set of Web pages, the last step is to copy them from your personal computer onto the public Internet, where anyone with a browser can see your pages.

Before you can upload your pages, you must first have a Web site that you can call home. Home is a spot on a computer connected to the Internet full time that lets you save your HTML files on it. To upload files, you must know the URL of your home page and have a username and password assigned to you, so that FrontPage can log in and send your Web to the Internet.

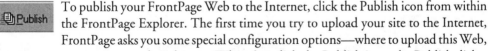

To publish your FrontPage Web to the Internet, click the Publish icon from within the FrontPage Explorer. The first time you try to upload your site to the Internet, FrontPage asks you some special configuration options—where to upload this Web, your username, password, and so on. When you click the Publish icon, the Publish dialog box appears (see Figure 24.12).

Figure 24.12.

Choose a spot to which to upload your site.

From the Publish dialog box, select a site onto which you want to upload your page. If you must create a new site, click the button labeled More Webs, and FrontPage steps you through building a new location to which you can send your files. Click OK, and FrontPage automatically begins to upload your pages.

CAUTION

> Before you click OK, make sure that you have started your Internet connection and can browse different pages using your browser. FrontPage needs a live Internet connection to properly upload your pages.

After your pages are uploaded, you can visit that site with your browser, and your entire personal Web site has been created.

JUST A MINUTE

> This section just glosses over the page publishing process. For more detailed information on uploading your pages to the WWW, read Hour 17, "Publishing to the WWW."

Summary

This hour stepped you through the entire process of creating a new personal Web site from scratch. By breaking down the difficult steps into a few manageable chunks, you learned how to build a site in under a few hours. FrontPage is such a useful and flexible tool, it enables you to build exciting and interactive sets of Web pages without doing much more than typing your own personal information.

Because this is the final hour in the book, you should now feel confident about using FrontPage to build your own Webs. This hour summarized some of the key points to building cool Web sites, but most of the material should have been familiar to you.

24

Q&A

Q **This hour focuses on using a template to create a FrontPage Web. When the new Web was created, you had me use the Personal Web template in step 2. Is there anything special I must know to use a different template or wizard?**

A The Personal Web template is the easiest to create and initially learn when first starting out with FrontPage 98. Feel free to use any of the other templates or wizards that come with FrontPage; however, they are more complicated. As a general rule, start out using the individual features you want by reading through the various hours in this book. Then create an entire site using the Personal Web template. When you understand these concepts, try to create a new site from the Project Web template. That template is an extension of the Personal Web template and adds several more pages and features you must learn. After that, you should be ready to handle just about anything FrontPage can throw at you.

Q **After looking at the different themes, I decided I'd rather edit the text and font appearance of my pages manually. How can I remove all pieces of a theme from my site?**

A You can easily remove themes from your site within the FrontPage Explorer. Click the Themes view, and select the radio button labeled This Web Does Not Use Themes. Then click the Apply button, and all traces of themes in this site are gone.

Of course, you can always edit and change the way your text appears, even with a theme assigned to your Web. Any font and text appearance changes you make take precedence over the defaults provided by a FrontPage theme.

Workshop

The Workshop contains quiz questions and an Activities section to help reinforce what you've learned in this hour. Try not to look at the quiz answers until you've tried to work them out yourself!

Quiz

1. What are three ways you can add large headlines to the top of your Web page?
2. How can you include a button bar in your site?

Answers

1. a) If your page uses themes, you can add a special FrontPage component called a page banner. This page banner matches your site theme and displays the text that appears in the Navigation view for the Web page.

    b) You can type a phrase of text and mark it as a Heading 1 style from the style bar within the FrontPage Editor.

    c) You can select the text you want to use as a headline and click the right mouse button. Choose Font Properties from the pop-up box that appears and set the attributes of this text. You can change the text size, color, and font from here.

2. Within the FrontPage Editor, choose Insert | Navigation Bar from the menu. FrontPage automatically adds a set of buttons to your page that links to a certain set of documents. FrontPage lets you configure whether hyperlinks are built to child files, parent documents, or other combinations of files in your current FrontPage Web.

Activities

1. Follow the steps associated in this chapter to build your complete Web site. Improve on the standard Personal Web template by adding a handful of additional pages to your Web. Then publish it to the Internet. Finally, stop by `http://www.shafran.com/frontpage98` to post your URL to other readers of this book so that you can showcase your creativity and Web talents.

2. Now that you've sucked all the useful information from this book, head to your local bookstore and pick up *FrontPage 98 Unleashed* by Sams.net Publishing, the huge tome of everything there is to know about Microsoft FrontPage. You'll learn intricate functionality and advanced features that couldn't be covered in this introductory book.

24

Appendix A

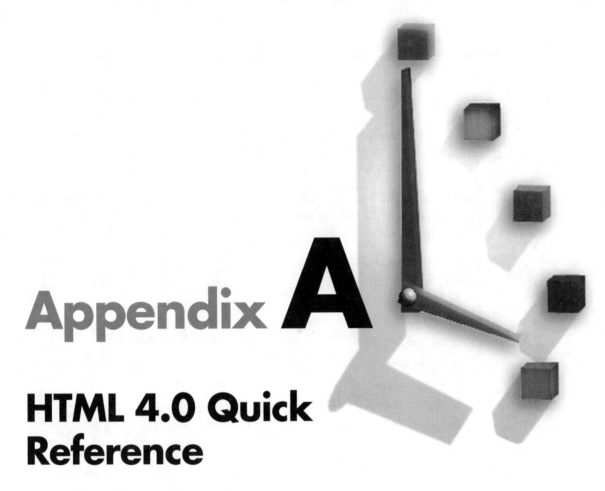

HTML 4.0 Quick Reference

by Bob Correll

HTML 4.0 is an ambitious attempt to meet the needs of Web developers worldwide, both casual and professional. This appendix provides a quick reference to all the elements and attributes of the language.

This appendix is based on the information provided in the *HTML 4.0 Specification W3C Working Draft 8-July-1997*, which can be found at `http://www.w3.org/TR/WD-html40/`.

In order to make the information readily accessible, this appendix organizes HTML elements by their function in the following order:

- ☐ Structure
- ☐ Text phrases and paragraphs
- ☐ Text font elements
- ☐ Lists
- ☐ Links
- ☐ Tables
- ☐ Frames
- ☐ Embedded content
- ☐ Style
- ☐ Forms
- ☐ Scripts

Within each section the elements are listed alphabetically and the following information is presented:

- ☐ Usage—A general description of the element
- ☐ Start/End Tag—Indicates whether these tags are required, optional, or illegal
- ☐ Attributes—Lists the attributes of the element with a short description of their effect
- ☐ Empty—Indicates whether the element can be empty
- ☐ Notes—Relates any special considerations when using the element and indicates whether the element is new, deprecated, or obsolete

Several elements and attributes have been *deprecated*, which means that they have been outdated by the current HTML version, and you should avoid using them. The same or similar functionality is provided using new features.

A

HTML 4.0 introduces several new attributes that apply to a significant number of elements. These are referred to as %coreattrbs, %i18n, and %events and are explained in the last section of the appendix.

Following this section, the common attributes (those with a % in front of them) and intrinsic events are summarized.

Structure

HTML relies upon several elements to provide structure to a document (as opposed to structuring the text within), as well as provide information that is used by the browser or search engines.

`<BDO>...</BDO>`

Usage	The bidirectional algorithm element is used to selectively turn off the default text direction.
Start/End Tag	Required/Required
Attributes	`lang="..."`—The language of the document.
	`dir="..."`—The text direction (`ltr`, `rtl`).
Empty	No
Notes	The `dir` attribute is mandatory.

`<BODY>...</BODY>`

Usage	Contains the content of the document.
Start/End Tag	Optional/Optional
Attributes	`%coreattrs, %i18n, %events`
	`background="..."`—Deprecated. URL for the background image.
	`bgcolor="..."`—Deprecated. Sets background color.
	`text="..."`—Deprecated. Text color.
	`link="..."`—Deprecated. Link color.
	`vlink="..."`—Deprecated. Visited link color.
	`alink="..."`—Deprecated. Active link color.
	`onload="..."`—Intrinsic event triggered when the document loads.
	`onunload="..."`—Intrinsic event triggered when document unloads.

Empty	No
Notes	There can be only one BODY and it must follow the HEAD. The BODY element can be replaced by a FRAMESET element. The presentational attributes are deprecated in favor of setting these values with style sheets.

Comments <!-- ... -->

Usage	Used to insert notes or scripts that are not displayed by the browser.
Start/End Tag	Required/Required
Attributes	None
Empty	Yes
Notes	Comments are not restricted to one line and can be any length. The end tag is not required to be on the same line as the start tag.

<DIV>...</DIV>

Usage	The division element is used to add structure to a block of text.
Start/End Tag	Required/Required
Attributes	%coreattrs, %i18n, %events align="..."—Deprecated. Controls alignment (left, center, right, justify).
Empty	No
Notes	Cannot be used within a P element. The align attribute is deprecated in favor of controlling alignment through style sheets.

<!DOCTYPE...>

Usage	Version information appears on the first line of an HTML document and is a Standard Generalized Markup Language (SGML) declaration rather than an element.

<H1>...</H1> through <H6>...</H6>

Usage	The six headings (H1 is the uppermost, or most important) are used in the BODY to structure information in a hierarchical fashion.
Start/End Tag	Required/Required

A

Attributes   %coreattrs, %i18n, %events
                  align="..."—Deprecated. Controls alignment (left,
                  center, right, justify).
Empty   No
Notes   Visual browsers will display the size of the headings in
                  relation to their importance, with H1 being the largest
                  and H6 the smallest. The align attribute is deprecated in
                  favor of controlling alignment through style sheets.

<HEAD>...</HEAD>

Usage   This is the document header and contains other ele-
                  ments that provide information to users and search
                  engines.
Start/End Tag   Optional/Optional
Attributes   %i18n
                  profile="..."—URL specifying the location of META
                  data.
Empty   No
Notes   There can be only one HEAD per document. It must
                  follow the opening HTML tag and precede the BODY.

<HR>

Usage   Horizontal rules are used to separate sections of a Web
                  page.
Start/End Tag   Required/Illegal
Attributes   %coreattrs, %events
                  align="..."—Deprecated. Controls alignment (left,
                  center, right, justify).
                  noshade="..."—Displays the rule as a solid color.
                  size="..."—Deprecated. The size of the rule.
                  width="..."—Deprecated. The width of the rule.
Empty   Yes

<HTML>...</HTML>

Usage   The HTML element contains the entire document.
Start/End Tag   Optional/Optional
Attributes   %i18n
                  version="..."—URL of the document type definition
                  specifying the HTML version used to create the
                  document.

Empty	No
Notes	The version information is duplicated in the `<!DOCTYPE...>` declaration and is therefore not essential.

\<META\>

Usage	Provides information about the document.
Start/End Tag	Required/Illegal
Attributes	`%i18n`
	`http-equiv="..."`—HTTP response header name.
	`name="..."`—Name of the meta information.
	`content="..."`—Content of the meta information.
	`scheme="..."`—Assigns a scheme to interpret the meta data.
Empty	Yes

\<SPAN\>...\</SPAN\>

Usage	Organizes the document by defining a span of text.
Start/End Tag	Required/Required
Attributes	`%coreattrs, %i18n, %events`
Empty	No

\<TITLE\>...\</TITLE\>

Usage	This is the name you give your Web page. The TITLE element is located in the HEAD element and is displayed in the browser window title bar.
Start/End Tag	Required/Required
Attributes	`%i18n`
Empty	No
Notes	Only one title allowed per document.

Text Phrases and Paragraphs

Text phrases (or blocks) can be structured to suit a specific purpose, such as creating a paragraph. This should not be confused with modifying the formatting of the text.

\<ACRONYM\>...\</ACRONYM\>

Usage	Used to define acronyms.
Start/End Tag	Required/Required
Attributes	`%coreattrs, %i18n, %events`
Empty	No

A

<ADDRESS>...</ADDRESS>

Usage	Provides a special format for author or contact information.
Start/End Tag	Required/Required
Attributes	%coreattrs, %i18n, %events
Empty	No
Notes	The BR element is commonly used inside the ADDRESS element to break the lines of an address.

<BLOCKQUOTE>...</BLOCKQUOTE>

Usage	Used to display long quotations.
Start/End Tag	Required/Required
Attributes	%coreattrs, %i18n, %events
	cite="..."—The URL of the quoted text.
Empty	No

Usage	Forces a line break.
Start/End Tag	Required/Illegal
Attributes	%coreattrs, %i18n, %events
	clear="..."—Sets the location where next line begins after a floating object (none, left, right, all).
Empty	Yes

<CITE>...</CITE>

Usage	Cites a reference.
Start/End Tag	Required/Required
Attributes	%coreattrs, %i18n, %events
Empty	No

<CODE>...</CODE>

Usage	Identifies a code fragment for display.
Start/End Tag	Required/Required
Attributes	%coreattrs, %i18n, %events
Empty	No

\<DEL\>...\</DEL\>

Usage	Shows text as having been deleted from the document since the last change.
Start/End Tag	Required/Required
Attributes	%coreattrs, %i18n, %events
	cite="..."—The URL of the source document.
	datetime="..."—Indicates the date and time of the change.
Empty	No
Notes	New element in HTML 4.0.

\<DFN\>...\</DFN\>

Usage	Defines an enclosed term.
Start/End Tag	Required/Required
Attributes	%coreattrs, %i18n, %events
Empty	No

\<EM\>...\</EM\>

Usage	Emphasized text.
Start/End Tag	Required/Required
Attributes	%coreattrs, %i18n, %events
Empty	No

\<INS\>...\</INS\>

Usage	Shows text as having been inserted in the document since the last change.
Start/End Tag	Required/Required
Attributes	%coreattrs, %i18n, %events
	cite="..."—The URL of the source document.
	datetime="..."—Indicates the date and time of the change.
Empty	No
Notes	New element in HTML 4.0.

\<KBD\>...\</KBD\>

Usage	Indicates text a user would type.
Start/End Tag	Required/Required
Attributes	%coreattrs, %i18n, %events
Empty	No

<P>...</P>

Usage	Defines a paragraph.
Start/End Tag	Required/Optional
Attributes	%coreattrs, %i18n, %events
	align="..."—Deprecated. Controls alignment (left, center, right, justify).
Empty	No

<PRE>...</PRE>

Usage	Displays preformatted text.
Start/End Tag	Required/Required
Attributes	%coreattrs, %i18n, %events
	width="..."—The width of the formatted text.
Empty	No

<Q>...</Q>

Usage	Used to display short quotations that do not require paragraph breaks.
Start/End Tag	Required/Required
Attributes	%coreattrs, %i18n, %events
	cite="..."—The URL of the quoted text.
Empty	No
Notes	New element in HTML 4.0.

<SAMP>...</SAMP>

Usage	Identifies sample output.
Start/End Tag	Required/Required
Attributes	%coreattrs, %i18n, %events
Empty	No

<STRONG>...</STRONG>

Usage	Stronger emphasis.
Start/End Tag	Required/Required
Attributes	%coreattrs, %i18n, %events
Empty	No

_{...}

Usage	Creates subscript.
Start/End Tag	Required/Required
Attributes	%coreattrs, %i18n, %events
Empty	No

`<SUP>...</SUP>`

Usage	Creates superscript.
Start/End Tag	Required/Required
Attributes	%coreattrs, %i18n, %events
Empty	No

`<VAR>...</VAR>`

Usage	A variable.
Start/End Tag	Required/Required
Attributes	%coreattrs, %i18n, %events
Empty	No

Text Formatting Elements

Text characteristics such as the size, weight, and style can be modified using these elements, but the HTML 4.0 specification encourages you to use style instead.

`<B>...</B>`

Usage	Bold text.
Start/End Tag	Required/Required
Attributes	%coreattrs, %i18n, %events
Empty	No

`<BASEFONT>`

Usage	Sets the base font size.
Start/End Tag	Required/Illegal
Attributes	size="..."—The font size (1 through 7 or relative, that is +3).
	color="..."—The font color.
	face="..."—The font type.
Empty	Yes
Notes	Deprecated in favor of style sheets.

`<BIG>...</BIG>`

Usage	Large text.
Start/End Tag	Required/Required
Attributes	%coreattrs, %i18n, %events
Empty	No

A

`<FONT>...</FONT>`

Usage	Changes the font size and color.
Start/End Tag	Required/Required
Attributes	`size="..."`—The font size (1 through 7 or relative, that is, +3).
	`color="..."`—The font color.
	`face="..."`—The font type.
Empty	No
Notes	Deprecated in favor of style sheets.

`<I>...</I>`

Usage	Italicized text.
Start/End Tag	Required/Required
Attributes	`%coreattrs, %i18n, %events`
Empty	No

`<S>...</S>`

Usage	Strikethrough text.
Start/End Tag	Required/Required
Attributes	`%coreattrs, %i18n, %events`
Empty	No
Notes	Deprecated.

`<SMALL>...</SMALL>`

Usage	Small text.
Start/End Tag	Required/Required
Attributes	`%coreattrs, %i18n, %events`
Empty	No

`<STRIKE>...</STRIKE>`

Usage	Strikethrough text.
Start/End Tag	Required/Required
Attributes	`%coreattrs, %i18n, %events`
Empty	No
Notes	Deprecated.

`<TT>...</TT>`

Usage	Teletype (or monospaced) text.
Start/End Tag	Required/Required
Attributes	`%coreattrs, %i18n, %events`
Empty	No

`<U>...</U>`

Usage	Underlined text.
Start/End Tag	Required/Required
Attributes	%coreattrs, %i18n, %events
Empty	No
Notes	Deprecated.

Lists

You can organize text into a more structured outline by creating lists. Lists can be nested.

`<DD>...</DD>`

Usage	The definition description used in a DL (definition list) element.
Start/End Tag	Required/Optional
Attributes	%coreattrs, %i18n, %events
Empty	No
Notes	Can contain block-level content, such as the `<P>` element.

`<DIR>...</DIR>`

Usage	Creates a multi-column directory list.
Start/End Tag	Required/Required
Attributes	%coreattrs, %i18n, %events
	compact—Deprecated. Compacts the displayed list.
Empty	No
Notes	Must contain at least one list item. This element is deprecated in favor of the UL (unordered list) element.

`<DL>...</DL>`

Usage	Creates a definition list.
Start/End Tag	Required/Required
Attributes	%coreattrs, %i18n, %events
	compact—Deprecated. Compacts the displayed list.
Empty	No
Notes	Must contain at least one `<DT>` or `<DD>` element in any order.

`<DT>...</DT>`

Usage	The definition term (or label) used within a DL (definition list) element.
Start/End Tag	Required/Optional
Attributes	%coreattrs, %i18n, %events
Empty	No
Notes	Must contain text (which can be modified by text markup elements).

`<LI>...</LI>`

Usage	Defines a list item within a list.
Start/End Tag	Required/Optional
Attributes	%coreattrs, %i18n, %events
	type="..."—Changes the numbering style (1, a, A, i, I), ordered lists, or bullet style (disc, square, circle) in unordered lists.
	value="..."—Sets the numbering to the given integer beginning with the current list item.
Empty	No

`<MENU>...</MENU>`

Usage	Creates a single-column menu list.
Start/End Tag	Required/Required
Attributes	%coreattrs, %i18n, %events
	compact—Deprecated. Compacts the displayed list.
Empty	No
Notes	Must contain at least one list item. This element is deprecated in favor of the UL (unordered list) element.

`<OL>...</OL>`

Usage	Creates an ordered list.
Start/End Tag	Required/Required
Attributes	%coreattrs, %i18n, %events
	type="..."—Sets the numbering style (1, a, A, i, I).
	compact—Deprecated. Compacts the displayed list.
	start="..."—Sets the starting number to the chosen integer.
Empty	No
Notes	Must contain at least one list item.

A

<UL>...</UL>

Usage	Creates an unordered list.
Start/End Tag	Required/Required
Attributes	%coreattrs, %i18n, %events
	type="..."—Sets the bullet style (disc, square, circle).
	compact—Deprecated. Compacts the displayed list.
Empty	No
Notes	Must contain at least one list item.

Links

Hyperlinking is fundamental to HTML. These elements enable you to link to other documents.

<A>...</A>

Usage	Used to define links and anchors.
Start/End Tag	Required/Required
Attributes	%coreattrs, %i18n, %events
	charset="..."—Character encoding of the resource.
	name="..."—Defines an anchor.
	href="..."—The URL of the linked resource.
	target="..."—Determines where the resource will be displayed (user-defined name, _blank, _parent, _self, _top).
	rel="..."—Forward link types.
	rev="..."—Reverse link types.
	accesskey="..."—Assigns a hotkey to this element.
	shape="..."—Enables you to define client-side imagemaps using defined shapes (default, rect, circle, poly).
	coords="..."—Sets the size of the shape using pixel or percentage lengths.
	tabindex="..."—Sets the tabbing order between elements with a defined tabindex.
Empty	No

<BASE>

Usage	All other URLs in the document are resolved against this location.
Start/End Tag	Required/Illegal

Attributes	href="..."—The URL of the linked resource.
	target="..."—Determines where the resource will be displayed (user-defined name, _blank, _parent, _self, top).
Empty	Yes
Notes	Located in the document HEAD.

<LINK>

Usage	Defines the relationship between a link and a resource.
Start/End Tag	Required/Illegal
Attributes	%coreattrs, %i18n, %events
	href="..."—The URL of the resource.
	rel="..."—The forward link types.
	rev="..."—The reverse link types.
	type="..."—The Internet content type.
	media="..."—Defines the destination medium (screen, print, projection, braille, speech, all).
	target="..."—Determines where the resource will be displayed (user-defined name, _blank, _parent, _self, _top).
Empty	Yes
Notes	Located in the document HEAD.

Tables

Tables are meant to display data in a tabular format. Before the introduction of HTML 4.0, tables were widely used for page layout purposes, but with the advent of style sheets this is being discouraged by the W3C.

<CAPTION>...</CAPTION>

Usage	Displays a table caption.
Start/End Tag	Required/Required
Attributes	%coreattrs, %i18n, %events
	align="..."—Deprecated. Controls alignment (left, center, right, justify).
Empty	No
Notes	Optional.

<COL>

Usage	Groups columns within column groups in order to share attribute values.
Start/End Tag	Required/Illegal
Attributes	%coreattrs, %i18n, %events

span="..."—The number of columns the group contains.

width="..."—The column width as a percentage, pixel value, or minimum value.

align="..."—Horizontally aligns the contents of cells (left, center, right, justify, char).

char="..."—Sets a character on which the column aligns.

charoff="..."—Offset to the first alignment character on a line.

valign="..."—Vertically aligns the contents of a cell (top, middle, bottom, baseline).

Empty	Yes

<COLGROUP>...</COLGROUP>

Usage	Defines a column group.
Start/End Tag	Required/Optional
Attributes	%coreattrs, %i18n, %events

span="..."—The number of columns in a group.

width="..."—The width of the columns.

align="..."—Horizontally aligns the contents of cells (left, center, right, justify, char).

char="..."—Sets a character on which the column aligns.

charoff="..."—Offset to the first alignment character on a line.

valign="..."—Vertically aligns the contents of a cell (top, middle, bottom, baseline).

Empty	No

<TABLE>...</TABLE>

Usage	Creates a table.
Start/End Tag	Required/Required
Attributes	%coreattrs, %i18n, %events

align="..."—Deprecated. Controls alignment (left, center, right, justify).

A

bgcolor="..."—Deprecated. Sets the background color.
width="..."—Table width.
cols="..."—The number of columns.
border="..."—The width in pixels of a border around
the table.
frame="..."—Sets the visible sides of a table (void,
above, below, hsides, lhs, rhs, vsides, box, border).
rules="..."—Sets the visible rules within a table (none,
groups, rows, cols, all).
cellspacing="..."—Spacing between cells.
cellpadding="..."—Spacing in cells.

Empty   No

`<TBODY>...</TBODY>`

Usage   Defines the table body.
Start/End Tag   Optional/Optional
Attributes   %coreattrs, %i18n, %events
align="..."—Horizontally aligns the contents of cells
(left, center, right, justify, char).
char="..."—Sets a character on which the column
aligns.
charoff="..."—Offset to the first alignment character
on a line.
valign="..."—Vertically aligns the contents of cells
(top, middle, bottom, baseline).

Empty   No

`<TD>...</TD>`

Usage   Defines a cell's contents.
Start/End Tag   Required/Optional
Attributes   %coreattrs, %i18n, %events
axis="..."—Abbreviated name.
axes="..."—axis names listing row and column
headers pertaining to the cell.
nowrap="..."—Deprecated. Turns off text wrapping in
a cell.
bgcolor="..."—Deprecated. Sets the background color.
rowspan="..."—The number of rows spanned by a cell.
colspan="..."—The number of columns spanned by a
cell.

A

align="..."—Horizontally aligns the contents of cells (left, center, right, justify, char).
char="..."—Sets a character on which the column aligns.
charoff="..."—Offset to the first alignment character on a line.
valign="..."—Vertically aligns the contents of cells (top, middle, bottom, baseline).

Empty   No

\<TFOOT>...\</TFOOT>

Usage   Defines the table footer.
Start/End Tag   Required/Optional
Attributes   %coreattrs, %i18n, %events
align="..."—Horizontally aligns the contents of cells (left, center, right, justify, char).
char="..."—Sets a character on which the column aligns.
charoff="..."—Offset to the first alignment character on a line.
valign="..."—Vertically aligns the contents of cells (top, middle, bottom, baseline).

Empty   No

\<TH>...\</TH>

Usage   Defines the cell contents of the table header.
Start/End Tag   Required/Optional
Attributes   %coreattrs, %i18n, %events
axis="..."—Abbreviated name.
axes="..."—axis names listing row and column headers pertaining to the cell.
nowrap="..."—Deprecated. Turns off text wrapping in a cell.
bgcolor="..."—Deprecated. Sets the background color.
rowspan="..."—The number of rows spanned by a cell.
colspan="..."—The number of columns spanned by a cell.
align="..."—Horizontally aligns the contents of cells (left, center, right, justify, char).

char="..."—Sets a character on which the column
aligns.
charoff="..."—Offset to the first alignment character
on a line.
valign="..."—Vertically aligns the contents of cells
(top, middle, bottom, baseline).

Empty   No

`<THEAD>...</THEAD>`

Usage   Defines the table header.
Start/End Tag   Required/Optional
Attributes   %coreattrs, %i18n, %events
                               align="..."—Horizontally aligns the contents of cells
                               (left, center, right, justify, char).
                               char="..."—Sets a character on which the column
                               aligns.
                               charoff="..."—Offset to the first alignment character
                               on a line.
                               valign="..."—Vertically aligns the contents of cells
                               (top, middle, bottom, baseline).
Empty   No

`<TR>...</TR>`

Usage   Defines a row of table cells.
Start/End Tag   Required/Optional
Attributes   %coreattrs, %i18n, %events
                               align="..."—Horizontally aligns the contents of cells
                               (left, center, right, justify, char).
                               char="..."—Sets a character on which the column
                               aligns.
                               charoff="..."—Offset to the first alignment character
                               on a line.
                               valign="..."—Vertically aligns the contents of cells
                               (top, middle, bottom, baseline).
                               bgcolor="..."—Deprecated. Sets the background color.
Empty   No

A

Frames

Frames create new "panels" in the Web browser window that are used to display content from different source documents.

\<FRAME\>

Usage	Defines a FRAME.
Start/End Tag	Required/Illegal
Attributes	name="..."—The name of a frame.
	src="..."—The source to be displayed in a frame.
	frameborder="..."—Toggles the border between frames (0, 1).
	marginwidth="..."—Sets the space between the frame border and content.
	marginheight="..."—Sets the space between the frame border and content.
	noresize—Disables sizing.
	scrolling="..."—Determines scrollbar presence (auto, yes, no).
Empty	Yes

\<FRAMESET\>...\</FRAMESET\>

Usage	Defines the layout of FRAMES within a window.
Start/End Tag	Required/Required
Attributes	rows="..."—The number of rows.
	cols="..."—The number of columns.
	onload="..."—The intrinsic event triggered when the document loads.
	onunload="..."—The intrinsic event triggered when the document unloads.
Empty	No
Notes	FRAMESETs can be nested.

\<IFRAME\>...\</IFRAME\>

Usage	Creates an inline frame.
Start/End Tag	Required/Required
Attributes	name="..."—The name of the frame.
	src="..."—The source to be displayed in a frame.
	frameborder="..."—Toggles the border between frames (0, 1).
	marginwidth="..."—Sets the space between the frame border and content.

A

marginheight="..."—Sets the space between the frame border and content.
scrolling="..."—Determines scrollbar presence (auto, yes, no).
align="..."—Deprecated. Controls alignment (left, center, right, justify).
height="..."—Height.
width="..."—Width.

Empty	No

<NOFRAMES>...</NOFRAMES>

Usage	Alternative content when frames are not supported.
Start/End Tag	Required/Required
Attributes	None.
Empty	No

Embedded Content

Also called inclusions, embedded content applies to Java applets, imagemaps, and other multimedia or programattical content that is placed in a Web page to provide additional functionality.

<APPLET>...</APPLET>

Usage	Includes a Java applet.
Start/End Tag	Required/Required
Attributes	codebase="..."—The URL base for the applet.
	archive="..."—Identifies the resources to be preloaded.
	code="..."—The applet class file.
	object="..."—The serialized applet file.
	alt="..."—Displays text while loading.
	name="..."—The name of the applet.
	width="..."—The height of the displayed applet.
	height="..."—The width of the displayed applet.
	align="..."—Deprecated. Controls alignment (left, center, right, justify).
	hspace="..."—The horizontal space separating the image from other content.
	vspace="..."—The vertical space separating the image from other content.
Empty	No
Notes	Applet is deprecated in favor of the OBJECT element.

A

\<AREA\>

Usage	The AREA element is used to define links and anchors.
Start/End Tag	Required/Illegal
Attributes	shape="..."—Enables you to define client-side imagemaps using defined shapes (default, rect, circle, poly).
	coords="..."—Sets the size of the shape using pixel or percentage lengths.
	href="..."—The URL of the linked resource.
	target="..."—Determines where the resource will be displayed (user-defined name, _blank, _parent, _self, _top).
	nohref="..."—Indicates that the region has no action.
	alt="..."—Displays alternative text.
	tabindex="..."—Sets the tabbing order between elements with a defined tabindex.
Empty	Yes

\<IMG\>

Usage	Includes an image in the document.
Start/End Tag	Required/Illegal
Attributes	%coreattrs, %i18n, %events
	src="..."—The URL of the image.
	alt="..."—Alternative text to display.
	align="..."—Deprecated. Controls alignment (left, center, right, justify).
	height="..."—The height of the image.
	width="..."—The width of the image.
	border="..."—Border width.
	hspace="..."—The horizontal space separating the image from other content.
	vspace="..."—The vertical space separating the image from other content.
	usemap="..."—The URL to a client-side imagemap.
	ismap—Identifies a server-side imagemap.
Empty	Yes

A

\<MAP\>...\</MAP\>

Usage	When used with the AREA element, creates a client-side imagemap.
Start/End Tag	Required/Required
Attributes	%coreattrs
	name="..."—The name of the imagemap to be created.
Empty	No

\<OBJECT\>...\</OBJECT\>

Usage	Includes an object.
Start/End Tag	Required/Required
Attributes	%coreattrs, %i18n, %events
	declare—A flag that declares but doesn't create an object.
	classid="..."—The URL of the object's location.
	codebase="..."—The URL for resolving URLs specified by other attributes.
	data="..."—The URL to the object's data.
	type="..."—The Internet content type for data.
	codetype="..."—The Internet content type for the code.
	standby="..."—Show message while loading.
	align="..."—Deprecated. Controls alignment (left, center, right, justify).
	height="..."—The height of the object.
	width="..."—The width of the object.
	border="..."—Displays the border around an object.
	hspace="..."—The space between the sides of the object and other page content.
	vspace="..."—The space between the top and bottom of the object and other page content.
	usemap="..."—The URL to an imagemap.
	shapes=—Enables you to define areas to search for hyperlinks if the object is an image.
	name="..."—The URL to submit as part of a form.
	tabindex="..."—Sets the tabbing order between elements with a defined tabindex.
Empty	No

A

<PARAM>

Usage	Initializes an object.
Start/End Tag	Required/Illegal
Attributes	`name="..."`—Defines the parameter name.
	`value="..."`—The value of the object parameter.
	`valuetype="..."`—Defines the value type (`data`, `ref`, `object`).
	`type="..."`—The Internet media type.
Empty	Yes

Style

Style sheets (both inline and external) are incorporated into an HTML document through the use of the STYLE element.

<STYLE>...</STYLE>

Usage	Creates an internal style sheet.
Start/End Tag	Required/Required
Attributes	`%i18n`
	`type="..."`—The Internet content type.
	`media="..."`—Defines the destination medium (`screen`, `print`, `projection`, `braille`, `speech`, `all`).
	`title="..."`—The title of the style.
Empty	No
Notes	Located in the HEAD element.

Forms

Forms create an interface for the user to select options and submit data back to the Web server.

<BUTTON>...</BUTTON>

Usage	Creates a button.
Start/End Tag	Required/Required
Attributes	`%coreattrs, %i18n, %events`
	`name="..."`—The button name.
	`value="..."`—The value of the button.
	`type="..."`—The button type (`button`, `submit`, `reset`).
	`disabled="..."`—Sets the button state to disabled.
	`tabindex="..."`—Sets the tabbing order between elements with a defined `tabindex`.

A

onfocus="..."—The event that occurs when the element receives focus.

onblur="..."—The event that occurs when the element loses focus.

Empty   No

\<FIELDSET>...\</FIELDSET>

Usage	Groups related controls.
Start/End Tag	Required/Required
Attributes	%coreattrs, %i18n, %events
Empty	No

\<FORM>...\</FORM>

Usage   Creates a form that holds controls for user input.

Start/End Tag   Required/Required

Attributes   %coreattrs, %i18n, %events

action="..."—The URL for the server action.

method="..."—The HTTP method (get, post). get is deprecated.

enctype="..."—Specifies the MIME (Internet media type).

onsubmit="..."—The intrinsic event that occurs when the form is submitted.

onreset="..."—The intrinsic event that occurs when the form is reset.

target="..."—Determines where the resource will be displayed (user-defined name, _blank, _parent, _self, _top).

accept-charset="..."—The list of character encodings.

Empty   No

\<INPUT>

Usage   Defines controls used in forms.

Start/End Tag   Required/Illegal

Attributes   %coreattrs, %i18n, %events

type="..."—The type of input control (text, password, checkbox, radio, submit, reset, file, hidden, image, button).

name="..."—The name of the control (required except for submit and reset).

value="..."—The initial value of the control (required for radio and checkboxes).

`checked="..."`—Sets the radio buttons to a checked state.

`disabled="..."`—Disables the control.

`readonly="..."`—For text password types.

`size="..."`—The width of the control in pixels except for text and password controls, which are specified in number of characters.

`maxlength="..."`—The maximum number of characters that can be entered.

`src="..."`—The URL to an image control type.

`alt="..."`—An alternative text description.

`usemap="..."`—The URL to a client-side imagemap.

`align="..."`—Deprecated. Controls alignment (`left`, `center`, `right`, `justify`).

`tabindex="..."`—Sets the tabbing order between elements with a defined `tabindex`.

`onfocus="..."`—The event that occurs when the element receives focus.

`onblur="..."`—The event that occurs when the element loses focus.

`onselect="..."`—Intrinsic event that occurs when the control is selected.

`onchange="..."`—Intrinsic event that occurs when the control is changed.

`accept="..."`—File types allowed for upload.

Empty	Yes

\<ISINDEX\>

Usage	Prompts the user for unput.
Start/End Tag	Required/Illegal
Attributes	`%coreattrs, %i18n`

`prompt="..."`—Provides a prompt string for the input field.

Empty	Yes
Notes	Deprecated.

\<LABEL\>...\</LABEL\>

Usage	Labels a control.
Start/End Tag	Required/Required
Attributes	`%coreattrs, %i18n, %events`

`for="..."`—Associates a label with an identified control.

A

`disabled="..."`—Disables a control.

`accesskey="..."`—Assigns a hotkey to this element.

`onfocus="..."`—The event that occurs when the element receives focus.

`onblur="..."`—The event that occurs when the element loses focus.

Empty   No

`<LEGEND>...</LEGEND>`

Usage   Assigns a caption to a `FIELDSET`.
Start/End Tag   Required/Required
Attributes   `%coreattrs, %i18n, %events`

`align="..."`—Deprecated. Controls alignment (`left`, `center`, `right`, `justify`).

`accesskey="..."`—Assigns a hotkey to this element.

Empty   No

`<OPTION>...</OPTION>`

Usage   Specifies choices in a `SELECT` element.
Start/End Tag   Required/Optional
Attributes   `%coreattrs, %i18n, %events`

`selected="..."`—Specifies whether the option is selected.

`disabled="..."`—Disables control.

`value="..."`—The value submitted if a control is submitted.

Empty   No

`<SELECT>...</SELECT>`

Usage   Creates choices for the user to select.
Start/End Tag   Required/Required
Attributes   `%coreattrs, %i18n, %events`

`name="..."`—The name of the element.

`size="..."`—The width in number of rows.

`multiple`—Allows multiple selections.

`disabled="..."`—Disables the control.

`tabindex="..."`—Sets the tabbing order between elements with a defined `tabindex`.

`onfocus="..."`—The event that occurs when the element receives focus.

`onblur="..."`—The event that occurs when the element loses focus.

A

onselect="..."—Intrinsic event that occurs when the
control is selected.

onchange="..."—Intrinsic event that occurs when the
control is changed.

| Empty | No |

<TEXTAREA>...</TEXTAREA>

Usage	Creates an area for user input with multiple lines.
Start/End Tag	Required/Required
Attributes	%coreattrs, %i18n, %events

name="..."—The name of the control.

rows="..."—The width in number of rows.

cols="..."—The height in number of columns.

disabled="..."—Disables the control.

readonly="..."—Sets the displayed text to read-only
status.

tabindex="..."—Sets the tabbing order between
elements with a defined tabindex.

onfocus="..."—The event that occurs when the
element receives focus.

onblur="..."—The event that occurs when the element
loses focus.

onselect="..."—Intrinsic event that occurs when the
control is selected.

onchange="..."—Intrinsic event that occurs when the
control is changed.

| Empty | No |
| Notes | Text to be displayed is placed within the start and end tags. |

Scripts

Scripting language is made available to process data and perform other dynamic events
through the SCRIPT element.

<SCRIPT>...</SCRIPT>

Usage	The SCRIPT element contains client-side scripts that are executed by the browser.
Start/End Tag	Required/Required
Attributes	type="..."—Script language Internet content type.

A

`language="..."`—Deprecated. The scripting language, deprecated in favor of the `type` attribute.

`src="..."`—The URL for the external script.

Empty	No
Notes	You can set the default scripting language in the META element.

`<NOSCRIPT>...</NOSCRIPT>`

Usage	The NOSCRIPT element provides alternative content for browsers unable to execute a script.
Start/End Tag	Required/Required
Attributes	None
Empty	No

Common Attributes and Events

Four attributes are abbreviated as `%coreattrs` in the preceding sections. They are

- ☐ `id="..."`—A global identifier
- ☐ `class="..."`—A list of classes separated by spaces
- ☐ `style="..."`—Style information
- ☐ `title="..."`—Provides more information for a specific element, as opposed to the TITLE element, which entitles the entire Web page

Two attributes for internationalization (i18n) are abbreviated as `%i18n`:

- ☐ `lang="..."`—The language identifier
- ☐ `dir="..."`—The text direction (`ltr`, `rtl`)

The following intrinsic events are abbreviated `%events`:

- ☐ `onclick="..."`—A pointing device (such as a mouse) was single-clicked
- ☐ `ondblclick="..."`—A pointing device (such as a mouse) was double-clicked
- ☐ `onmousedown="..."`—A mouse button was clicked and held down
- ☐ `onmouseup="..."`—A mouse button that was clicked and held down was released
- ☐ `onmouseover="..."`—A mouse moved the cursor over an object
- ☐ `onmousemove="..."`—The mouse was moved
- ☐ `onmouseout="..."`—A mouse moved the cursor off an object
- ☐ `onkeypress="..."`—A key was pressed and released
- ☐ `onkeydown="..."`—A key was pressed and held down
- ☐ `onkeyup="..."`—A key that was pressed has been released

A

INDEX

Maximum Internet Security: A Hacker's Guide to Protecting Your Internet Site and Network

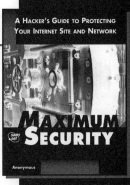

—Anonymous

Now more than ever, it is imperative that users be able to protect their systems from hackers trashing their Web sites or stealing information. Written by a reformed hacker, this comprehensive resource identifies security holes in common computer and network systems, allowing system administrators to discover faults inherent within their networks and work toward solutions to those problems. This book explores the most commonly used hacking techniques so users can safeguard their systems and includes step-by-step lists and discussions of the vulnerabilities inherent in each operating system on the market.

The CD-ROM is loaded with source code, technical documents, system logs, utilities, and other practical items for understanding and implementing Internet and computer system security.

Price: $49.99 USA/$70.95 CAN   *User level: Accomplished–Expert*
ISBN: 1-57521-268-4   *650 pages*

Creating Killer Interactive Web Sites

—Adjacency with Ibanez

Creating Killer Interactive Web Sites is a one-of-a kind look into the secrets of one of the world's most preeminent Web design firms: Adjacency. Providing the most in-depth analysis of Web design ever published, this guide brings a new standard to the integration of design and interactivity in creating successful sites. It explains the art of integrating interactivity into a well-designed Web site, offers proven techniques to entice site visitors, and gives detailed case studies of sites that successfully integrate design and interactivity.

Price: $49.99 USA/$70.95 CAN   *User level: Intermediate–Advanced*
ISBN: 1-56830-373-4   *256 pages*

HTML 4 Unleashed

—Rick Darnell, Michael Larson, et al.

A comprehensive guide and reference to the foundation language of the World Wide Web, *HTML 4 Unleashed* provides an exhaustive resource devoted to the language of Web development. The Web's explosive growth continues to give us an expanding market of Web authors ranging from casual home hobbyists to the professional Web developer. *HTML 4 Unleashed* gives these readers the information they need to grow with an ever-changing technology. This book covers all the latest proprietary extensions, including Microsoft's Active HTML and Netscape's JavaScript style sheets. It includes information on integrating HTML with other technologies such as Java and ActiveX and details new HTML technologies such as the experimental "Cougar" specification, cascading style sheets, and Extensible Markup Language (XML).

The CD-ROM contains a wide variety of HTML development tools, a collection of examples from the authors, and two electronic books in HTML format.

Price: $49.99 USA/$70.95 CAN   *User level: Accomplished–Expert*
ISBN: 1-57521-299-4   *1,100 pages*

Teach Yourself Web Publishing with HTML 4 in 14 Days, Second Professional Reference Edition

—Laura Lemay and Arman Danesh

A thoroughly revised version of the best-selling book that started the whole HTML/Web publishing phenomenon, *Teach Yourself Web Publishing with HTML 4 in 14 Days, Second Professional Reference Edition* is easy for the beginner yet comprehensive enough that even experienced Web authors will find it indispensable for reference. It includes 16 more chapters than the softcover edition, plus a 300-page HTML reference section. It covers the new "Cougar" specification for the next version of HTML and the new Netscape and Microsoft technologies like style sheets, absolute positioning, and dynamic HTML.

The CD-ROM includes an electronic version of the reference section, plus additional Web publishing tools for Windows and Macintosh platforms.

Price: $59.99 USA/$84.95 CAN   *User level: New–Casual–Accomplished*
ISBN: 1-57521-305-2   *1,100 pages*

Add to Your Sams.net Library Today
with the Best Books for Internet Technologies

ISBN	Quantity	Description of Item	Unit Cost	Total Cost
1-57521-268-4		Maximum Internet Security: A Hacker's Guide to Protecting Your Internet Site and Network	$49.99	
1-56830-373-4		Creating Killer Interactive Web Sites	$49.99	
1-57521-299-4		HTML 4 Unleashed	$49.99	
1-57521-305-2		Teach Yourself Web Publishing with HTML 4 in 14 Days, Second Professional Reference Edition	$59.99	
		Shipping and Handling: See information below.		
		TOTAL		

Shipping and Handling: $4.00 for the first book, and $1.75 for each additional book. If you need to have it NOW, we can ship product to you in 24 hours for an additional charge of approximately $18.00, and you will receive your item overnight or in two days. Overseas shipping and handling adds $2.00. Prices subject to change. Call between 9:00 a.m. and 5:00 p.m. EST for availability and pricing information on latest editions.

201 W. 103rd Street, Indianapolis, Indiana 46290

1-800-428-5331 — Orders   1-800-835-3202 — FAX   1-800-858-7674 — Customer Service

Book ISBN 1-57521-367-2

MACMILLAN COMPUTER PUBLISHING USA

A VIACOM COMPANY

Technical

Support:

If you need assistance with the information in this book, please access the Knowledge Base on our Web site at **http://www.superlibrary.com/ general/support**. Our most Frequently Asked Questions are answered there. If you do not find the answer to your questions on our Web site, you may contact Macmillan Technical Support **(317) 581-3833** or e-mail us at **support@mcp.com**.